Henry Varnum Poor

The money question

A handbook for the times

Henry Varnum Poor

The money question
A handbook for the times

ISBN/EAN: 9783744723251

Printed in Europe, USA, Canada, Australia, Japan

Cover: Foto ©Suzi / pixelio.de

More available books at **www.hansebooks.com**

THE MONEY QUESTION

A HANDBOOK FOR THE TIMES

BY

HENRY V. POOR

Author of "Money and its Laws," "Resumption and the Silver
Question," "Twenty-two Years of Protection,"
"Poor's Manual of the Railroads
of the United States,"
etc., etc.

NEW YORK
H. V. & H. W. POOR
44 Broad Street
1897

PREFACE.

In the following pages money is treated as a subject coming within the range of the exact sciences, every proposition, if properly elaborated, having all the force of demonstration.

Three kinds of money are in use in the United States :

I. Metallic money, the universal equivalent, and consequently the standard of value, its value being measured by its weight.

II. The notes and credits of banks and bankers, issued or assumed to be issued, in the discount of merchants' bills.

III. Notes of the Government, for the redemption of which, previous to their issue, no adequate means are provided.

The first kind need not be considered at any length, as its value is measured by its cost and the demand therefor, the insignia of Government adding nothing to its value.

The value of the second kind of money depends on the provision made for its retirement previous to its issue. If the institutions issuing it are restricted to the discount of bills representing merchandise prepared for, or in process of distribution, it will be retired by its use, being accepted equally with metallic money by the holders of merchandise, and by the issuers in the payment of bills in the discount of which it was issued. As it is safer and more convenient in use than metallic money it will have the preference, its use discharging capital from the exchanges. It has become the money of all commercial communities, metallic money having with them little other function than the discharge of balances arising in their foreign or domestic trade.

At the foundation of our Government provision for the second kind of money, that of commerce, was made through the instrumentality of a National Bank which served as the custodian of the public revenues collected and discharged by means of its notes. The Bank was restricted in its issues to bills of exchange representing merchandise in the process of distribution, its issues being a part of the machinery therefor. They could not be in excess, as they were presently used in the place of metallic money to reach their constituent, being retired by their use. No restriction was imposed as to the amount of notes that might be issued other than the limit to the discount of merchants' bills.

At the foundation of the Government State Banks were in operation. Their number was rapidly increased and to such an extent that they always supplied the greater part of the currency. Their issues were received by the National Bank in the payment of the revenues, as in the ordinary course of business. As the Bank had to account to Government, at the par of coin, for the notes, received in the payment of the revenues, of the State Banks, it required the daily discharge of all balances found against their issuers. In this way the restriction imposed upon the National Bank was imposed upon all others, so that there could be no excess of issue either by the National or State Banks. The result was a currency perfect in its kind, convenient in use, and always of the value of the merchandise which it represented, and consequently of metallic money, being accepted equally with this in the sale or purchase of merchandise.

The Bank, upon which the whole monetary system of the country necessarily rested, was overthrown, being, as was alleged, a menace, through the vast capital wielded by it, to the liberties and welfare of the people. The State Banks took its place as the custodian of the public revenues received and disbursed in its notes. As they were not restricted in their issues to the discount of merchants' bills, and as with most of the States the object was an increase of money, whatever the kind, they were speedily compelled to suspend specie payments. As the National Bank was not to be restored, and as the State Banks could be no longer used, the only alternative to the Government was to collect the revenues in metallic money to be held in its own strong box, leaving the people, always to use paper money in some form, to take care of themselves. In time measures were gradually adopted by them for the improvement of the currency, among the most important of which were Clearing Houses, at which the rule of the stronger became that of the weaker. In spite of all this the banks of the newer States, from the want of any adequate restraint, continued to flood the country with their worthless issues.

While the operations of the Government were on a small scale, not exceeding $100,000 daily, the payment of the revenues in metallic money did not cause any great inconvenience, as only small balances remained in the Treasury. When suddenly its expenses rose from $150,000 to $3,000,000 daily, the alternative presented to the Government was a return to the money of the banks, or an issue of one of its own notes. At the breaking out of the war of the Rebellion the amount of metallic money in sight, that is, in the banks of the cities of Boston, New York, and Philadelphia, equalled about $63,000,000. The Secretary of the Treasury undertook to carry on the operations of the Government, on the enormous scale which they had assumed, wholly by the use of metallic money. The result was a speedy suspension of specie payments by the banks which, in a most patriotic manner, had placed their means wholly at the disposal of the Government. As no return was to be made to the notes of banks, and as metallic money — then gold — was not to be had, the only alternative of the Government was an issue on a vast scale of its own notes. To make way for these the issue of notes by the State Banks was prohibited. A National Safety Fund System was indeed created, but the issue of notes under it was made so onerous that only a limited amount was supplied.

Soon after the close of the war the Government undertook the retirement of its notes, a process arrested from the stringency created. If they were allowed to remain in any quantity it was inevitable that the amount would be largely increased. If the notes of the Government were proper money, they should be issued to an amount equal to the assumed wants of Government and people. In the process of their retirement the amount was reduced from $700,000,000 to $346,000,000. It has since been increased so that it now stands at $830,000,000. They have produced, and are producing, all the effects of a currency based upon debt instead of capital; vast expenditures without any adequate means for their support, and great apprehension and alarm that any considerable run upon it may force the Government into a suspension of specie payments, in which, as its currency is the basis of all other issuers, every industry in the land will be involved. To avert such a calamity a return to the system established at the foundation of the Government is now urged, a system which would provide all the money that could be properly issued ; a money always reflecting the means of the people ; a money everywhere of the value of metallic money, the latter being almost wholly discharged from the exchanges. To urge such a return is the purpose of the following pages. The method is alike simple and obvious — the funding of the notes of the Government, and the creation of a National Bank as the custodian of the public revenues, receivable and disbursed by means of its notes, the issues of all other institutions to be left free, with the certainty that the restrictions imposed upon the National Bank will be imposed upon all. Such a return is inevitable; the only question being whether it be made to avert, or be the necessary result of a great catastrophe.

MONEY.

I N every age the most valued possession has necessarily been the money of the race, the standard of value, the universal equivalent. At an early stage cowries and wampum served as money. As man rose in the scale, with increased transactions, copper, from the wider range of its uses, became his most valued possession, consequently his money. For the same reason, with his continued advance, copper gave place to silver, and silver to gold, with nations whose exchanges, from the extent of their productions, are on a very large scale. As every form of life that has existed still exists, copper is still the money of races on a comparatively low plane; silver with races highly civilized, but whose transactions, large in the aggregate, are inconsiderable in ratio to their numbers; and gold with all the great commercial nations of the world. In the substitution of one metal for another as money the rule of convenience was alone followed, precisely as it has been in the substitution of the railway for the ordinary earth-road, of ships driven by steam instead of wind, and of power for hand looms. Every one throughout history has sought to convert his products into the article in most general request, into money, or into promises to pay money, certain of being able, by direct exchange, to obtain anything of which he might stand in need. Such article became money by common preference, in which neither governments nor concert had more to do than with the selection of articles of food or clothing.

The qualities fitting a metal to serve as money are a high relative value; a capacity of subdivision without impairing its value; of resisting the action of the elements; of receiving, no matter how minute the piece, an impress denoting the weight of pure metal it contains, consequently its value; and a uniformity in value through long periods of time due to a uniformity in the cost of its production, and in the demand therefor based upon a sense of beauty as well as use. Gold would not make a good tool or railroad bar, but were it in sufficient abundance it would be in the greatest demand for structures, furniture, and domestic utensils, as well as in the arts. As it is not abundant, it is chiefly used for decoration or ornaments for which a high price is paid, as for other choice articles, food, drink, or clothing. Diamonds which have a high relative value, due chiefly to their rarity and use as ornaments, are for obvious reasons unfit to serve as money. The greater its relative value the better fitted, other things being equal, is an article to serve as such. It is plain that without some article for which a supreme preference was felt, and which consequently became the universal equivalent and the solvent of all transactions, man could never have risen above that condition in which all exchanges are in kind, a condition alike incompatible with progress or wealth.

The capacity of an article to serve as reserves adds to its value over and above that due to it from the demand for it in the arts. Unlike other articles of merchandise, money has two functions, — one, like that of iron, in the arts and industries of life; the other as reserves by means of which one may, in small compass, safely treasure up his accumulations for future use, certain that under all conditions they will retain the value at which they were received. Unlike metallic money articles of food may have no value unless consumers can be presently found. Of two kinds of wood, each equally well adapted to certain uses, the most durable would have the preference as to price.

Of the value of an article fitted to serve as money it would be fruitless to inquire the proportion due to its use in the arts and that due to its use as the money, or reserves, of individuals or society. The proportion, however, of the amount used as money or reserves is regularly decreasing from the steady increase in the use of instruments or symbols by which the greater part of the exchanges of society are now carried on.

FUNCTION OF GOVERNMENTS IN THE MATTER OF METALLIC MONEY.

As it is inconvenient, or impossible, for individuals to determine the degree of fineness, or weight, of any piece of metal serving as money, one of the most obvious and important duties of governments is, by assay, to determine such fineness, and to impose upon each piece issued evidence of the weight of pure metal it contains, to be ready alike for present or future use. It is a duty akin to that of providing standards of extension or weight. The action of a government no more affects the value of the metal subject to it than does the provision of weights and measures affect the value of articles measured thereby. When a metal used as money is to be used in the arts, it is usually in the form of coin or stamped bars, the amount used being thereby easily determined. Coinage established, all contracts are assumed to be payable in the unit, or its multiples, which, by agreement of the parties thereto, as well as by the action of the government, become legal tender between them.

METALLIC MONEY OF THE UNITED STATES.

Gold Coins. The coinage of the eagle, having a value of $10, was authorized by the act of April 2, 1792. Its weight was 270 grains; its fineness, 916⅔ grains. The weight was changed by the act of June 28, 1834, to 258 grains; the fineness to 899.225 grains. By the act of January 18, 1837, the fineness was changed to 900 grains. The act of April 2, 1792, also authorized the coinage of the half and quarter eagles of proportional weight and fineness. Double eagles and coins of one dollar were authorized by the act of March 3, 1849; the three-dollar piece by the act of February 21, 1853. All the coins were to be of the standard weight and fineness.   .

Silver Coins. The silver dollar was authorized by the act of April 2, 1792. Its weight was 416 grains; fineness, 892.4. The weight was changed by the act of January 18, 1837, to 412½ grains; its fineness to 900 grains. By the act of 1792 the ratio was 1 of gold to 15 of silver. By the act of 1837 the ratio established was 1 to 16. By the ratio of 1792 gold was undervalued, and was not used as money. The object of the act of 1834 changing the ratio was to bring gold into use. As by it silver was undervalued the small amount coined went out of use, being more valuable for export as merchandise than as money. By the act of February 12, 1873, the coinage of silver was discontinued, to be restored by the act of February 28, 1878, at the ratio of 1 to 16. By the act of November 1, 1893, the coinage of silver dollars was discontinued.

SYMBOLIC MONEY. BANKS OF ISSUE.

Metallic money being the equivalent, in value, of articles sought in exchange, so far as it can be dispensed with a corresponding amount of capital is discharged from use. It is to-day almost wholly so discharged by means of what may be termed " symbolic money," consisting of bankers' bills drawn against merchandise moving between different countries and widely separated sections of the same country, such bills entitling their holder to that which they represent ; of merchants' bills drawn against merchandise moving from producer to consumer in the same country, and of the notes and credits of banks and bankers issued in the discount of the same. An importer of merchandise into the United States, for example, remits in the payment thereof a banker's bill drawn ordinarily upon his correspondent in London, the Clearing House of the world. To provide the means for its payment the banker purchases bills drawn against exports of merchandise equal in value to his own. So far as that exported equals in value that imported no metallic money interposes in the foreign commerce of a country, imports and exports offsetting one another. If the imports exceed the exports in value, both alike being the ordinary subjects of consumption, the banker himself becomes an exporter of merchandise in the form of coin, of the universal equivalent, now gold, equal in value to such excess, all commerce between solvent nations and communities being reciprocal in amount or value. If the exports exceed the imports in value, the excess comes back in merchandise in the form of the universal equivalent, which, in international commerce, interposes as a rule only in discharge of balances, the transfers of merchandise being almost wholly effected by symbols. These are always payable, whether so expressed or not, in metallic money, in case the holder prefers this to the merchandise they represent, and as a guarantee that such merchandise has a value in gold equal to its nominal amount.

In the exchanges of merchandise between widely separated parts or sections of the same country, as in the exchanges between different nations, metallic money ordinarily interposes only in the payment of balances. The merchandise, for example, moving from Chicago to New York is accompanied by a bill or bills representing its value, the proceeds of which are to serve for the payment of merchandise of equal value moving from New York to Chicago. Remittances on either side are made by bills of bankers who, to provide the means for their payment, purchase, as in the foreign trade of the country, merchants' bills equal in amount to their own. If the amount, in value, of merchandise moving from one city equals that moving to it from the other, the proceeds on either side serve for the payment of the bills drawn, no metallic money interposing. Bills representing merchandise moving in gross are ordinarily drawn on such time as experience has shown to be required for the distribution to consumers of that which they represent. As they serve for the transfer of the title of their constituent, they perform, as instruments of exchange, all the functions of metallic money.

The instruments for the distribution of merchandise represented by bills from merchants to consumers are the notes, and credits in the form of deposits to be drawn by cheques, of banks and bankers, issued in the discount of such bills. The two differ only in the manner in which the proceeds of discounts are taken. They are accepted by the holders of merchandise, the makers of the bills discounted, as they will pay their bills at bank equally with coin. As they are convertible into merchandise they are accepted as money by those who have occasion to purchase the same, the use of metallic money, as such, being to reach some other article of merchandise. They are consequently paid out by producers, in whose favor the bills given were discounted, in the purchase of labor and material to be used in new creations of merchandise to take the place, as fast as it is consumed, of that upon the market. By their use by consumers, in the purchase of merchandise, they fall into the hands of the makers of the bills discounted and are returned to the issuers in the payment of the same. As the process of discount at bank consists of a mutual exchange of obligations, so the process of payment consists of the mutual cancellation of the same, but not until they have been instrumental in the distribution of merchandise represented thereby equal in value to their nominal amount. Such illustrations cannot be too often repeated, as they serve to show why metallic money is no longer used, and that it is impossible it ever should be used in considerable amounts except in the discharge of balances, unless indeed a return be made to barbarism in which all methods by which the operations of society are now carried on are forgotten. They also serve to show what an elastic currency is

— one that measures the means of the people to consume. If merchandise be plenty, its symbol, money, will be plenty. If scarce, money will be scarce, the remedy being an increase of merchandise, always to have its symbol, the possession of which entitles the holder to that which it represents.

In the sale of merchandise, the holders of the same, the makers of the bills discounted, receive alike the notes and credits of all banks of good standing, as these will be received at all equally with their own in the payment of their bills. A bank, in fact, prefers to receive in payment of its bills the notes and credits of other banks rather than its own, as, in ratio to the amount so received, specie can be demanded, its own issues remaining in circulation.

The exchanges taking place in the United States afford a striking illustration, the best probably that could be produced, of the degree of the substitution of symbolic for metallic money — capital — and of the advantages resulting therefrom. In 1892 the railroads of the country moved, say, 750,000,000 tons of merchandise, the value of which, at $20 the ton, equalled $15,000,000,000. A portion of this, say one-half, was duplicated, but the value of the net tonnage equalled fully $40 the ton. The value of the tonnage of the Erie Canal, of which a careful record is kept, little or no portion of which is duplicated, and which consists of freight having the lowest relative value, averages $30 the ton. If it be assumed that the water-borne tonnage of the country and that over ordinary highways equals one-quarter the whole, the aggregate for the year equalled 1,000,-000,000 tons, having a value of $20,000,000,000. For the transfer of the title of such tonnage two sets of instruments, as has been shown, were used : one of bills for its movement, in gross, from the producer to the merchant; and one of notes and credits issued in the discount of such bills for its distribution, piece by piece, from merchant to consumer. The amount of symbolic money, merchants' bills for distribution in gross, and the notes and credits issued by banks and bankers for distribution, piece by piece, employed in the movement of merchandise from producers to consumers for the year, in the United States, and performing so far all the functions of metallic money, equalled $40,000,000,000, no metallic money directly interposing except in the form of subsidiary coins.

The provision of symbolic money by banks and bankers in the United States, September 30, 1892, according to the Comptroller

of the Currency, equalled $3,100,943,227, as follows: Deposits
with National banks, $1,775,251,128; with State banks, $648,-
513,809; with Trust companies, $411,654,996; with private banks
and bankers, $93,091,148; notes of National banks, October 31,
1892, $172,432,146. The whole arose out of the discount of bills
to the amount of $3,217,738,732, as follows: Discounts by National
banks, $2,153,498,826; by State banks, $654,654,490; by Loan
and Trust companies, $330,174,726; by private bankers, $79,310,-
684. If it be assumed that the bills discounted were drawn for
periods averaging fifty days, the total amount under discount for the
year was very nearly $20,000,000,000, a sum equalling very nearly
the value of the merchandise moving, in gross, during the year, from
producer to consumer. Interest, at the rate of 4 per cent., upon
a sum of metallic money equal to the provision of the symbolic
money, the notes and credits of banks and bankers, would
amount to $124,000,000 annually. The saving effected in the
matter of interest, whatever it may be, is by no means
the chief advantage resulting from the substitution of symbolic
for metallic money. Were metallic money to interpose in all
transactions, the expense, inconvenience, and risk attending
its care and movement would be so great as to reduce transactions in all commercial countries to one-tenth their present
volume. Symbolic money is so much more convenient in use that
no one, not even the warmest advocate of silver money in the
United States, would, if he could get the former, touch a dollar of
the latter, or of gold even, if there were piles of it as high as
Pike's Peak at every station on every line of railroad between the
mining districts of the continent and the Atlantic coast. He would
greatly prefer to have his money in the form of bits of paper which
he could carry securely on his person, no matter the amount or
value, these being convertible into metallic money at his pleasure,
or into any other form of merchandise, to be held and cared for by
others without cost or annoyance to himself till he had occasion for
their use. Metallic has given place to symbolic money for the same
reason that cowries or wampum gave place to copper, copper to
silver, and silver to gold, as instruments of exchange. It is hardly
too much to say that should a merchant in New York accompany
an order for 10,000 barrels of flour upon a manufacturer in Minne-
apolis with gold, an inquest *de lunatico inquirendo* would soon be
held to determine his sanity.

The difference between the notes of a bank and credits granted by it to take the form of deposits is one of form only. The notes, which are promises to pay to the holder an equal amount of coin, are what may be termed *subsidiary* paper money — pocket money, for transactions inconsiderable in amount ; or where it is not known that the person offering cheques is entitled to draw them ; or where a person having occasion to make payments has not his cheque-book by him. The tendency everywhere in commercial countries is to cheques in preference to notes, from the greater safety and convenience of their use ; cheques, in addition to their use as money, serving as valuable records of the transactions to which they relate. The proportion in amount, or value, of cheques to notes in the United States, were the issue of each alike free, is of course a matter of conjecture ; but it is probable that the use of the former as money would be tenfold greater than that of the latter, the proportion of cheques constantly increasing from the establishment of banks in every considerable place of trade, with which every one in affairs opens accounts for the safe keeping, as well as the convenient use, of his money. As it is, while the deposits in the national banks equalled $1,775,251,128, the notes of the same in circulation October 31, 1892, equalled only $143,423,298. At the same time, however, the notes of the United States — greenbacks, equalled $346,681,016 ; silver certificates and notes circulating as money, $487,744,654 ; the two equalling $834,425,670. Should the United States ever return to a normal and healthy monetary system, its notes, except such as might be used as instruments, never legal tender, for the collection of the revenues, evidences of debt, not of capital, would be wholly retired.

So great has been the progress in the instrument, symbolic money, by which the exchanges of all commercial countries are now carried on, that metallic money, except in the form of subsidiary coins, is almost wholly discharged from use. When it interposes, and then only in inconsiderable amounts, it is in the discharge of balances arising between nations and widely separated districts of the same country, and between banks and bankers, issuers of symbolic money, for distribution from hand to hand. Its chief use is in the discharge of balances arising between the latter. If all bills discounted represented merchandise certain to be taken for consumption within the period in which they were to mature, and if all had the same time to run, balances arising between issuers of symbolic, or bank money, would be only nominal. The amount daily arising between issuers of such money in the United States is well shown in the operations of Clearing Houses[1] now established in every considerable

[1] *Statement showing the number of Banks, members of the New York Clearing House established in 1853; their aggregate capital; clearings; balances; average daily clearings; daily balances, and percentage of balances to clearings at the same, for thirty-nine years, 1854 to 1892, inclusive.*

Year.	No. of banks	Capital.	Clearings.	Balances paid in money.	Average daily clearings.	Average daily balances paid in money.	Balances to clearings.
1854	50	$47,044,900	$5,759,455,987	$297,411,494	$19,104,505	$988,078	5.2
1855	48	48,884,180	5,362,912,098	289,694,137	17,412,052	940,565	5.4
1856	50	52,883,700	6,906,213,328	384,714,489	22,278,108	1,079,724	4.8
1857	50	64,420,200	8,333,226,718	365,313,902	26,968,371	1,182,246	4.4
1858	46	67,146,018	4,756,664,386	314,238,911	15,393,736	1,016,954	6.6
1859	47	67,921,714	6,448,005,956	363,984,693	20,807,333	1,777,944	5.6
1860	50	69,907,435	7,321,143,057	380,603,438	23,401,757	1,232,018	5.3
1861	50	68,900,605	5,915,742,758	353,383,944	19,269,520	1,151,088	6.0
1862	50	68,375,820	6,871,443,591	415,530,331	22,237,682	1,344,758	6.0
1863	50	68,972,508	14,868,597,849	677,626,483	48,428,657	2,207,252	4.6
1864	49	68,586,763	24,097,196,926	885,719,205	77,984,455	2,866,405	3.7
1865	55	80,363,013	26,932,384,342	1,035,765,108	84,796,040	3,373,628	4.0
1866	58	82,370,200	28,717,146,914	1,060,135,106	93,541,195	3,472,753	3.7
1867	58	81,770,200	28,675,129,472	1,144,963,451	93,101,167	3,717,414	4.0
1868	59	81,270,200	28,484,288,637	1,125,455,237	92,182,164	3,645,250	4.0
1869	59	82,720,200	37,407,028,987	1,120,318,308	121,451,303	3,637,397	3.0
1870	61	83,620,206	27,804,539,400	1,036,484,822	90,274,479	3,365,210	3.7
1871	62	84,420,200	29,300,986,682	1,209,721,029	95,133,074	3,827,666	4.1
1872	61	84,420,200	33,844,369,568	1,428,582,707	109,884,317	4,636,632	4.2
1873	59	83,370,200	35,461,052,826	1,474,508,025	115,885,764	4,818,654	4.1
1874	59	81,635,200	22,855,927,636	1,286,758,176	74,692,574	4,205,076	5.7
1875	59	80,455,200	25,061,237,902	1,408,608,777	81,899,470	4,693,297	5.6
1876	59	81,731,200	21,397,274,247	1,595,042,029	79,349,428	4,218,378	5.9
1877	58	71,085,200	23,259,243,701	1,373,996,302	76,358,176	4,504,906	5.9
1878	57	63,611,500	22,508,438,442	1,307,843,857	73,555,988	4,274,000	5.8
1879	59	60,800,200	25,178,770,691	1,400,111,063	82,015,540	4,560,622	5.6
1880	57	60,475,200	37,182,128,621	1,516,538,631	121,510,224	4,956,009	4.1
1881	60	61,162,700	48,565,818,212	1,776,018,162	159,232,191	5,823,010	3.5
1882	61	60,902,700	46,552,846,161	1,595,000,024	151,637,935	5,195,440	3.4
1883	63	61,162,700	40,293,165,258	1,568,983,166	132,543,307	5,161,129	3.9
1884	61	60,412,700	34,092,037,338	1,524,930,994	111,048,982	4,967,202	4.5
1885	64	58,612,700	25,250,791,440	1,295,355,252	82,789,480	4,247,069	5.1
1886	63	59,312,700	33,374,682,216	1,519,565,395	109,067,589	4,965,000	4.5
1887	64	60,362,700	34,572,848,786	1,569,627,325	114,337,209	5,142,316	4.5
1888	63	60,762,700	30,863,686,609	1,570,198,528	101,192,415	5,148,195	5.1
1889	63	60,762,700	34,796,465,529	1,757,637,473	114,839,820	5,800,782	5.0
1890	64	60,812,700	37,660,686,572	1,753,040,145	123,074,139	5,728,889	4.7
1891	63	60,772,700	34,053,608,770	1,584,635,500	111,051,471	5,195,526	4.6
1892	64	68,233,500	36,279,905,236	1,861,500,575	118,561,782	6,083,335	5.1
Total	..	†68,515,265	†986,597,212,585	‡43,410,277,328	†82,470,719	†3,701,883	†4.4

† Yearly average for 39 years.   ‡ Totals for 39 years.

The Clearing-House transactions of the Assistant Treasurer (a member of it), of the United States at New York, for the year ending October 1, 1892, were as follows:

Exchanges received from Clearing House $330,904,236 19
Exchanges delivered to Clearing House 124,324,688 45

Balances paid to Clearing House $206,579,547 74

The balances, $206,579,547.74, were paid to the Clearing House as follows:

United States gold certificates $83,355,000 00
United States Treasury notes 75,275,000 00
Legal tenders and change 47,949,547 74

place of trade. The exchanges at the fifty-seven Clearing Houses
in the United States in 1892 equalled $61,017,839,067 ; the daily
average being about $200,000,000. The balances daily arising
averaged about $16,000,000, or about 8 per cent. of the exchanges
taking place. In the city of New York the exchanges at the Clearing House for 1892 equalled $36,279,905,236, the daily average
being $118,561,782 ; the daily balances, $6,083,335, a sum equalling 5.1 per cent. of the exchanges. Clearing Houses, enforcing
daily settlements between all their members, are now the great
correctives to any tendency to over-issues of currency. No greater
amount of metallic money (not including subsidiary coin) would be
required in the internal commerce of the country, equalling $40,-
000,000,000 annually, than that now required at the Clearing
Houses, as at these the debtors one day are creditors the next,
but for extraordinary calls to which issuers are exposed
from disturbances arising alike in our domestic and foreign
trade. The amount of reserves, gold, held by the Bank of
England, ending with 1892, for its own issues, as well as for those
of all other issuers in the United Kingdom, the aggregate averaging
$3,000,000,000, equalled about £23,000,000,[1] or $115,000,000.
London, the Clearing House of the world, is first called upon to
supply the lack of capital in every part of it. It has to consider
quite as much the political and military as the financial and industrial situation the world over. When peace is menaced the first
care of the belligerents is to provide plentiful supplies of gold, the
only kind of money to be depended upon as having the same value
in all countries and in all emergencies. Were the monetary system
of the United States a normal one, a sum not exceeding one-half
that maintained by the Bank of England, the greater part to be held
in New York, the Clearing House of the country, would be ample
as reserves for all the issuers of symbolic money within it, and for
the discharge of all balances arising in the domestic and foreign

---

[1] *Statement showing the amount in pounds of gold held by the Bank of England near
the first day of January of each year, for twenty years, ending with 1892.*

Year.	Amount.	Year.	Amount.
1883	£22,355,000	1888	£19,455,412
1884	20,360,721	1889	19,712,368
1885	20,826,856	1890	17,782,374
1886	19,929,836	1891	23,465,534
1887	20,238,539	1892	22,468,478

The average amount at the beginning of each year was £20,659,541, the average amount
held being somewhat larger, but not exceeding that given.

trade of a country subject to very few of the disturbing influences to which Great Britain is exposed. The United States is usually, and always, with a proper monetary system, would be, the creditor nation. With a proper monetary system and with Clearing Houses in all the great business centres, it would be impossible that there should be any considerable fluctuations in trade, or that any large balance should be found due abroad, or from one section to another, or between issuers of symbolic money. But assuming that the reserves of the issuers of symbolic money in the United States should be in the same ratio to their liabilities as are those held by the Bank of England, the amount required by them would not exceed $100,000,000, to increase with the increase of the exchanges. We are consequently paying an enormous penalty for our unnatural and fantastic system. According to the report of the director of the mint, the amount of gold in the public treasury, November, 1893, was $162,683,854 ; in the hands of the public, $498,121,679 ; in both, $660,805,533. The amount of silver in the public treasury was $488,318,428 ; in the hands of the public, $58,834,149 ; in both, $547,152,577 ; the total of the two being $1,207,958,110. It will thus be seen that we are carrying as dead weight more than $1,000,000,000 in the form of silver and gold, counting silver at its nominal value, which, as capital, might, but for our vicious monetary system, be made the basis of new industries, increasing vastly our production of merchandise and with it the amount of the symbolic money of the country.

As the issues of a bank made in the discount of bills of exchange are ordinarily returned to it through the purchase for consumption of the merchandise they represent, its share capital which constitutes its reserves may be wholly paid in in bills, a portion of them to mature in season to provide the coin necessary to take in such of their issues as are not returned to it in the manner described. If pressed for gold this can ordinarily be had by a pledge of bills the constituents of which have ordinarily the value of an equal nominal amount of gold. No small portion of treatises upon money is taken up with the discussion of the proportion of reserves in coin to liabilities, such proportion, in the books, to be all the way from a quarter to one-half of liabilities, plenty of illustrations being offered. The proportion depends upon the constituents of the bills discounted. If it be merchandise, the liabilities of the issuer are returned without any intervention on his part.   If not merchandise, the borrower ordinarily will be unable to meet his loans. No empyrical rule, consequently, can be laid down.   Little or no coin may be necessary to the entire solvency of a bank.   In case of a suspension on a large scale provision for resumption is not necessarily that of coin, but that the bills of a bank should represent merchandise, the ordinary subjects of consumption.   In such case no greater amount of gold may be required when banks resume than when they suspended specie payment.   Resumption is not the taking in in coin of the liabilities of a bank, but that its issues should represent merchandise having a value in gold equal to their nominal amount.   The process of resumption on an extended scale may not involve the use or movement of a dollar of coin.   The capital of new banks is ordinarily paid in in the form of cheques upon other banks against deposits which grow out of the discount of merchants' bills.   Every one possessed of merchandise is capable of issuing instruments for its distribution entitled to circulate at the par of gold.   Such methods have been frequently resorted to, but are no longer necessary, banks standing ready to discount all bills given for merchandise, supplying a higher form of currency than that issued by a single producer whose credit, no matter his means, is limited to a narrow circle.

As already shown, the only difference between bills discounted and the notes and credits issued in their discount, both being alike at the option of the holder payable in coin, is in the time in which they are respectively to mature; the bills being payable on such time as is assumed to be necessary for the distribution for consumption of their constituent; the notes and credits presently, it being assumed that provision therefor has been made in the merchandise put upon the market which the bills, and notes and credits, issued in their discount, alike represent.   If no such provision is made the issuer has to supply the merchandise in the form of the universal equivalent.   Credit, as expressed by bills, is the necessary condition of the issue of symbolic money.   But for it metallic money, as an equivalent, would be required alike for the movement of merchandise in gross as for its distribution, piece by piece, to consumers.   It is the essential quality of symbolic money that previous to its issue provision be made for its return to the issuer in the merchandise which such money represents.   If the public are solvent the banks must be, although unable to meet upon the instant any considerable demand for specie. If called upon they may have no alternative but to suspend payment. Their bills paid, no new loans being made, they would again have all their capital in hand in its original form. Under such conditions, suspension of specie payments may be a matter of a few days only. The consumption of merchandise would go on as before, the liabilities on either side being discharged by mutual offset until they are wholly retired. A suspension of specie payments may have hardly any other injurious effect than to arrest for a time the operations of production and trade. It is a common thing to speak of the issues of banks as "paper money based upon specie." The exact reverse is the fact. Paper money is based, not upon specie, but upon merchandise, and is retired thereby, specie interposing, as a rule, not between producer and consumer, but only between issuers of symbolic money.

The proceeds of bills discounted are ordinarily taken in the form of credits to remain on deposit with the issuers, to be drawn according to the wants of those in whose favor they are granted. Notes, subsidiary paper money, find their way into circulation chiefly by means of cheques against deposits for the payment of wages, current expenses, and the like. As they are drawn for specific purposes they presently return in greater part to the issuers, a small amount as pocket money remaining in the hands of the public.

As the capital of banks when first established may be largely paid in in bills, these supplying in their payment, which may be demanded in coin, the reserves proper to be held, to the extent that the proceeds of loans made by them are undrawn, these may be treated, in part, as reserves for new loans. Issues so made do not inflate the currency, as they have behind them the proper constituent for their redemption. The owners of undrawn proceeds of loans well understand the use that is to be made of them and do not object, the banks being strengthened instead of weakened thereby. When demanded in large sums, all that the banks have to do is to call in their loans, or negotiate new ones for themselves, payable in coin, for gold is always to be had at prices not ordinarily much above those demanded for other kinds of merchandise. It is to be remembered that nearly all the issues of symbolic money, though nominally payable in gold, are resolved by merchandise, the ordinary subjects

of consumption. The holder of a barrel of flour is just as potential
in money as the possessor of gold who has to purchase and consume
flour as the condition of existence. Gold, however, has the advantage that it is not subject to decay, while the uses to which it can be
put are always certain to maintain its value the world over. It has
the same significance everywhere. There can be no overstock of
it, while flour may be largely in excess of demand, the consumption
of it on a large scale being restricted to a few races. Ordinarily,
however, the supply of merchandise for consumption, and of gold,
keep an even pace, so that the holder of gold has no advantage
over a holder of merchandise, even of the kind which, to maintain
its value, must be presently consumed.

The greater part of the issues of banks and bankers in all commercial countries is based upon the undrawn proceeds of loans.
On the 30th of September, 1892, the loans of the National banks of
the United States equalled $2,153,498,829. Their own loanable
capital equalled $1,029,077,041, made up of $686,573,115 of share
capital, $238,871,425 of surplus funds, and $103,632,501 of undivided profit. Their deposits equalled $1,775,251,128. Their
loans consequently exceeded their own means by $1,124,421,788.
The loans and discounts of the State banks equalled $654,654,490;
of Trust companies, $310,174,726; of private banks and bankers,
$69,310,687; the total being $1,034,139,903. The share capital of
the State banks equalled $233,751,171; the surplus funds and un-
divided profits, $90,358,080. The capital of the Trust companies
equalled $80,645,972; their surplus and undivided profits,
$60,768,148. The capital of the private banks and bankers
equalled $34,590,227; their surplus funds and reserved profits,
$11,259,164. The total loanable capital of the three equalled
$510,372,762. Their loans in excess of their capital equalled
$513,767,141. Their deposits equalled $1,153,264,953, made up
of $648,513,809 with State banks, $411,659,996 with Trust companies, and $93,091,148 with private banks and bankers. The loans
of all classes of issuers equalled $3,187,637,732, a sum $1,648,187,-
929 in excess of their loanable capital, amounting to $1,539,649,-
903. Their deposits equalled $2,928,516,081. By the means
described the whole available capital of the country is made the
basis of reproduction, not a dollar that can be spared remaining
unused. The advantage inures chiefly to workmen, as their

wages are in ratio to the amount of capital employed, while the prices of all articles of consumption are reduced in like ratio.[1]

As all issues of currency properly made are retired automatically and within brief periods by the consumption of their constituent, their denomination or amount is to be suited to the means or wants of the humblest as well as the largest consumers. There is the same reason for the issue of notes of one dollar as of ten or fifty dollars. No bank, however, would on the score of convenience and economy issue notes for less than one dollar. It is often urged that no notes should be issued for less than ten dollars, in order to force specie into use, so that in the event of a breakdown in paper money the people shall have something to fall back upon. The same reason might be used against the use of cheques of less amount than fifty dollars. It is to be remembered that the purpose of symbolic money is to take the place of metallic money, which is to be wholly discharged from the exchanges, except as subsidiary coins. There can be no more inflation with a symbolic currency, properly issued, than with a metallic currency, as the purpose of each as money is to reach some article of consumption. The amount of specie to be held is a matter of experience, the issuer, where the capital of a bank is fully paid, always inclining, as a matter of caution, to an excess, as much to maintain a high credit as to be always prepared for any emergency. With a proper system no considerable adverse balance could arise in the foreign trade of the country, as the instruments could never be in excess of the means of expenditure.

[1] *Statement showing the number ; amount of share capital ; loans and discounts ; surplus funds ; undivided profits, and deposits of the National banks of September 30, 1892, and of the State banks, Loan and Trust companies, and private banks and bankers at the close of the fiscal year 1892.*

	3,773 National banks.	3,191 State banks.	168 Loan and Trust companies.	1,161 Private banks and bankers.
Share capital	$686,573,115	$233,751,171	$80,645,972	$32,590,227
Surplus funds	238,871,425	66,725,191	45,824,747	7,730,587
Undivided profits	103,632,501	23,632,989	15,943,401	3,528,577
	$1,029,077,041	$324,109,351	$142,414,120	$43,849,391
Loans and discounts . . .	2,153,498,829	654,654,490	310,174,726	69,310,687
Deposits	1,775,251,128	648,513,809	411,659,996	93,091,148

SAVINGS BANKS.

In addition to the deposits with banks and bankers which, as capital, are made the basis of increased issues of symbolic money, are
deposits with savings banks, the accumulated earnings, or reserves,
of those who, having no adequate means of investing their earnings
or savings, intrust them to institutions especially equipped for such
purpose. As the deposits with savings banks are ordinarily made
in the notes of banks of issue, or in cheques upon the same, they
represent capital in a form fitted to serve as a basis of reproduction,
for the prosecution of enterprises of all kinds, or for permanent investment. Deposits with savings banks, as with banks of issue, are
payable presently in gold, as an undertaking, or guarantee, that the
property upon which they are loaned, or into which they are converted, has a value equal to that of an equal amount of gold, — of
the universal equivalent. There is this difference between deposits
with banks of issue and those with savings banks. The former,
arising out of the discount of bills, are used as the instruments for
the distribution of the merchandise which such bills represent, and
are retired by their use. If not returned to the issuer, through the
purchase of merchandise, they are to be taken in by paying out
a corresponding amount of specie. However issued, they are certain to pass into the hands of the holders of merchandise by whom
they are presently deposited in a bank which, if not the issuer, to
strengthen itself, immediately demands from the issuers payment in
specie. On the other hand, deposits in savings banks, though payable on demand in coin, represent accumulations to be invested, their
owners having no present use for the same. As they will be drawn
only to meet the occasional wants of the depositors, the aggregate
amount, with a healthy state of affairs, steadily increases so that the
whole mass at any one time may be safely treated as a proper subject for investment. Of course in the event of disturbance or apprehension there may be runs upon savings banks for specie, to be
ordinarily returned, as the apprehension subsides, to the banks from
which it was drawn, or to some other institutions of the kind. As
the purpose of savings banks is to invest the money of the laboring
classes, or of those who cannot well invest for themselves, and as
it is always understood that the deposits are to be invested in property which cannot be immediately converted into gold, in the case

of a run upon them they are allowed to defer payment for such time
as is assumed to be necessary for the conversion of their assets. The
amount of deposits in all the savings banks of the United States,
September 30, 1892, equalled $1,712,769,626, of which $705,777,-
557 were held by the savings banks of the New England States, the
amount averaging $150 per head of their population. As in these
States savings banks may make loans to manufacturing corporations,
they are of great aid in carrying large stocks of merchandise for
which there may be no present remunerative demand, as the money
of these banks for such purposes, and in any amounts, can be had
at the lowest current rates. The manufacturers in these consequently have a great advantage over those in other States who
have no such facility for borrowing. In the State of New York the
deposits in the savings banks equalled $588,425,421. The depos-
its in the savings banks of the State of California equalled $127,-
000,000. Had all the States deposits in savings banks at the rate
of those in New England, the total for the country would reach
$10,000,000,000. There are few manufacturing establishments and
no savings banks in the States of Mississippi and Texas, which may
largely account for their hostility to interests in which they have
little or no share, but out of which deposits in savings banks chiefly
arise.

MONEY BY LAW.

There are two kinds of money by law — a debased coinage, and
notes payable at the pleasure of the issuer ; both to be received at
their nominal value in the discharge of debts. The latter is by far
the more dangerous and disastrous expedient, as debased coins
have, ordinarily, no other support than the value of the metal they
contain ; and by no sophistry can one be persuaded that a coin of a
half an ounce of silver has the value of a full ounce. New contracts will be made in them only at the value of the metal they
contain. So soon, therefore, as those existing are discharged the
mischief resulting from the debasement is substantially at an end.

Notes issued to serve as money are a very different affair. They
may be issued and accepted in entire good faith, being promises

of a government for which, through its taxing power, the whole means of its people are assumed to be pledged. They are at the outset always well received from the credit attached to them, from the increased activity they impart to all the operations of society, and as a facile expedient for meeting any great emergency. The occasion of their issue is usually one which has roused the spirit of the people to the highest pitch, so that little attention is paid to any voice of warning, the great mass being content to forego present payment for the good of the cause, confident that, the crisis passed, abundant provision for their redemption will be made. As the community among whom they are issued is impoverished in ratio to their amount, as they are instruments in excess of the means of expenditure, each succeeding issue, no matter how great has been the depreciation, is, consequently, always more eagerly welcomed than the preceding one. The Continental currency, though resting on very feeble foundations, the joint action of the several States over which Congress had no control, was well received, and circulated for nearly two years at the par of coin. As the contest was prolonged the amount was necessarily rapidly increased, prices, from the distrust created, being inflated in far greater ratio. Still no one hesitated to take them at a price, as the greater the depreciation the greater the gain, should it turn out that the Government would eventually provide the means for their redemption. They were as readily taken at one-fifth as at their par value. Nothing, however, could arrest the decline as issue followed issue till the amount equalled $250,000,000. At last their worthlessness became so patent that they fell a vast and lifeless mass to the ground. The histories of the time are full of pictures of the sufferings from the extravagance and waste necessarily resulting from the possession of vast sums which, at a rate, served all the purposes of money; and from the losses to the holders when the final crash came. To greatly aggravate the catastrophe the several States vied with the National Government in vast issues of notes for the common cause, all of which shared a common fate. The terrible disasters that were suffered were held up as warnings for all time, and led to the insertion in the Constitution of the new National Government of an article forbidding the States to emit "bills of credit;" that is, notes to serve as money, a restriction which on several occasions has been held to be as imperative upon the National Government

as upon those of the States. When the former turned its attention
to the subject of the indebtedness contracted for the prosecution
of the war, it provided, by way of recognition only, for the funding
of the notes at the rate of one per cent. of their nominal value,
although they were still held in great amounts by persons who
received them at the value of coin, and although they contributed
essentially to the success of the great cause. Not a word of remonstrance was raised at the meagre provision made for them. It was
felt on all hands that no plan could render substantial justice to the
holders; that the notes were obligations very different in kind from
other forms of indebtedness, and that they had about them a taint
of fraud in which the people and the Government were alike
involved. They were consequently virtually repudiated, while debts
contracted by the ordinary methods were funded at their full value,
interest added, those of the several States contracted by similar
methods for the common cause being also assumed, no provision
whatever being made for their notes issued to serve as money.

The occasion of the issue of notes to serve as money by our
National Government was the war of the Rebellion. Although
nearly thirty-five years have elapsed since their issue, we have not
yet had the hardihood to repudiate, nor the manliness, honesty, or
sense to retire them. They still remain, in vast mass, the pest and
menace of the nation. An explanation of their issue after we had
become a great, prosperous and powerful nation, possessed of
ample means for every emergency, and of the failure to retire them,
involves a monetary history, in brief compass, of the United States.

BANK OF THE UNITED STATES.

Upon the formation of the National Government four matters of
paramount importance were committed for his consideration to
General Hamilton, Secretary of the Treasury: Provision proper
to be made for the public debt contracted for the prosecution of the
war; a protective tariff; the coinage; and a symbolic money as the
ordinary instrument of exchange. The latter, the only one that here
concerns us, was to be provided by a Bank of the United States
upon which three prime conditions were imposed — a paid-up
capital (of $10,000,000); that it should take interest at a rate not
exceeding 6 per cent., and that it should deal with nothing but bills
of exchange and gold and silver bullion. A double guarantee for

the safety of the holders of its issues was thus provided — capital, the preservation of which would be the first care of its managers; and loans only upon evidences of merchandise the speedy consumption of which would return its issues automatically, and without any interposition on its part. It might make losses by the discount of bills for the constituent of which there was no present demand, such bills, however, to bear only a very small proportion to those properly based, and which, consequently, were certain to be paid, the losses being too inconsiderable to affect the general result. The exchanges, of merchandise, *in gross*, are almost wholly effected by the use of bankers' and merchants' bills, the holders being entitled to that which they represent, or to the proceeds of the same. There is no occasion for the interposition of the Government in such issues. Those receiving the same can easily ascertain whether they have their proper constituent. As those who are to receive the issues of banks, for the distribution of merchandise, *piece by piece*, are further removed from the original transaction, the making of the bills, and have no means of ascertaining the adequacy of the security on which they are based, it is proper for Government to see that it be adequate by provision of merchandise, as well as of coin reserves. If it assumed no such duty a currency, the instruments of distribution, *piece by piece*, would, in time, equally with bills of exchange for its distribution, *in gross*, be issued by individuals or firms, every one possessed of capital being competent to issue instruments for its distribution. Such currency would in many respects be superior to that of corporations from the greater uniformity of issue, more abundant provision of capital, and more competent and trustworthy management, the chief care of the issuers being the preservation of their capital; and as no issues would be accepted by the public but those of concerns of undoubted standing and solvency. Railroads could be constructed at less cost and operated far more economically by individuals than by corporations, from the keener sense of personal interest that would always be present, but such advantages have to be foregone from the amount of capital often involved, and for the reason that, being institutions, their management must be intrusted to bodies having perpetual existence. The advantages of banks are that they are the only means by which, in numerous places, capital dedicated to a specific object, and subject to few risks, can be combined. A currency alike for distribution of merchandise *in gross*, and *piece by piece*, should be issued where it is produced.   As the issues of banks should always and everywhere have the same value, it is proper that they be under the supervision of a common authority.   The newer States will never, in such matters, adopt proper precautions, so strong with them will be the temptation to create banks for the purpose of borrowing instead of lending money.

The Bank of the United States was the custodian of the public revenues which were made receivable in its notes (never legal tender).   As it received in the ordinary course of business, for whatever purpose drawn, the notes of the State Banks, of which great numbers were speedily created, it had to account to the Government at the par of coin for such as were received in the payment of the revenues.   The bank consequently, for its protection, enforced daily settlements, all balances on either side being payable in coin, unless, as the stronger institution, it extended credits, as was often the case, on balances in its favor.   By such provision a Clearing House was in effect established of which every bank in the country, as the necessary condition for securing circulation of its issues, was, whether willingly or not, a member.   With such provision it was impossible that there could be any inflation of the currency, or that any considerable balances, to be discharged in coin, could arise either in domestic or foreign trade, the currency in use being wholly one of symbols, every issue being discharged by the purchase for consumption of its constituent within a period of, say, sixty days, no new issues to follow but to represent new creations of merchandise.   As for the Government it never had the custody of a dollar of its funds. All accumulations of these, beyond its immediate wants, were loaned by the bank, and remained in the channels of production and trade.   The coin for which it had any occasion was supplied by the bank.   All remittances abroad on its account were made by the bills of the bank as a drawer of foreign exchange, to cover which, as in ordinary affairs, merchants' bills were remitted.   The relation of the Government to the bank was precisely that of any other customer, the bank loaning the balances, for which they had no immediate use, of all its customers.   Thus at the very beginning of our history, and for the first time in history, a new and gratifying spectacle was presented of a currency always perfect in its kind, always equal in amount to the subjects of consumption, specie being discharged _from the ordinary operations alike of

Government and people. The nation, consequently, at the very outset entered upon a career of prosperity which, considering the lack of artificial highways, and of those improvements in the mechanic arts which have since changed the whole face of society, was without a parallel. During the whole period of its existence there was never a moment in which the bank was pressed for metallic money, nor in which there was not an abundance of it for every use to which it might be called. The result speedily disarmed all constitutional objections which had been raised, Mr. Jefferson himself when he came to the Presidency approving an act for the establishing of a branch in New Orleans upon the acquisition of Louisiana from France, as much an original act as that creating the bank.

Although the bank had been the instrument for the creation of a currency, perfect in its kind, by means of which capital was almost wholly discharged from the exchanges, the rates of interest being thereby greatly reduced, the extension of its charter, strange as it may seem, was refused. As the greater part of the currency had been supplied by the State banks, it was assumed that they were competent for the issue of all that was required. The fact was overlooked that their currency was maintained at the par of coin wholly through the control exercised over them by the National Bank. The organized opposition came from these institutions chafing under the supervision which the bank exercised over them. Several of the Eastern States, among them Massachusetts and Pennsylvania, memorialized Congress against the extension of the charter. There was still a lingering opposition to it on constitutional grounds.

Upon the winding up of the bank the Government from necessity was compelled to place itself in the same relation to the State banks that it had previously occupied to that of the United States. No sooner was it seen that the latter was to go into liquidation than the former, subject to no adequate control, began to increase largely their issues to fill the vacuum about to be made in the circulation. Great numbers of new banks were created for the same purpose. The object of the establishment of the Bank of the United States was to provide a currency always the symbol of capital. The States left to themselves were certain to create banks the issues of which were to supply the place of capital instead of being the representatives of it. No restrictions consequently were imposed as to their loans. Borrowers were always eager for accommodations which were freely extended, as great numbers of banks, without capital, had little to lose but much to gain by exchanging their issues, bearing no interest, for those of borrowers bearing interest, and often at a high rate. The moment therefore that the strong arm of the National Bank which, for its own preservation, had always to be outstretched, was withdrawn, then a great inflation of the currency was the immediate result. So long as distrust was not aroused there was little thought of demanding coin for notes, these being far more convenient in use. The Continental currency, worthless at the start, circulated, as has been shown, for nearly two years, from the confidence felt in it, at the par of coin.

In 1812 came the war with Great Britain. For its prosecution the Government was not only forced to increase greatly taxes of all kinds, but to make large loans, all payable, and distributed, by means of the issues of the State banks. Distrust at last excited led to a run upon them, and, in 1814, the greater part suspended specie payments. Released even from a pretence of making good their issues, these were so enormously increased that, in 1816, according to the statement of Mr. Calhoun, in a speech in advocacy of a new National Bank, they reached the enormous sum of $200,000,000, a sum more than sixfold greater than the aggregate for 1811 when the first National Bank went out of operation. During the whole period between the first and second banks the Government had no money but the issues of the State banks. At that early day it was forced into the adoption of the " Pet Bank System," so notorious in later times, and over which it could exercise no control. There was no thought, nor was there any possibility, of carrying on its operations in coin. The loans negotiated by it, and payable at a future day in coin, equalled nominally $80,000,000. The aggregate amount received therefor in the notes of the banks equalled $68,000,000, its securities payable in coin, commanding, in bank notes, only 85 per cent. of their nominal value. From the rise in prices due to the inflation of the currency, the value, in coin, of the articles and services which the Government had to purchase did not exceed $34,000,000. The total loss suffered by it consequently, from a disordered currency, equalled $48,000,000. The whole subject was carefully considered in 1830 by a Committee of Ways and Means of the House of Representatives, of which Mr. McDuffie, of

South Carolina, was chairman, which, in a report submitted by him, said :

> The Government borrowed during the short period of the war $80,000,000, at an average discount of 15 per cent., giving certificates of stock, amounting to $80,000,000, in exchange for $68,000,000, in such bank paper as could be obtained. Upon the very face of the transaction, therefore, there was a loss of $12,000,000, which would, in all probability, have been saved if the Treasury had been aided by such an institution as the Bank of the United States. But the sum of $68,000,000, received by the Government, was in a depreciated currency, not more than half as valuable as that in which the stock given in exchange for it has been and will be redeemed. Here, then, is another loss of $34,000,000, resulting, incontestibly and exclusively, from the depreciation of the currency, and making, with the sum lost by the discount, $46,000,000. — *History of the Bank*, p. 734.

The banks suspended specie payment in August, 1814. A meeting of Congress was presently called to consider the situation. On the 17th of October following the Committee of Ways and Means of the House, of which Mr. J. W. Eppes, of Virginia, was chairman, " having under consideration the support of public credit," addressed a communication to Hon. A. J. Dallas, Secretary of the Treasury, " in order to afford you an opportunity of suggesting any other, or such additional provisions as may be necessary to revive and maintain unimpaired the public credit." To this communication Mr. Dallas, on the 17th of October, replied :

> The condition of the circulating medium of the country presents a copious source of mischief and embarrassment. The recent exportations of specie have considerably diminished the fund of gold and silver coin ; and another considerable portion of that fund has been drawn, by the timid and the wary, from the use of the community, into the private coffers of individuals. On the other hand, the multiplication of banks in the several States has so increased the quantity of paper currency that it would be difficult to calculate its amount, and still more difficult to ascertain its value, with reference to the capital on which it has been issued. But the benefit of even this paper currency is, in a great measure, lost, as the suspension of payments in specie, at most of the banks, has suddenly broken the chain of accommodation that previously extended the credit and the circulation of the notes which were emitted in one State into every State of the Union. It may, in general, be affirmed, therefore, that there exists, at this time, no adequate circulating medium common to the citizens of the United States. The moneyed transactions of private life are at a stand, and the fiscal operations of the Government labor with extreme inconvenience. It is impossible that such a state of things should be long endured ; but, let it be fairly added, that, with legislative aid, it is not necessary that the endurance.

should be long. Under favorable circumstances, and to a limited extent, an emission of treasury notes would, probably, afford relief ; but treasury notes are an expensive and precarious substitute, either for coin or for bank notes, charged as they are with a growing interest, productive of no countervailing profit or emolument, and exposed to every breath of popular prejudice or alarm. The establishment of a national institution, operating upon credit, combined with capital, and regulated by prudence and good faith, is, after all, the only efficient remedy for the disordered condition of our circulating medium. While accomplishing that object, too, there will be found, under the auspices of such an institution, a safe depository for the public treasure, and a constant auxiliary to the public credit. But, whether the issues of a paper currency proceed from the national treasury, or from a national bank, the acceptance of paper in a course of payments and receipts must be forever optional with the citizens. *The extremity of that day cannot be anticipated when any honest and enlightened statesman will again venture upon the desperate expedient of a tender law.* — *History of the Bank*, p. 481.

In 1815 a bill which passed both Houses of Congress for the creation of a new bank failed to receive the signature of the President, Mr. Madison, from its inadequacy to the object sought to be accomplished.

The condition of the country in 1816 had become so desperate that by common consent the only escape was a new bank upon the model of the old, the capital to be increased to $35,000,000 that it might be better able to cope with the difficulties it was to encounter. In its advocacy Mr. Calhoun, who had charge of the measure in the House, said :

That the currency of the nation was extremely depreciated, and in degrees varying according to the different sections of the country, all would assent. That this state of the currency was a stain on the public and private credit and injurious to the morals of the community was so clear a position as to require no proof. There were, however, other considerations arising from the state of the currency, not so distinctly felt nor so generally assented to. The state of our circulating medium was opposed to the principles of the Federal Constitution. The power was given to Congress by that instrument in express terms to regulate the currency of the United States. In point of fact, that power, though given to Congress, is not in their hands. The power is exercised by banking institutions no longer responsible for the correctness with which they manage it. Gold and silver have disappeared entirely; there is no money but paper money, and that money is beyond the control of Congress. No one who referred to the Constitution could doubt that the money of the United States was intended to be placed entirely under the control of Congress. The only object the framers of the Constitution could have had in view in giving to Congress the power "to coin money, regulate the value thereof, and of foreign coin," must have been to give a steadiness and fixed value to the currency of the United States. The state of things at the time of the adoption of the Constitution afforded an argument in support of such construction. There then existed a depreciated paper currency which could only be regulated and made uniform by giving a power for that purpose to the general government. I contend, therefore, taking into view the prohibition against the States issuing bills of credit, that there was a strong presumption this power was intended to be exclusively given to Congress. There was no provision in the Constitution by which States were prohibited from creating the banks which now exercise this power; but banks were then but little known. There was but one, the Bank of North America, with a capital of only $400,000 ; and the universal opinion was that bank notes represented gold and silver, and that there could be no necessity to prohibit banking institutions under this impression, because their notes always represented gold and silver, and they could not be multiplied beyond the demands of the country. I draw the distinction between banks of deposit and banks of discount, the latter of which were then but little understood — and their abuse not conceived until demonstrated by recent experi- ence. No man in the convention, much talent and wisdom as it contained, could possibly have foreseen the course of these institutions ; that they would have multiplied from one to two hundred and sixty ; from a capital of $400,000 to $80,000,000 ; that from being consistent with the provisions of the Constitu- tion and the exclusive right of Congress to regulate the currency they would be directly opposed to it; that, so far from their credit depending on their punctu- ality in redeeming their bills with specie, they might go on, *ad infinitum*, in vio- lation of their contracts, without a dollar in their vaults. There has, indeed, been an extraordinary revolution in the currency of the country. By a sort of under-current the power of Congress to regulate the money of the country has caved in, and upon its ruin have sprung up those institutions which now exercise the right of making money for and in the United States ; for gold and silver are not the only money, but whatever is the medium of purchase and sale, in which bank paper alone is now employed, and has, therefore, become the money of the country.

A change great and wonderful has taken place, which divests you of your rights and turns you back to the condition of the Revolutionary War, in which every State issued " bills of credit " which were made a legal tender and were of various value.

This, then, is the evil. We have, in lieu of gold and silver, a paper medium, unequally but generally depreciated, which affects the trade and industry of the nation, which paralyzes the national arm, which sullies the faith both public and private of the United States, — a paper no longer resting on gold and silver as its basis. We have, indeed, laws regulating the currency of foreign coin ; but they are, under present circumstances, a mockery of legislation, because there is no coin in circulation. The right of making money — an attribute of sovereign power, a sacred and important right — is exercised by two hundred and sixty banks, scattered over every part of the United States, not responsible to any power whatever for their issues of paper. The next and great inquiry was, How was this evil to be remedied? Restore these institutions to their original use; cause them to give up their usurped power; cause them to return to their legitimate office of places of discount and deposit; let them be no longer mere paper machines; restore the state of things which existed anterior to 1813, which was consistent with the just policy and interests of the country ; cause them to fulfil their contracts ; to respect their broken faith ; resolve that everywhere there shall be an uniform value to the national currency. Your constitutional control will then prevail.

In the United States, according to the best estimation, there were not, in the vaults of all the banks, more than $15,000,000 of specie, with a capital amount-ing to about $82,000,000; hence the cause of the depreciation of bank notes — the excess of paper in circulation beyond that of specie in their vaults. This excess was visible to the eye, and almost audible to the ear; so familiar was the fact, that this paper was emphatically called trash, or rags. According to esti-mation, there are in circulation within the United States $200,000,000 of bank notes, credits, and bank paper, in one shape or other. Supposing $30,000,000 of these to be in possession of the banks themselves, there were perhaps $170,000,000 actually in circulation, or on which the banks drew interest. — *History of the Bank of the United States*, p. 631.

The speech of Mr. Calhoun was unsurpassed alike in statement and in fervid eloquence, as he was describing scenes of disaster wit-nessed on every side. The currency of the country, through the neglect of the Government, had completely broken down. Under the first bank it was all that could be desired. A similar institution would restore the situation. The Constitution gave to Congress the power to "regulate the value of money." That in use, and to be used, was not coin, but paper. Currency of coin needed no regula-tion, its value being determined by weight. But little inconvenience would be felt should the United States, as it often had done, adopt the coins of other countries instead of issuing its own, as the former would, for all the purposes for which metallic money was used in considerable sums, the discharge of balances arising between the issuers of symbolic money, and in international trade, be just as con-venient as the latter. The commercial value of bullion always regu-lates that of the coins into which it is converted. The only function of government in the matter of coinage is to affix names or titles to certain weights and metals. Its great duty was not the regulation of the coinage, as that would take care of itself, but of the money in use. For this all that was requisite was a second bank upon the model of the first.

The new bank went into operation March 3, 1816. At the time there were 260 State banks, the issues of which in various forms equalled $200,000,000, a large part of which was almost wholly valueless. The first thing for the bank was to clear the field of the worthless stuff encumbering it by assisting such banks as were solvent, time being given, and by driving those insolvent out of existence by supplying a sound currency adequate to the wants of the people who always prefer the best instruments to given ends. It began its operations by assuming, by the permission of the National Government, balances to the amount of $10,804,112, due from the State banks to it, allowing long credits therefor. In its efforts to restore the currency it made, as was inevitable, heavy losses on every side, one of $1,600,000 by the mismanagement of the Baltimore branch. Upon the tumultuous sea upon which the new institution embarked, it barely escaped disastrous shipwreck. So excessive were its losses that for the first thirteen years of its existence its dividends averaged only 4.88 per cent., against nearly twice that rate by the first bank, which, when it began its operations, had a clear field before it. It was not until 1820 that affairs in the Northern and Eastern States were substantially restored. In the Southern States a large number of banks were still unable to resume. These were forced out of existence as soon as the national one was able, through its branches, to supply a currency adequate in amount, and of the value of coin.

In 1811 eighty-eight State banks were in operation, having a capital of $42,610,605, and a note circulation of $22,700,000. The deposits, not given in Mr. Gallatin's "Considerations on the Currency," our only source of information, did not probably exceed $7,000,000, the total of the two being about $30,000,000. In 1820 the number of banks was 307, the nominal capital of which equalled $102,110,611, their notes in circulation equalling $40,641,574. A great number of these were subsequently wound up. The issues of those that weathered the storm did not probably exceed $40,000,-000, an amount only $10,000,000 greater than that of 1811. The increase of the currency from $30,000,000 in 1811 to $200,000,000 in 1816, and its reduction to $40,000,000, before order was fully restored, were attended by disasters which can only be imagined, not expressed. If the National Government from a disordered currency, in transactions equalling nominally $80,000,000, made a loss of $46,000,000, how vast must have been those of the people, with transactions a hundredfold greater! The value in coin of the merchandise and service received by it, $34,000,000, was a trifling sum to be taken in the form of domestic products for the purchase of which the notes received were used. Had the bank been in existence such products could have been far more easily reached by a currency purely symbolic, consequently of the value of coin, than by one greatly inflated, as with the former the industries of the country would have remained undisturbed, while the people, from the sense of patriotism which was aroused, would have promptly anticipated every want of the Government. A vicious currency so impaired the vigor and energy, as well as the morale, of the people, that the period between the two banks was one of the most disastrous and discreditable in our history. Had there been no break between them there would have been no suspension of specie payments, and none of the terrible disasters that followed. Such was the deliberate judgment of Mr. Gallatin, Secretary of the Treasury from 1802 to 1814 continuously, a most competent authority. In his "Considerations on the Currency" he said:

We have stated all the immediate and remote causes within our knowledge which concurred in producing that event [the suspension of the specie payments]; and although the effects of a longer continuance of the war cannot be conjectured, it is our deliberate opinion that the suspension might have been prevented, at the time when it took place, had the former Bank of the United States been still in existence. The exaggerated increase from 88 to 260 of State banks, occasioned by the dissolution of that institution, would not have occurred. That bank would, as before, have restrained within proper bounds, and checked their issues; and, through the means of its offices, it would have been in possession of the earliest symptoms of the approaching danger. It would have put the Treasury Department on its guard; both acting in concert would certainly have been able at least to retard the event; and, as the treaty of peace was ratified within less than six months after the suspension took place, that catastrophe would have been altogether avoided.

We have already adverted to the unequivocal symptoms of renewed confidence shown by the rising value of bank notes, which followed the peace. This would have greatly facilitated an immediate resumption of specie payments, always more easy, and attended with far less evils, when the suspension has been of short duration. The banks did not respond to that appeal made by public opinion; nor is there any evidence of any preparations, or disposition on their part, to pay their notes in specie, until after the act to incorporate the new Bank of the United States had passed.[1] — *Considerations on the Currency*, p. 46.

[1] In his "Considerations on the Currency" Mr. Gallatin gave the names of 165 banks which failed, chiefly in the period that immediately followed the attempt to resume specie payments.

Order restored, the country again entered upon a period of prosperity, which rivalled that which had prevailed throughout the whole period of the first bank, the currency being perfectly adapted in amount and kind to the wants of the people.

In 1828 General Jackson was elected to the Presidency. In his first annual message, December 8, 1829, he referred to the bank in the following terms :

The constitutionality and expediency of the law creating the Bank of the United States are well questioned by a large portion of our fellow-citizens, and it must be admitted by all that it has failed in the great end of establishing a uniform currency.

The assault of General Jackson upon the bank came upon the nation like a clap of thunder from a clear sky. The language of a madman, it was received with amazement rather than indignation. Under the two banks the country had enjoyed the priceless boon of a currency perfect in its kind, by means of which capital had been almost wholly discharged from the exchanges — a currency the nominal value of which always measured that of the subjects, whether domestic or foreign, of consumption, and with which no considerable balances to be paid in coin could arise either in foreign or domestic trade. The sentiment everywhere in reference to the bank was one of profound satisfaction and content.

Not a moment was lost in reply. On the 10th of March, so soon as it could be appointed, that part of the message relating to the bank was referred to the Committee of Ways and Means of the House, consisting of Mr. McDuffie, of South Carolina, Chairman ; Mr. Verplanck, of New York ; Mr. Dwight, of Massachusetts ; Mr. Smyth, of Virginia ; Mr. Ingersoll, of Connecticut ; Mr. Gilmore, of Pennsylvania, and Mr. Overton, of Louisiana. On the 10th of April following, the committee submitted an elaborate and unanimous report in which it considered chiefly two questions — 1st, Has Congress the power to incorporate such a Bank of the United States? and, 2d, Whether it is expedient to establish and maintain such an institution? In support of the constitutionality of the bank the committee, among other things, said :

If the concurrence of all the departments of the Government at different periods of our history, under every administration, and during the ascendency of both the great political parties into which the country was divided soon after the adoption of the present Constitution, shall be regarded as having the authority ascribed to such sanctions by the common consent of all well-regulated communities, the constitutional power of Congress to incorporate a bank may be assumed as a postulate no longer open to controversy. In little more than two years after the Government went into operation, and at a period when most of the distinguished members of the Federal Convention were either in the executive or legislative councils, the Act incorporating the first Bank of the United States passed both branches of Congress by large majorities, and received the deliberate sanction of President Washington, who had then recently presided over the deliberations of the convention. The constitutional power of Congress to pass the Act of Incorporation was thoroughly investigated, both in the executive Cabinet and in Congress, under circumstances in all respects propitious to a dispassionate decision. There was at that time no organization of political parties; and the question was, therefore, decided by those who, from their knowledge and experience, were peculiarly qualified to decide correctly, and who were entirely free from the influence of that party excitement and prejudice which would justly impair, in the estimation of posterity, the authority of a legislative interpretation of the constitutional charter. No persons can be more competent to give a just construction to the Constitution than those who had a principal agency in framing it; and no administration can claim a more perfect exemption from all those influences which sometimes pervert the judgments even of the most wise and patriotic, than that of the Father of his Country during the first term of his service. . . .

In less than two years after the expiration of the charter, — the war with Great Britain having taken place in the meantime, — the circulating medium became so disordered, the public finances so deranged, and the public credit so impaired, that the enlightened patriot, Mr. Dallas, who then presided over the Treasury Department, with the sanction of Mr. Madison, and as it is believed every member of the Cabinet, recommended to Congress the establishment of a National Bank, as the only measure by which the public credit could be revived and the fiscal resources of the government redeemed from a ruinous and otherwise incurable embarrassment; and such had been the impressive lesson taught by a very brief but fatal experience, that the very institution which had been so recently denounced and rejected by the Republican party, being now recommended by a Republican administration, was carried through both branches of Congress as a Republican measure by an overwhelming majority of the Republican party. It is true that Mr. Madison did not approve and sign the bill which passed the two Houses, because it was not such a bill as had been recommended by the Secretary of the Treasury, and because the bank it proposed to create was not calculated, in the opinion of the President, to relieve the necessities of the country. But he premised his objections to the measure " by waiving the constitutional authority of the Legislature to establish an incorporated bank, as being precluded, in his opinion, by repeated recognitions, under varied circumstances, of the validity of such an institution, in Acts of the legislative, executive, and judicial branches of the government, accompanied by indications, in different modes, of a concurrence of the general will of the nation." Another bill was immediately introduced; and would, in all probability, have become a law, had not the news of peace, by doing away with the pressure of the emergency, induced Congress to suspend further proceedings on the subject until the ensuing session. At the commencement of that session, Mr. Madison invited the attention of Congress to the subject; and Mr. Dallas again urged the necessity of establishing a bank, to restore the currency, and facilitate the collection and disbursement of the public revenue; and so deep and solemn was the conviction upon the minds of the public functionaries that such an institution was the only practicable means of restoring the circulating medium to a state of soundness, that, notwithstanding the decided opposition to all the State Banks and their debtors, — and, indeed, the whole debtor class of the community, — the Act incorporating the present Bank of the United States was passed by considerable majorities in both branches of Congress, and approved by Mr. Madison.

In reference to the question of the expediency of the bank, the committee said :

The question really presented for determination is not between a metallic and a paper currency, but between a paper currency of uniform value, and subject to the control of the only power competent to its regulation, and a paper currency of varying and fluctuating value, and subject to no common or adequate control whatever. On this question, it would seem that there could hardly exist a difference of opinion; and that this is substantially the question involved in considering the expediency of a national bank will satisfactorily appear by a comparison of the state of the currency previous to the establishment of the present bank and its condition for the last ten years.

Human wisdom has never effected, in any other country, a nearer approach to uniformity of the currency than that which is made by the use of the precious metals. If, therefore, it can be shown that the bills of the United States Bank are of equal value with silver at all points of the Union, it would seem that the proposition is clearly made out that the bank has accomplished the great end of establishing a uniform and sound currency. It is not denied that the bills of the mother bank, and of all its branches, are invariably and promptly redeemed in specie whenever presented at the offices by which they have been respectively issued, and at which, upon their face, they purport to be payable. Nor is it denied that the bills of the bank, and of all its branches, are equal to specie in their respective spheres of circulation. . . .

But it is impossible to exhibit anything like a just view of the beneficial operations of the bank without adverting to the great reduction it has effected, and the steadiness it has superinduced in the rate of the commercial exchanges of the country. . . . It has been already stated that it has saved the community from the immense losses resulting from a high and fluctuating state of the exchanges. It now remains to show its effect in equalizing the currency. In this respect, it had been productive of results more salutary than were anticipated by the most sanguine advocates of the policy of establishing the bank. *It has actually furnished a circulating medium more uniform than specie.* This proposition is susceptible of the clearest demonstration. If the whole circulating medium were specie, a planter of Louisiana who should desire to purchase merchandise in Philadelphia would be obliged to pay one per cent. either for a bill of exchange on this latter place, or for the transportation and insurance of his specie. His specie at New Orleans, where he had no present use for it, would be worth one per cent. less to him than it would be in Philadelphia, where he had a demand for it. But, by the aid of the Bank of the United States, one-half of the expense of transporting specie is now saved to him. The bank for one-half of one per cent. will give him a draft upon the mother bank at Philadelphia, with which he can draw either the bills of that bank, or specie, at his pleasure. In like manner, the bank and its branches will give drafts from any point of the Union to any other where offices exist, at a percentage greatly less than it would cost to transport specie, and, in many instances, at par. If the merchant or planter, however, does not choose to purchase a draft from the bank, but prefers transmitting bills of the office where he resides to any distant point, for commercial purposes, although these bills are not strictly redeemable at the point to which they are transmitted, yet, as they are receivable in payment of all dues to the Government, persons will be generally found willing to take them at par, and always at a discount much less than would pay the expense of transporting specie. The fact that the bills of the bank and its branches are indiscriminately receivable at the custom houses and land offices, in payment of duties, and for the public lands, has an effect in giving uniformity to the value of these bills.

For all the purposes of the revenue, it gives to the national currency that perfect uniformity, that ideal perfection, to which a currency of gold and silver, in so extensive a country, could have no pretensions. A bill issued at Missouri is of equal value with specie at Boston, in payment of duties, and the same is true of all other places, however distant, where the bank issues bills, and the Government collects its revenue. When it is, moreover, considered that the bank performs, with the most scrupulous punctuality, the stipulation to transfer the funds of the Government to any point where they may be wanted, free of expense, it must be apparent that the committee are correct, to the very letter, in stating that the bank has furnished, both to the Government and to the people, a currency of absolutely uniform value in all places, for all the purposes of paying the public contributions, and disbursing the public revenue. And when it is recollected that the Government annually collects and disburses more than $23,000,000, those who are at all familiar with the subject will at once perceive that bills, which are of absolute uniform value for this vast operation, must be very nearly so for all the purposes of general commerce. — *History of the Bank*, p. 735.

A matter upon which the committee especially dwelt was the services which the bank rendered in facilitating the exchanges, *in gross*, of the country. Commerce between different countries, and widely separated districts of the same country, must, in the end, be reciprocal in amount, or value. An immense advantage consequently is gained when the indebtedness contracted between two points can be discharged by the credits, corresponding in amount, arising between the two, avoiding thereby the use of metallic money in their discharge. Between New York and New Orleans at the time was a very large reciprocal movement of merchandise represented by merchants' bills. These, drawn in the commerce between them, were, by means of the bank, offset, the one against the other, so that no capital in the form of coin had to move, except in the case of excess of indebtedness on one side or the other. Where the bills were equal in amount the price of exchange between the two cities was *nominal*, as no movement of coin by the drawers on either side was involved. This illustration will serve for the commerce between all cities in which the bank had branches, as was the case at all points of commercial importance. By the methods described the bank constituted a clearing house for the drawers of merchants' bills throughout the country, precisely as it had established a clearing house for the issuers of currency for the distribution of merchandise *piece by piece*, specie only interposing to make good balances, never considerable in amount. In the entire absence at the time of internal means of communication, except that of rivers never to be relied on, the advantages resulting from the manner in which the exchanges *in gross* were effected, without the use of coin, was second only to those by which, by means of its issues of banks, they were effected *piece by piece*.

On the 29th of March, 1829, the Committee on Finance of the Senate, of which Mr. Smith, of Maryland, was chairman, the other members being Mr. Silsbee, of Massachusetts; Mr. King, of New York; Mr. Smith, of South Carolina, and Mr. Johnson, of Louisiana, to which was referred so much of the message of the President as related to the bank, submitted a unanimous report, from which the following extracts are given:

The currency of the United States, in its relation to the Government, consists of gold and silver, and of notes equivalent to gold and silver. And the inquiry which naturally presents itself is, whether this mass of currency is sound and uniform for all the practical purposes of the Government, and the trade of the Union. That it is so, will appear from the following facts:

1st, The Government receives its revenue from —

   343 Custom Houses.
    42 Land Offices.
8,004 Post Offices.
   134 Receivers of Internal Revenue.
    37 Marshals.
    33 Clerks of Courts.

These, with other receiving officers, who need not be specified, compose an aggregate of more than nine thousand persons, dispersed through the whole of the Union, who collect the public revenue. From these persons the Government has, for the ten years preceding January 1, 1830, received $230,068,855.17. This sum has been collected in every section of this widely extended country. It has been disbursed at other points, many thousand miles distant from the places where it was collected; and yet it has been so collected and distributed, without the loss, as far as the committee can learn, of a single dollar, and without the expense of a single dollar to the Government. That a currency by which the Government has been thus enabled to collect and transfer such an amount of revenue to pay its army and navy, and all its expenses, and the national debt, is unsafe and unsound, cannot readily be believed, for there can be no surer test of its sufficiency than the simple fact that every dollar, received in the form of a bank note, in the remotest parts of the interior, is, without charge, converted into a silver dollar, at every one of the vast number of places where the service of the Government requires its disbursement. The Secretary of the Treasury, in his report of the 6th of December, 1828, declares that, during the four years preceding, the receipts of the Government had amounted to more than $97,000,000, and that " all payments on account of the public debt, whether for interest or principal; all on account of pensions; all for the civil list; for the army; for the navy; or for whatever purpose wanted, in any part of the Union, have been punctually met." The same officer states that " it is the preservation of a good currency that can alone impart stability to property, and prevent those fluctuations in its value, hurtful alike to individuals and to national wealth. This advantage the bank has secured to the community, by confining within prudent limits, its issues of paper."

It cannot be doubted that, throughout the whole country, the circulating bank notes are equal to specie, and convertible into specie. There may be and probably are exceptions; because among banks as among men there are some who make a show of unreal strength. But it is a fact so familiar to the experience of every citizen in the community as to be undeniable that, in all the Atlantic and commercial cities, and generally speaking throughout the whole country, the notes of the State banks are equal to gold and silver. The committee do not mean to say that there may not be too many banks, or that insolvencies do not occasionally occur among them; but as every bank which desires to maintain its character must be ready to make settlements with the Bank of the United States as the agent of the Government, or be immediately discredited, and must therefore keep its notes equal to gold and silver, there can be little danger to the community while the issue of the banks is restrained from running to excess by the salutary control of the Bank of the United States, whose own circulation is extremely moderate compared with the amount of its capital. Accordingly, the fact is, that the general credit of the banks is good, and that their paper is always convertible into gold and silver, and for all local purposes forms a local equivalent to gold and silver. There is, however, superadded to this currency a general currency more known, more trusted, and more valuable than the local currency which is employed in the exchanges between different parts of the country. These are the notes of the National Bank. These notes are receivable for the Government by the 9,000 receivers scattered throughout every part of the country. They are in fact in the course of business paid in gold or silver, though they are not legally, or necessarily, so paid by the branches of the bank in every section of the Union. In all commercial places they are received in all transactions without any reduction in value, and never, under any circumstances, does the paper from the remotest branches vary beyond a quarter of one per cent. in its actual exchange for silver. Here, then, is a currency as safe as silver, more convenient and more valuable than silver; which, through the whole western and southern and interior parts of the Union, is eagerly sought in exchange for silver; which in those sections often bears a premium paid in silver; which is, throughout the Union, equal to silver in payment to the Government and payments to individuals in business; and which, whenever silver is needed in any part of the country, will command it without the charge of the slightest fraction of a percentage. By means of this currency funds are transmitted at an expense less than in any other country. In no other country can a merchant do what every citizen of the United States can do — deposit, for instance, his silver at St. Louis or Nashville or New Orleans, and receive notes which he can carry with him 1,000 or 1,500 miles to the Atlantic cities, and there receive for them an equivalent amount of silver without any expense whatever; and in no possible event an expense beyond a quarter of one per cent. If, however, a citizen does not wish to incur the anxiety of carrying these notes with him, or to run the hazard of the mail, he may instead of them receive a draft, payable to himself or his agent alone, so as to insure the receipt of an equal amount at an expense of not one-half, and often not one-fourth, of the actual cost of carrying the silver. The owner of the funds, for instance, at St. Louis or Nashville can transfer them to Philadelphia for one-half per cent.; from New Orleans generally without any charge at all, at most one-half per cent.; from Mobile from par to one-half per cent.; from Savannah at one-half per cent.; and from Charleston at from par to one-quarter per cent.

This seems to present a state of currency approaching as near to perfection as could be desired; for here is a currency issued (through branches) at twenty-four different parts of the Union, obtainable by any citizen who has money or credit. When in his possession, it is equivalent to silver in all its dealings with the 9,000 agents of the Government throughout the Union. In all his dealings with the interior it is better than silver; in all his dealings with the commercial cities, equal to silver; and if, for any purpose, he desires the silver with which he bought it, it is at his disposal almost universally without any diminution, and never more than a diminution of one-quarter per cent. It is not easy to imagine, it is scarcely necessary to desire, any currency better than this.

The preceding extracts should be read and reread by every one who would get an adequate idea of the nature, and extent of use, in the United States, of symbolic money, rendered such by a stroke of the pen, — by restrictions, imposed upon a single institution, the fiscal agent of the Government, of discounts to bills of exchange. For the distribution of merchandise all that is required in the agent is capacity and integrity, supplemented by a due provision of reserves, to be maintained by every one in affairs. The producer in the sale of his wares does not demand from the merchant, the distributor of them, any security other than his bills supported by a proper provision of reserves. When he offers them for discount he is not required, for their payment, to put up any security additional to their constituent supported by the reserves of their maker, supplemented by his own. The provision made is regarded by the bank discounting the bills as ample for its protection. Losses may be suffered, but they are incident to, and make up a part of, the charge or cost of distribution. Those to whom the issues of the bank discounting the bills are paid, as money, have not only the security described, — the merchandise represented by the bills, in the discount of which the issues they hold were made, supplemented by the reserves of all the parties thereto, all alike responsible for their payment, — but, in addition, the reserves, ordinarily ample, of the issuers. They are entitled to the additional security, being removed one step farther from, and having little knowledge of, the transactions out of which the issues they are to receive arose. With such cumulative security, the issues of banks are properly preferred by all as money to gold. All provision beyond that described would be a needless addition of capital to the process of distribution, the burden to be borne alike by producer and consumer.

Such was the currency, alike of the Government and the people, under the two banks. With it, at the end of each year, the Government, with all its engagements fulfilled and all its wants supplied through the instrumentality of bank money, was precisely in the position in which it would have been had metallic money been used in every one of its transactions — a very great additional advantage resulting from the use by it of the money of commerce, that of the people, instead of one of capital involving a heavy outlay in its provision as well as for its transportation and safe keeping. With no other currency on any considerable scale but that of the banks with which all the operations of the Government as well as of the people were carried on for a period of forty years, not a dollar of loss was suffered by the Government, and very little by the people from the failure of State banks which supplied the greater part of the currency. With a National Bank upon the model of the old, the Government might to-day, as in the past, with entire safety turn its back wholly upon the currency, the greater part of it to be supplied by

other banks, State or National, certain that the issues of these, to
gain circulation, must be up to any standard it might provide for
a single institution of its own, the custodian of its revenues. With
such an institution the issues of all other banks, State or National,
with no other security behind them but the constituents of the bills
discounted, and of the ordinary reserves of the parties thereto, and
of the issuers, the amount of such reserves to be left to the discretion of those who were to provide them, might well be received in
the payment of all the Government revenues, and for their disbursement. Governments, like individuals, use money as an instrument,
not as an end, to reach food, clothing, material, and the like ; and it
may well accept as money whatever represents the objects for which
it has use, whether it be issued by banks of the States of Montana,
Colorado, Massachusetts, or New York. Subject to proper restrictions the issues of all would have the same value and be as proper
for Government to receive in the payment of its revenues, and
without any further security or provision for their solvency than those
described, as gold. To require more would be disadvantageous
alike to producer, distributor and consumer, including the Government. By means of them producers of cotton, rice, wheat, sugar,
tobacco, corn, and fabrics would, in effect, pay their debts, public and
private, *in kind*, their products being turned into money at their own
doors, a money proper to be accepted by every one in affairs. If
what one receives does not represent merchandise wanted, it can be
readily exchanged for the kind that does, or, in default of this, for
the universal equivalent in which all issues are, *in terms*, liable to be
discharged, and for which the reserves of the issuers are provided.
With such a currency, should any apprehension arise, a crisis could
not be precipitated, as the monetary and industrial situation would
be perfectly sound. The only effect would be an arrest of operations
until the sky was clear. If no new discounts were made, one-half of
the currency outstanding, symbolizing articles for consumption,
would be automatically retired by their purchase for use within a
period of, say, thirty days. The pause at worst would be but
a momentary one, as the alarm could not be due to any disorder in
monetary or industrial affairs ; nor could it create a run upon the
banks to any considerable extent for their reserves, as their issues
would, in great measure, be in the hands of the makers of their
bills, to be presently used in their payment.

The Government is exercised for the welfare of the people ; money that is good enough for them is good enough for those charged with its administration. . In affairs it is a part of the people, and should take its chances with the people. Governments, like individuals, must, in affairs, carry on their operations through intermediaries. They are liable to lose or be defrauded ; still, they must all the same be employed. But no guarantee can be exacted by our Government for the faithful and competent discharge of the duties of those employed by it so far-reaching and effective as those exacted, through the instrumentality of an institution of its own creation, from banks over which it has no legislative control. The Government should adopt the methods employed by the people, not only for its own convenience, but to lessen the burdens of the people. It should use symbolic money precisely as it uses railroads. The two contrivances have precisely the same purpose. Gold, capital, should be as much discharged from its operations as from those of the people. A symbolic currency, made such by the oversight of the Government, would not only be the greatest boon alike to it and the people, but would create a profound sense of nationality, long lost ; would be evidence of a paramount and beneficent authority present in almost every transaction, and affording the strongest possible guarantee of domestic order, and of the integrity of the national life, so frequently and often rudely assailed. Its tendency to the creation of a strong and intelligent sense of nationality may prove the great obstacle to its provision. A government which could establish and maintain it would be regarded as possessed of power capable of subjecting the discordant elements included in our system to its control. The refusal to extend the charter of the second bank was upon the ground that its creation transcended the power of the National Government. There can be no doubt but that, at the time, a considerable majority of the people of the United States were in favor of subordinating the authority of the National Government to that of the States. One cause of discord removed by the Civil War, others of still greater magnitude may come to the front. For such abundant elements still exists. While the opportunity favors no time should be lost in establishing a monetary system which, by its excellence, would create such a sense of its value that the authority behind it would at all hazards be upheld.

The picture here drawn is not a fancy sketch, but history through

a period of forty years, now as much forgotten as if the events re-
corded had taken place before the construction of the pyramids, so
completely did the irruption of barbarians into the fair field of
civilization efface, even from memory, the most remarkable and
beneficent monument of the fathers.

Among the distinguished citizens who replied to General Jackson's attack upon the bank was Mr. Albert Gallatin, who, from 1802
to 1814, was continuously Secretary of the Treasury, serving during
the greater part of the terms of Mr. Jefferson and Mr. Madison, and
for the greater part of the War of 1812. From his eminent ability,
the long period in which he presided over the Treasury, and his wide
experience in affairs, being subsequently president of a bank in the
city of New York, he was of all men best qualified to speak author-
itatively upon the subject of the currency, and the services rendered
by the bank alike to the government and the people.   His reply was
his "Considerations on the Currency and the Banking System of
the United States," an elaborate monetary history of the country
from the formation of the Government to 1830. From that work
extracts have been given designed to show that, had the bank been
in operation, suspension of specie payments in 1814 would have
been averted. Those that follow relate chiefly to the constitutionality, from its usefulness, of the bank :

> The Act incorporating the bank is sanctioned exclusively by that clause which
> gives to Congress power to make all laws which shall be "necessary and
> proper" for carrying into execution any of the powers vested in the government
> of the United States. . . .
>
> Experience has confirmed the great utility and importance of a Bank of the
> United States in its connection with the Treasury. The first great advantage
> derived from it consists in the safe keeping of the public moneys, securing, in
> the first instance, the immediate payment of those received by the principal col-
> lectors, and affording a constant check on all their transactions; and afterwards
> rendering a defalcation in the moneys once paid, and whilst nominally in the
> Treasury, absolutely impossible. The next, and not less important, benefit is to
> be found in the perfect facility with which all the public payments are made by
> cheque or treasury drafts, payable at any place where the bank has an office ; all
> those who have demands against government are paid in the place most conven-
> ient to them; and the public moneys are transferred through our extensive terri-
> tory, at a moment's warning, without any risk or expense, to the places most
> remote from those of collection, and wherever public exigencies may require.
> From the year 1791 to this day, the operations of the Treasury have, without

interruption, been carried on through the medium of banks; during the years 1811 to 1816, through the State banks; before and since, through the Bank of the United States. Every individual who has been at the head of that department, and, as we believe, every officer connected with it, has been made sensible of the great difficulties that must be encountered without the assistance of those institutions, and of the comparative ease and great additional security to the public with which their public duties are performed through the means of the banks. To insist that the operations of the Treasury may be carried on with equal facility and safety through the aid of the State banks, without the interposition of a Bank of the United States, would be contrary to fact and experience. That great assistance was received from the State banks while there was no other has always been freely and cheerfully acknowledged. But it is impossible in the nature of things that the necessary concert could be made to exist between thirty different institutions; and in some instances heavy pecuniary losses, well known at the seat of government, have been experienced. To admit, however, that State banks are necessary for that purpose is to give up the question. To admit that banks are indispensable for carrying into effect the legitimate operations of government is to admit that Congress has the power to establish a bank. The General Government is not made by the Constitution to depend, for carrying into effect powers vested in it, on the uncertain aid of institutions created by other authorities, and which are not at all under its control. It is expressly authorized to carry those powers into effect by its own means, by passing the laws necessary and proper for that purpose; and in this instance by establishing its own bank, instead of being obliged to resort to those which derive their existence from another source, and are under the exclusive control of the different States by which they have been established.

It was not at all anticipated, at the time when the former Bank of the United States was first proposed, and when constitutional objections were raised against it, that bank notes issued by multiplied State banks, gradually superseding the use of gold and silver, would become the general currency of the country. The effect of the few banks then existing had not been felt beyond the three cities where they had been established. The States were forbidden by the Constitution to issue bills of credit; bank notes are bills of credit to all intents and purposes; and the State could not do, through others, what it was not authorized to do itself; but the bank notes, not being issued on the credit of the States, nor guaranteed by them, were not considered as being, under the Constitution, bills of credit emitted by the States. Subsequent events have shown that the notes of State banks, pervading the whole country, might produce the very effect which the Constitution had intended to prevent, by prohibiting the emission of bills of credit by any State. The injustice to individuals, the embarrassments of government, the depreciation of the currency, its want of uniformity, the moral necessity imposed on the community, either to receive that unsound currency or to suspend every payment, purchase, sale, or other transaction incident to the wants of society, all the evils which followed the suspension of specie payments, have been as great, if not greater, than those which might have been inflicted by a paper currency, issued under the authority of any State. We have already adverted to the several provisions of the Constitution which gave to Congress the right and imposed on it the duty to provide a remedy; but there is one which deserves special consideration.

Whatever consequences may have attended the suspension of specie payments in Great Britain, there still remained one currency which regulated all the others. All the country bankers were compelled to pay their own notes, if not in specie, at least in notes of the Bank of England. These notes were, as a standard of value, substituted for gold; and if the currency of the country was depreciated, and fluctuating in value from time to time, it was at the same uniform value throughout the country. There was but one currency for the whole, and every variation in its value was uniform as to places, and at the same moment operated in the same manner everywhere. But the currency of the United States, or, to speak more correctly, of the several States, varied during the suspension of specie payments, not only from time to time, but at the same time from State to State, and in the same State from place to place. In New England, where those payments were not discontinued, the currency was equal in value to specie; it was at the same time at a discount of 7 per cent. in New York and Charleston, of 15 in Philadelphia, of 20 and 25 in Baltimore and Washington, with every other possible variation in other places and States.

The currency of the United States, in which the public and private debts were paid and the public revenue collected, not only was generally depreciated, but was also defective in respect to uniformity. Independent of all the other clauses in the Constitution which relate to that subject, it is specially provided, 1st, that all duties, imposts, and excises shall be uniform throughout the United States; 2d, that representative and direct taxes shall be apportioned among the several States according to their respective numbers, to be determined by the rule therein specified; and that no capitation or other direct tax shall be laid, unless in proportion to the enumeration. Both these provisions were violated whilst the suspension of specie payments continued. It is clear that after the quota of the direct tax of each State had been determined according to the rule prescribed by the Constitution, it was substantially changed by being collected in currencies differing in value in the several States. It is not less clear that the clause which prescribes a uniformity of duties, imposts, and excises was equally violated by collecting every description of indirect duties and taxes in currencies of different value. The only remedy existing at that time was the permission to pay direct and indirect taxes in treasury notes. But those notes did not pervade every part of the country in the same manner as bank notes; they were of too high denomination to be used in the payment of almost any internal tax; they were liable also to vary in value in the different States; and they could operate as a remedy only as long as their depreciation was greater than that of the most depreciated notes in circulation.

We will now ask whether, independent of every other consideration, Congress was not authorized and bound to pass the laws necessary and proper for carrying into effect with good faith those provisions of the Constitution, and whether that could or can be done in any other manner than either by reverting to a purely metallic, or by substituting a uniform paper currency to that which had proved so essentially defective in that respect, and which from its not being subject to one and the same control is, and forever will be, liable to that defect. The uniformity of duties and taxes of every description, whether internal or external, direct or indirect, is an essential and fundamental principle of the Constitution. It is self-evident that that uniformity cannot be carried into effect without a corresponding uniformity of currency. Without laws to this effect, it is absolutely impossible that the taxes and duties should be uniform, as the Constitution prescribes; such laws are therefore necessary and proper, in the most strict sense of the words. There are but two means of effecting the object, — a metallic or a uniform paper currency. Congress has the option of either, and either of the two which may appear the most eligible will be strictly constitutional, because strictly necessary and proper for carrying into effect the object. If a currency exclusively metallic is preferred, the object will be attained by laying prohibitory stamp duties on bank notes of every description, and without exception. If it is deemed more eligible, under existing circumstances, instead of subverting the whole banking-system of the United States, and depriving the community of the accommodations which bank notes afford, to resort to less harsh means; recourse must be had to such as will ensure a currency sound and uniform itself, and at the same time check and regulate that which will continue to constitute the greater part of the currency of the country.

Those statements also show that the Bank of the United States, wherever its operations have been extended, has effectually checked excessive issues on the part of the State banks, if not in every instance, certainly in the aggregate. They had been reduced, before the year 1820, from sixty-six to less than forty millions. At that time, those of the Bank of the United States fell short of four millions. The increased amount required by the increase of population and wealth during the ten ensuing years has been supplied in a much greater proportion by that bank than by those of the States. With a treble capital, they have added little more than eight millions to their issues. Those of the Bank of the United States were nominally twelve, in reality about eleven millions greater in November, 1829, than in November, 1819. The whole amount of the paper currency has, during those ten years, increased about forty-five per cent., and that portion which is issued by the State banks only twenty-two and a half per cent. We have indeed a proof, not very acceptable perhaps to the bank, but conclusive of the fact, that it has performed the office required of it in that respect. The general complaints, on the part of many of the State banks, that they are checked and controlled in their operations by the Bank of the United States, that, to use a common expression, it operates as a *screw*, is the best evidence that its general operation is such as had been intended. It was for that very purpose that the bank was established. We are not, however, aware that a single solvent bank has been injured by that of the United States, though many have undoubtedly been restrained in their operations much more than was desirable to them. This is certainly inconvenient to some of the banks, but in its general effect is a public benefit to the community.

As respects the past, it is a matter of fact that specie payments were restored, and have been maintained, through the instrumentality of that institution. It gives a complete guarantee that under any circumstances its notes will preserve the same uniformity that they now possess. Placed under the control of the General Government, relying for its existence on the correctness, prudence and skill with which it shall be administered, perpetually watched and occasionally checked by both the Treasury Department and rival institutions, and without a monopoly, yet with a capital and resources adequate to the object for which it was established, the bank also affords the strongest security which can be given with respect to paper, not only for its ultimate solvency, but also for the uninterrupted solvency of its currency. The statements we have given of its progressive and present situation show how far those expectations have heretofore been realized.

The manner in which the bank checks the issues of the State banks is equally simple and obvious. It consists of receiving the notes of all those which are solvent, and requiring payment from time to time, without suffering the balance due by any to become too large. We think that we may say that, on this operation, which required particular attention and vigilance, and must be carried on with great firmness and due forbearance, depends almost exclusively the stability of the currency of the country.

The President of the United States has expressed the opinion that the bank has failed in the great end of establishing a uniform and sound currency, and has suggested the expendiency of establishing " a National Bank, founded upon the credit of the Government and its revenues." He has clearly seen that the uniformity of the currency was a fundamental principle derived from the Constitution, and that this, unless the United States reverted to a purely metallic currency, could not be effected without the aid of a National Bank. But it appears to us that the objection of want of uniformity, which may be supported in one sense, though not in the constitutional sense of the word, applies generally to a paper currency, and not particularly to that which is issued by the Bank of the United States. And although we are clearly of opinion that the United States at large are entitled to the pecuniary profit arising from the substitution of a paper for a metallic currency, we are not less convinced that this object cannot be attained in a more eligible way, and more free of objections, than through the medium of a National Bank, constituted on the same principles as that now existing. (Page 78, *et seq.*)

With Mr. Gallatin the constitutionality of the bank was to be inferred from its usefulness in the exercise of the powers expressly enumerated. Whatever was useful and not prohibited was constitutional. The bank was of great use as the custodian, without expense to the Government, of the public moneys. It was of great use in the collection of the revenues, rendering losses by collectors almost impossible. It was of great use in the transfer of the public moneys, without loss or expense to the Government. "From 1791 to this day the operations of the Treasury have been carried on through the medium of banks, and every public officer has been made sensible of the great difficulty that must be encountered without the assistance of these institutions." The great assistance received from the State banks within the period between the two banks was acknowledged, although heavy losses had been made by employing them. As banks were necessary for carrying into effect the powers vested in it, the Government was not, for carrying into effect those granted, to depend upon the uncertain aid of institutions created by other authorities and over which it had no control.

The States were forbidden to issue " bills of credit," but the notes of banks created by them were " bills of credit to all intents and purposes." A State could not do indirectly, through instruments created by itself, what it could not do directly. " Bills of credit " were issued by the States notwithstanding, some of them providing capital therefor and appointing the staff to conduct them. The prohibition in the Constitution during the period between the two banks was almost wholly nugatory. Within it " injustice to individuals, the embarrassment of the Government, the depreciation of the currency, the want of uniformity, the moral necessity imposed on the community either to receive an unsound currency or to suspend every payment, purchase, sale, or other transaction incident to the wants of society; all the evils which followed the suspension of specie payments, were as great, if not greater," said Mr. Gallatin, " than those which might have been inflicted by a paper currency issued under the authority of any State." Fortunately, by means of a National Bank, " bills of credit" issued by the State banks, from the restrictions imposed upon them, were subsequently not only equal in value to the issues of the national one, but proved to be of the greatest advantage, State banks being established in numerous places in which the National Bank had no branch, so that " bills of credit " of the State banks, which seemed to be palpable infractions of the Constitution, proved efficient instruments for the promotion of the general welfare.

In the period between the two banks the National Government was compelled to accept the notes, the value of which differed greatly, of the State banks, in all its operations. The value of the notes of the banks, which did not suspend specie payments, of the New England States, was equal to that of specie. Those of the banks of the State of New York were at a discount of 15 per cent.; of Philadelphia, 20 per cent.; of Baltimore, 25 per cent. Away from the great centres of trade the depreciation was still greater. Still all revenues of the Government, wherever collected, had to be paid in notes issued in the different sections of the country. The people of the New England States, consequently, were far more heavily taxed that those of other sections, in violation of the provision of the Constitution that " all duties, imposts, and excises shall be uniform throughout the United States." During the suspension of specie payments in Great Britain the value, though greatly depreciated, of the notes of the Bank of England in which the revenues were paid was the same throughout the kingdom. " Taxes, imposts and excises " everywhere were at the same standard as to value. The remedy in the United States was a National Bank, the notes of which were everywhere of the same value, the notes of the State banks subject, in effect, to the restrictions imposed upon the National Bank, being everywhere of the same value, that of specie. Without such an institution it was impossible that the taxes should be levied as the Constitution prescribed. " If a currency exclusively metallic is preferred, the object will be obtained," said Mr. Gallatin, " by levying prohibitory stamp duties on bank notes of every description," precisely as similar duties were levied, but with a very different purpose, during the War of the Rebellion. A resort to a measure so harsh was greatly to be deprecated. The fact that specie payments were restored and had been maintained through the instrumentality of the bank " gives a complete guarantee," said Mr. Gallatin, " that under any circumstances its notes will preserve the same uniformity they now possess. Placed under the control of the Government, relying for its existence upon the correctness, prudence and skill with which it shall be maintained ; perpetually watched and occasionally checked both by the Secretary and rival institutions ; without a monopoly, and yet with a capital and resources adequate for the object for which it was established ; the bank affords the strongest possible security which can be given in respect to paper, not only for its ultimate solvency, but for the uninterrupted solvency of the currency."

The manner in which the National Bank, vested with no authority over them by law, checked the issues of the State banks was very obvious and simple. It consisted of receiving the issues of all in good credit, such issues to be presently made good either by offset or in coin, proper forbearance being extended by the national as the stronger institution, but bound to protect itself, as the issues of the State banks were received by it equally with its own in the payment of the revenues. "The general complaint on the part of many of the State banks that they were controlled in their operations by the Bank of the United States, that, to use a common expression, it operates as a screw, is the best evidence that its general operation is such as has been intended." For the bank to refuse to receive on deposit or in the payment of its bills or of the public revenues the issues of any of the State banks would be to throw such discredit upon them that the public would not receive them. The effect was the same as the expulsion at the present time of a bank from the New York Clearing House. With such a menace always over them, their issues, limited to bills of exchange, could no more inflate the currency than those of the Bank of the United States.

To the assertion of General Jackson that the bank had failed in establishing a sound and uniform currency, Mr. Gallatin replied that a sound and uniform currency could be provided only through the medium of a National Bank the same in kind as that which existed.

The reply of Mr. Madison was in vindication chiefly of the constitutionality of the bank. He had been President from 1809 to 1817, for the whole period between the two banks and for that of the war, and had been witness of the terrible disasters resulting from the neglect to extend the charter of the first, and had earnestly favored and signed the bill for the second, as the only escape therefrom. He left seclusion, the solace of his declining years, to combat with all the force of his long experience, his great abilities, his fervent patriotism and unsullied name, the doctrine of anarchy now first proclaimed by a President of the United States. In a communication addressed, under date of June 25, 1831, to Mr. Charles J. Ingersoll, he said :

I have received your letter of the 18th instant. The few lines which answered your former one of the 21st of January last were written in haste and in bad health; but they expressed, though without the attention in some respects due to the occasion, a dissent from the views of the President as to the Bank of the United States and a substitute for it, to which I cannot but adhere. The objections to the latter have appeared to me to predominate greatly over the advantages expected from it, and the constitutionality of the former I still regard as sustained by the considerations to which I yielded in giving my assent to the existing bank.

Some obscurity has been thrown over the question, by confounding it with the respect due from one legislature to laws passed by preceding legislatures. But the two cases are essentially different. A constitution being derived from a superior authority is to be expounded and obeyed, not controlled or varied, by the subordinate authority of a legislature. A law, on the other hand, resting on no higher authority than that possessed by every successive legislature, its expediency as well as its meaning is within the scope of the latter.

The case in question has its true analogy in the obligation arising from judicial expositions of the law on succeeding judges; the Constitution being a law to the legislator, as the law is a rule of decision to the judge. And why are judicial precedents, when formed on due discussion and consideration, and deliberately sanctioned by reviews and repetitions, regarded as of binding influence, or rather of authoritative force, in settling the meaning of a law? It must be answered, 1st, because it is a reasonable and established axiom that the good of society requires that the rules of conduct of its members should be certain and known, which would not be the case if any judge, disregarding the decisions of his predecessors, should vary the rule of law according to his individual interpretation of it. *Misera est servitus ubi jus est aut vagum aut incognitum ;* 2d, because an exposition of the law publicly made and repeatedly confirmed by the constituted authority carries with it by fair inference the sanction of those who, having made the law, through their legislative organs, appear under such circumstances to have determined its meaning through their judiciary organ.

Can it be of less consequence that the meaning of a constitution should be fixed and known than that the meaning of a law should be so? Can, indeed, a law be fixed in its meaning and operation, unless the Constitution be so? On the contrary, if a particular legislature, differing in the construction of the Constitution from a series of preceding constructions, proceed to act on that difference, they not only introduce uncertainty and instability in the Constitution, but in the laws themselves; inasmuch as all laws preceding the new construction and inconsistent with it are not only annulled for the future, but virtually pronounced nullities from the beginning. But it is said that the legislator, having sworn to support the Constitution, must support it in his own construction of it, however different from that put on it by his predecessors, or whatever be the consequences of the construction. And is not the judge under the same oath to support the law? Yet has it ever been supposed that he was required or at liberty to disregard all precedents, however solemnly repeated and regularly observed; and, by giving effect to his own abstract and individual opinions, to disturb the established course of practice in the business of the community? Has the wisest and most conscientious judge ever scrupled to acquiesce in decisions in which he has been overruled by the mature opinions of the majority of his colleagues, and subsequently to conform himself thereto, as to the authoritative expositions of the law? And is it not reasonable that the same view of the official oath should be taken by a legislator acting under the Constitution, which is his guide, as is taken by a judge acting under the law, which is his ?

There is in fact, and in common understanding, a necessity of regarding a course of practice, as above characterized, in the light of a legal rule of interpreting a law; and there is a like necessity of considering it a constitutional rule of interpreting a constitution. . . .

It was in conformity with the view here taken of the respect due to deliberate and reiterated precedents that the Bank of the United States, though on the original question held to be unconstitutional, received my executive signature in the year 1816. The Act originally establishing a bank had undergone ample discussions in its passage through the several branches of the Government. It had been carried into execution throughout a period of twenty years, with annual legislative recognitions; in one instance, indeed, with a positive ramification of it into a new State; and with the entire acquiescence of all the local authorities, as well as of the nation at large, to all of which may be added a decreasing prospect of any change in the public opinion adverse to the constitutionality of such an institution. A veto from the Executive, under these circumstances, with an admission of the expediency and almost necessity of the measure, would have been a defiance of the obligations derived from a course of precedents amounting to the requisite evidence of the national judgment and intention.

It has been contended that the authority of precedents was in that case invalidated by the consideration that they proved only a respect for the stipulated duration of the bank with a toleration of it until the law should expire, and by the casting vote given in the Senate by the Vice-President, in the year 1811, against a bill for establishing a National Bank, the vote being expressly given on the ground of unconstitutionality. But, if the law itself was unconstitutional, the stipulation was void, and could not be constitutionally fulfilled or tolerated. And as to the negative of the Senate, by the casting vote of the presiding officer, it is a fact well understood at the time that it resulted not from an equality of opinions in that assembly on the power of Congress to establish a bank, but from a junction of those who admitted the power, but disapproved the plan, with those who denied the power. On a simple question of constitutionality, there was a decided majority in favor of it.

Mr. Madison inferred the constitutionality of the bank from long use — from precedent, the strongest argument that could be adduced, for the object of all construction is to adapt their organic law to the life of a people. It may seem strange that neither Mr. Madison nor Mr. Gallatin referred, in terms, to the authoritative decision in 1819 of the Supreme Court, affirming the constitutionality of the Act creating the bank. Both took higher ground. The construction given to the Constitution by long practice or habit expressed, so far, the life of the people. An exposition by the Supreme Court might not be in harmony with such life. It might be in violation of it. An exposition at one time might be overruled by another. It is the duty of a court to correct its own misconceptions, or the inadequacy of its former renderings. But a construction by the people long concurred in must be in such harmony with their welfare as not to be overruled. Mr. Madison and Mr. Gallatin placed themselves upon more authoritative ground — upon natural law. When the construction is by the people, the law is neither "*vagum*," nor "*incognitum;*" it is a part of their daily life. The decision of a supreme tribunal may, to the ordinary mind, be both "*vagum*" and "*incognitum.*" There is a life of society as well as individuals. It must with both be harmonious to have its highest value, or to have any value. It is the old story — the minority must submit to the will of the majority. To dissenting justices the law as laid down by the majority is their rule of conduct. So with all holding official position. Mr. Madison, as a member of Congress, earnestly opposed the charter of the first bank. His convictions, most emphatically expressed, were overruled by the popular judgment. If not over-ruled, it would have been his duty to approve the charter of the second bank. But not only were the convictions once entertained overruled, but from a sense of the value and usefulness of the first bank he earnestly recommended the creation of the second one.

On the twenty-third day of December, 1830, the House of Rep-resentatives directed a special committee of that body "to inquire into the expediency of providing by law that dollars of the new (Spanish) American governments and five-franc pieces shall be a legal tender in the payment of all debts and demands; and, also, whether any additional regulations are necessary relative to the recoinage of foreign silver coined at the mint." On the 23d of February, 1831, the committee, of which Mr. Campbell P. White, of New York, was chairman, submitted a report, from which the fol-lowing extracts are given:

In countries where gold and silver coin compose exclusively, or chiefly, the currency, it is a general and very convenient practice to use national coins. The public seal is a satisfactory evidence of their value, and the money unit and its parts, being uniformly exhibited, facilitate computation. This usual practice did not, however, obtain when our circulation was principally metallic; and the motives of convenience, which recommend an extensive issue of standard coins, cease to have influence in our present circumstances. Our currency is bank notes, to the exclusion of the precious metals, except as change. The money unit of the United States, or its concurrent tender, "Spanish milled dollars," is rarely, if ever, seen in circulation. The currency differs from that of all other nations extensively commercial, in being truly and effectively paper, secured by a specie fund, held by its issuers, the banks.

Gold and silver, whether coined or not, are viewed in the commercial world as bullion, and valued according to their quantity of fine metal. The stamp of the United States adds nothing to the value of the precious metals abroad; and, as it is a costly impression, it should only be applied when necessary to the general convenience of the community.   It is not perceived in what respect the public convenience is promoted by the coinage of silver, which passes temporarily into the vaults of the banks, and is soon afterwards again melted by refiners in foreign nations.

The director of the mint states that the American coin possessed by the Bank of the United States and its branches is less than $2,000,000, or about one-sixth part of its specie.   Assuming a similar ratio for the State banks (which is a liberal estimate, considering the advantageous position of the former institution), the entire amount of American coin held by the banks does not, likely, much exceed $4,000,000.   Taking the issues of one, two, and three dollar notes in the Eastern States as a guide, it does not seem probable that there is a greater amount of silver in general circulation, of all denominations, than $5,000,000, of which perhaps $3,000,000 or $4,000,000 are American coin.

According to this estimate, the national coins do not, likely, exceed $7,000,000 or $8,000,000 in silver.   The mint has fabricated $37,000,000, of which $9,000,-000 were of gold.   Considering that $20,000,000 of silver coins have been issued since 1817, and about $11,000,000 within the last five years, the inutility and inexpediency of extensive operations at the mint are manifest.

The silver coins of the banks should be viewed as the money of commerce, the value of which is determined by its quantity of fine metal.   This course is in accordance with sound mercantile principles, and with former usage.

Congress has repeatedly sanctioned it, by regulating the value of British, Portuguese, French, and Spanish gold, and also of five-franc pieces and crowns of France, giving them currency according to their weight when tendered, at rates calculated to minute fractions, varying with the standard of their respective mints — a course of policy which is equitable to all in its effects, and beneficial as well as accommodating to commercial operations.

If these coins were a legal tender on the principle of regulation applied to other coins noted, being current by weight, at the correct value ascertained by mint experiments (that of 116.10 cents per ounce), justice would be rendered to the importing merchant, a heavy annual expense would be saved to the United States, and banking and commercial transactions would be greatly facilitated. If our currency was metallic, public convenience might reasonably demand and properly discharge the expense of coining all silver previous to its being tendered in payments.

In conformity with these views, the committee recommend that the dollars of Mexico, Central America, Peru, Chili, and also the dollars restamped in Brazil, of the denomination of 960 reas, shall be a legal tender in all payments above the sum of $100, at the rate of 116.10 cents per ounce troy, provided the aforesaid coins shall be of the usual standard fineness of 10 ounces 15½ pennyweights of fine silver to the pound troy of 12 ounces; and that the five-franc pieces of France, of the standard of 10 ounces 16 pennyweights fine to the pound troy, shall likewise be a legal tender in all payments exceeding $100, at the rate of 116.40 cents per ounce troy.

If the total quantity of coins in general circulation be correctly estimated at

$5,000,000, the wear and necessary supply for an increasing population cannot, under our present system of money, create a yearly demand for more than $200,000 or $300,000 of new coins, in addition to the amount in circulation.

The deposit of silver bullion for five years past appears to be increasing; and its annual average being $600,000, there is no reason to doubt but the mint will be abundantly supplied with silver for every useful and desirable object.

The conclusions to which the committee came were :

1. That the operations of commerce will assuredly dispense to every country its equitable and useful proportion of the gold and silver in currency, if it is not repulsed by paper or subjected to legal restrictions.

2. That it cannot be of essential importance to any State whether its proportion of the money of commerce thus distributed consists of gold or of silver, or of both metals, it being the instrument of exchange, but not the commodity really wanted.

3. That there are inherent and incurable defects in the system which regulates the standard of value in both gold and silver: its instability as a measure of contracts, and mutability as the practical currency of a particular nation, are serious imperfections; whilst the impossibility of maintaining both metals in concurrent, simultaneous, or promiscuous circulation appears to be clearly ascertained.

4. That the standard being fixed in one metal is the nearest approach to invariableness, and precludes the necessity of further legislative interference.

5. That gold and silver will not circulate promiscuously and concurrently for similar purposes of disbursement. Nor can coins of either metal be sustained in circulation with bank notes, possessing public confidence, of the like denominations.

6. That, if the national interest or convenience should require the permanent use of gold eagles and their parts, and also of silver dollars, the issue of bank bills of one, two, three, five, and ten dollars must be prohibited.

7. That, if it should hereafter be deemed advisable to maintain both gold and silver coins in steady circulation, and to preserve silver as the measure of commerce and contracts, gold must be restricted to small payments.

8. That if it is the intention to preserve silver as the principal measure of exchange, permanently and securely, it will be necessary to estimate the relative value of gold under [below] its present average or probable future value in general commerce.

The report of the committee is important in showing, from what may be called an independent standpoint, as it was not intended as a reply to General Jackson's attack upon the bank, the condition or state of the currency at the time, whether symbolic or metallic, and of the views universally held as to the laws which regulate the value and circulation of the latter. The currency, except in the form of change, was wholly of paper, the amount of metallic money in the hands of the people not exceeding $5,000,000, or about 30 cents per head. As with an adequate provision of paper money, metallic money would not enter into circulation, the nation, the committee declared, should not be burdened with the coinage of an amount exceeding the wants of the people, that for such purpose being from $200,000 to $300,000 annually, of small coins, no silver dollars having been coined since 1808, of which, up to the date of the committee's report, only about 1,400,000 had been issued. As the value of metallic money is measured by weight, the coinage of other countries was as good as our own and as appropriate for reserves, the only use to which, on any considerable scale, it was put. At the time, foreign coins were almost the only kind in use, the value of those in the hands of the people and the banks, coming from our mint, not exceeding $7,000,000 or $8,000,000 of a total coinage, of silver, of $28,000,000. The amount of specie, all silver, in the hands of the people and the banks was about $22,000,000, the sum averaging about $1.70 per head of population. The recommendation of the committee, therefore, was well made, " that the silver dollars of Mexico, Peru, Chili, and Brazil, and the crowns and five-franc pieces of France, all of standard value, be legal tender in the United States in all contracts exceeding $100," repeating the precedent established at the foundation of the Government, for the reason, to use the words of the committee, that " the operations of commerce will assuredly disburse to every country its equitable proportion of gold and silver in currency," and without any provision of its own, — a recommendation exhaustive of the whole subject under discussion.

The report of the committee is also important in showing the probable amount of metallic money that would, with a proper system, interpose in the domestic exchanges at the present time. The amount of the loans at bank, January 1, 1830, was $200,541,214. The amount of symbolic money provided at the time equalled $116,883,826, consisting of $61,323,898 of notes and $55,559,928 of deposits. Assuming that the bills discounted ran for sixty days, the average amount daily falling due equalled $4,000,000. So small was the amount of metallic money in circulation, and so scattered was it, that no considerable amounts could be massed for any purpose whatever. It is not probable that silver, the only kind of money in circulation, and that in the form of subsidiary coins, interposing in the payment of bills exceeded 1 per cent. of their amount, or $40,000 daily. Were we now on a similar basis, it is not probable that a larger proportional amount of metallic money would be required. That a much larger amount interposes is due to the vicious monetary system which prevails. Under the two banks the loans made were almost all time-loans. The aggregate amount of issues of banks and bankers at the present time equals about $3,200,000,000. The exchanges at the Clearing House, showing the amount daily maturing at the great centres of trade, average about $200,000,000 daily, the whole amount of loans and discounts at any one time outstanding running off within a period of, say, sixteen days. The exchanges at the Clearing Houses make up the greater part of those of the country. The balances daily arising at these average about 8 per cent., or $16,000,000. Were no loans made but upon bills of exchange, it is not probable that the balances daily arising would exceed one-quarter their present amount, or $4,000,000. Banks now exercise two functions — they are lenders of capital as well as discounters of bills. The two are wholly different in kind, and should never be exercised by the same institution unless it be composed of two independent departments. A lender of capital parts with it. The capital of an issuer of currency is always to remain in hand. To part with it is to weaken his power of issue and contract the volume of currency in an equal degree. Loans of capital at bank are ordinarily demand loans liable to be called in at any moment, often requiring large sums of coin in their payment, in want of other provision. Another reason for the very large balances now daily arising at the Clearing Houses is that a greater part of the currency, that of the Government, does not represent merchandise in process of distribution, and is not discharged by its use. It is neither capital, nor the symbol of capital. Its effect, consequently, is to excite speculative operations in which large balances necessarily arise. With the retirement of such currency, and with proper restrictions upon the issues by banks, the amount daily interposing would not exceed the amount named, a much larger sum to be provided to meet demands other than those arising in the ordinary operations of commerce and trade.

The system created by Hamilton was an ideal one, as by it no issues could be made, either by the National or State Banks, except for the distribution of merchandise, there being no difference be-tween them and the bills of exchange out of which they arose, except that the former, to serve as money, were payable presently; the latter being drawn for the time necessary, in theory at least, for the movement of merchandise from producers to distributers for con-sumption; the purpose and effect of both kinds of instruments being to discharge capital from the processes of distribution, both being retired by their use, the value of each depending upon that of its constituents, merchandise, and the reserves of the issuers. So long as the issues, whether of the National or State Banks, were sym-bolic there could be no inflation of the currency, as the amount meas-ured the value of the subjects of consumption. As from their representative capacity they were to their holders the equivalent of specie, they were preferred to it as money, from the greater safety and convenience of their use. There could be no run upon the issuers for coin, as no considerable balances to be paid in it could arise either in foreign or domestic trade. Such balances arise in domestic trade only when " accommodation paper," as it is termed, is discounted; and in foreign trade only when imports exceed ex-ports of merchandise, in which case gold goes forward as the universal equivalent for their discharge.

Although the act establishing the bank provided that, during its existence, there should be no other of the kind, no monopoly of issue was or could be created, as the State Banks which already ex-isted, with the great number of new ones which speedily followed, were capable of supplying, and did supply, by far the greater part of the currency, precisely the same in kind as that issued by the National one to which the public would naturally give preference, unless the issues of the former were equally well based. The State Banks, consequently, without any provision in their charters there-for, were forced to observe the restrictions imposed upon the National one; the manner in which they were enforced having been already sufficiently described. The National Bank received the notes and credits of the State Banks, not only in the ordinary course of business, but in the payment of the public revenues. As it was responsible for these to the Government, at the value of coin, it compelled all other issuers to make good daily in coin all balances arising against them. The notes and credits of the State Banks, over which the National Government had no other control but that described, could, consequently, no more inflate the currency, could no more be in excess than those of the National Bank, all being alike the same in kind. For the further protection of the public the national institution was restricted to a rate of interest not exceeding six per cent., a rate never regarded as excessive, being less than that prescribed by many of the States to their own institutions. From the abundance of capital it was seldom that such rate could be obtained. That prescribed to the National could not be exceeded by the State Banks, as the former, like the Bank of England, held itself, with its branches established at every considerable place of trade, bound to discount all good bills that were offered. By the means described a perfect currency, the greater part of it supplied by the State Banks, was provided alike for the Government and people, specie, except in the form of subsidiary coins, being wholly discharged from ordinary use. As the bank was the custodian of the public revenues the Government was relieved of all charge of their keeping, transfer and distribution. If metallic money was wanted, either by the people or the Government, it was supplied by the bank, remittances abroad being made by its bills as the great drawer of " foreign exchange."

OVERTHROW OF THE BANK AND THE INFLATION OF THE CURRENCY.

In 1832 a bill passed both Houses of Congress for the extension of the charter, to expire in 1836, of the bank. The bill was vetoed by General Jackson. Among the reasons therefor, set forth in a message of great length, were the following :

To the extent of its practical effect, the bank is a bond of union among the banking establishments of the nation, erecting them into an interest separate from that of the people, and its necessary tendency is to unite the Bank of the United States and the State banks in any measure which may be thought conducive to their common interest.

By documents submitted to Congress at the present session, it appears that on the first of January, 1832, of the $28,000,000 of private stock in the corporation, $8,405,500 were held by foreigners, mostly of Great Britain. The amount of stock held in the nine Western and Southwestern States is $140,200, and in the four Southern States is $5,623,100, and in the Middle and Eastern States is about $13,522,000. The profits of the bank in 1831, as shown in a statement to Congress, were about $3,455,598 ; of this there accrued in the nine Western

States about $1,640,048; in the four Southern States, about $352,507; and in the Middle and Eastern States, about $1,463,041. As little stock is held in the West, it is obvious that the debt of the people in that section to the bank is principally a debt of the Eastern and foreign stockholders; that the interest they pay upon it is carried into the Eastern States and into Europe; and that it is a burden upon their industry and a drain of their currency, which no country can bear without inconvenience and occasional distress. To meet this burden and equalize the exchange operations of the bank, the amount of specie drawn from those States through its branches, within the last two years, as shown by its official reports, was about $6,000,000. More than half a million of this amount does not stop in the Eastern States, but passes on to Europe, to pay the dividends of the foreign stockholders. In the principle of taxation recognized by this act, the Western States find no adequate compensation for this perpetual burden on their industry and drain of their currency. The branch bank at Mobile made, last year, $95,140; yet, under the provisions of this act, the State of Alabama can raise no revenue from these profitable operations, because not a share of the stock is held by any of her citizens. Mississippi and Missouri are in the same condition, in relation to the branches at Natchez and St. Louis ; and such, in a greater or less degree, is the condition of every Western State. The tendency of the plan of taxation which this act proposes will be to place the whole United States in the same relation to foreign countries which the Western States now bear to the Eastern. When, by a tax on resident stockholders, the stock for this bank is made worth ten or fifteen per cent. more to foreigners than to residents, most of it will inevitably leave the country. . . .

In another of its bearings, this provision is fraught with danger. Of the twenty-five directors of this bank, five are chosen by the government and twenty by the citizen stockholders. From all voice in these elections the foreign stockholders are excluded by the charter. In proportion, therefore, as the stock is transferred to foreign holders, the extent of suffrage in the choice of directors is curtailed.

Already is almost a third of the stock in foreign hands, and not represented in elections. It is constantly passing out of the country, and this act will accelerate its departure. The entire control of the institution would necessarily fall into the hands of a few citizen stockholders; and the ease with which the object would be accomplished, would be a temptation to designing men to secure that control in their own hands, by monopolizing the remaining stock. There is danger that a president and directors would then be able to elect themselves from year to year, and, without responsibility or control, manage the whole concerns of the bank during the existence of its charter. It is easy to conceive that great evils to our country and its institutions might flow from such a concentration of power in the hands of a few men irresponsible to the people.

Is there no danger to our liberty and independence in a bank that in its nature has so little to bind it to our country? . . .

Should the stock of the bank principally pass into the hands of the subjects of a foreign country, and we should unfortunately become involved in a war with that country, what would be our condition? Of the course which would be pursued by a bank almost wholly owned by the subjects of a foreign power, and managed by those whose interests, if not affections, would run in the same direction, there can be no doubt. All its operations within would be in aid of the hostile fleets and armies without. Controlling our currency, receiving our public moneys, and holding thousands of our citizens in dependence, it would be more formidable and dangerous than the naval and military power of the enemy.

It is maintained by the advocates of the bank that its constitutionality, in all its features, ought to be considered as settled by precedent, and by the decision of the Supreme Court. To this conclusion I cannot assent. Mere precedent is a dangerous source of authority, and should not be regarded as deciding questions of constitutional power, except where the acquiescence of the people and the States can be considered as well settled.

If the opinion of the Supreme Court covered the whole ground of this act, it ought not to control the coördinate authorities of this government. The Congress, the executive, and the court must each for itself be guided by its own opinion of the Constitution. Each public officer who takes an oath to support the Constitution swears that he will support it as he understands it, and not as it is understood by others. It is as much the duty of the House of Representatives, of the Senate, and of the President to decide upon the constitutionality of any bill or resolution which may be presented to them for passage or approval, as it is of the supreme judges when it may be brought before them for judicial decision. The opinion of the judges has no more authority over Congress than the opinion of Congress has over the judges; and, on that point, the President is independent of both. The authority of the Supreme Court must not, therefore, be permitted to control the Congress or the executive when acting in their legislative capacities, but to have only such influence as the force of their reasoning may deserve. . . .

This act authorizes and encourages transfers of its stock to foreigners, and grants them an exemption from all State and national taxation. So far from being "necessary and proper" that the bank should possess this power to make it a safe and efficient agent of the government in its fiscal operations, it is calculated to convert the Bank of the United States into a foreign bank; to impoverish our people in time of peace; to disseminate a foreign influence through every section of the republic; and, in war, to endanger our independence.

General Jackson in his veto message proceeded upon the assumption that the issues of the bank were mere forms of credit, costing nothing in themselves, but for the use of which interest was charged. If its loans equalled $50,000,000, at five per cent., the profit was $2,500,000, less the trifling expense involved. A privilege so valuable, if not originally obtained by corruption, was to be maintained by corruption. As an illustration of its oppressions, "hardly a dollar of the share capital of the bank," he said, "was held in the Southern and Western States; yet from the former the bank in 1831 drew $1,640,048; from the latter, $352,507," — all pure plunder. In 1830 and 1831, specie, to the amount of $6,000,000,

for which no return was received, was, he declared, drawn from the
South and West, the greater part of it going to pay dividends on the
share capital of the bank held abroad, — "a burden that no people
could bear." As a further illustration: the profits of the branch at
Mobile, Ala., in 1831, equalled $95,148, — all sheer robbery, "not a
share of the stock of the bank being held by citizens of that State."
It was the same with the States of Mississippi and Missouri. These
charges and many others the same in kind, by their mere statement,
were held at the time to be fully proved. A mighty wave of
"populism" swept with resistless force over the nation. There
were no great commercial and manufacturing interests, so potent in
the contest just passed, capable of making headway against it. At
the time no other evidence was wanted of the robberies of the
issuers of paper money than that they lived in expensive abodes,
rode in fine carriages, and fared well; the great mass being obliged
to content themselves with humble dwellings, with walking instead of riding and with homely fare. In vain it was urged that
if Alabama and Mississippi had not a dollar of the share capital of
the bank it was for the very good reason that they had a better use
for their money; that without the capital of others their products
could not be moved and would, consequently, be worthless; that
the use of instruments of distribution, whatever the kind, always
carries with it an obligation to pay a proper consideration therefor;
that issuers of paper money could have no motive to oppress, as
their welfare was in ratio to the prosperity of the people; that, from
competition, their returns were no greater upon the capital that had
to be/ provided by way of reserves and for expenses necessarily
involved, than upon equal amounts of capital and service dedicated
to other modes of distribution, or to production; that their profits
could not be excessive, as they were all restricted in rates to six per
cent.; that they were no more a class separated from the people
than were producers of merchandise to be distributed by means of
the instruments described; that there could be no monopoly of
issue, as charters for State Banks (the great issuers) could be had
for the asking; that capital always tends to flow in the direction that
promises the best return, and that those who had most to lose from
any great convulsion or disaster would be the most earnest and self-
sacrificing in averting it. But "Down with the monster!" was
the mighty cry that came from every quarter of the land.

It is hardly necessary to refer to the absurd charge that in the event of a foreign war the share capital of the bank, being in the hands of the enemy, would be a source of danger greater than that of a hostile army thundering at our gates. All the means of the bank would be within the country, directly under the control of the government, and subject to seizure and forfeiture should the shareholders be in league with the enemy.

Precedent with a progressive people has the force of law, being the record of their habits or life as to the matters to which it relates. The purpose of all constitutional and legislative enactments is the general welfare. Common law, that of precedent, precedes constitutional and statute law, one of the great functions of judicial tribunals being to declare and give it form. It constituted the great part of the law inherited by the United States from England. It was the source of Roman Law which, having for its groundwork the sense of fitness and right, excelled all systems which preceded or followed. Not to allow precedent to ripen into law is to defeat the purpose, the general welfare of constitutional or positive law. Mr. Jefferson earnestly opposed the proposition for the first bank on the ground that its creation transcended the powers of the National Government, there being no express warrant therefor. Upon the acquisition of Louisiana he approved of the bill to establish a branch of the bank in that territory, as much an original act as the creation of the bank itself, his objections yielding to the general voice. Mr. Madison, who with Mr. Jefferson opposed the first bank, earnestly advocated the second, from a sense of its utility, declaring that precedent had overruled the objections he once held. With General Jackson the fact that the two banks had been in operation for a period of thirty-six years was no evidence of the assent thereto of the people. With him precedent could not bind the States as, in relation to the United States, they were sovereign. To deny the force of precedent in the interpretation of the Constitution and the life of the people is to deal a fatal blow to society itself, a blow which would have been delivered by General Jackson, but for the appeal to the final arbiter in affairs — the sword.

It would naturally be supposed that from such an extreme and revolutionary measure as the striking by General Jackson of the Supreme Court from our system, the people would have recoiled with horror. Instead of this, they rushed to the support of the President, North and South, with a wilder acclaim than that which followed his assault upon the bank and credit system of the country. What is the explanation of such a strange and revolutionary outburst?

At the time of General Jackson's attack upon the bank and the Supreme Court, civil liberty in the United States was on trial — to be achieved rather than already established — the great struggle being the War of the Rebellion, which, at the outset, was one for power on the part of the North and independence on that of the South. At the time the highways of the country were the old earthways, wholly inadequate to the distribution of merchandise or to intercommunication upon a large scale. The great mass of the people were agriculturists living upon their own products. Although the assault upon the bank, if successful, threatened the security of all property, the danger with the great mass seemed too remote to create alarm. Very few had ever seen a note of it, or had any relation with it. All that they could be made to see was its great wealth, contrasted with their humble means, and they were quite willing, from envy or jealousy, to see it overthrown, no matter how violent or revolutionary the process. From the slow increase of their own they were very easily made to believe that its immense possessions were unfairly acquired. The great mass were equally indifferent to the attack upon the Supreme Court, which, if successful, was certain to be followed by anarchy, from which the country could only be rescued by the strong arm of a single despot. They hardly knew any other than their own State governments which enacted their laws, protected them, and maintained social order. They saw no more danger in the attack upon a tribunal so remote as the National Judiciary than upon the National Bank. They seldom or never had the occasion to invoke the service or protection of either. They could get on as well, apparently, without one as the other. Having consciously little at stake and but a feeble conception of the basis upon which, upon the broad scale of a continent, social order must rest, they viewed with suspicion and dread a tribunal to whose mysterious power there seemed to be no limit or control, which had overthrown the legislation of States, and which some day might be directed against themselves. Under such conditions appeals of demagogues to the people, flattered as possessing every manly grace and virtue, the strength of the nation, the source of its wealth in peace, its defence from foreign aggression, but overreached and robbed by the crafty and unscrupulous few, were sure to carry the day. They will always carry the day in republics where suffrage is free, until the people, the working-classes, are conscious of having their chief stake in the maintenance of social order. At the time of General Jackson there was no such consciousness; hence the ease with which he swayed the masses at his will. Why, in the recent crisis, did not appeals as inflammatory as those of Jackson carry the day?

At the era of Jacksonism no internal commerce worthy the name existed. Earthways were the nation's highways. The railway was little other than a proposition. The telegraph, with which one may converse with another a thousand miles distant, was not even a proposition. From 1832, when the old methods still prevailed, to 1895 a mighty change had taken place. In the latter year 179,000 miles of railway were in operation, the share capital and indebtedness of which equalled $11,000,000,000; every section of the country was penetrated by them. They moved that year 750,000,000 tons of freight, having a value of $15,000,000,000, the daily movement equalling 2,500,000 tons, having a value of $50,000,000. Their earnings for the year equalled $1,100,000,000, of which $750,000,000 were paid out in their working. For this nearly 1,000,000 of picked men were employed. The merchandise moved the same year over ordinary highways, and water borne, equalled 250,000,000 tons, the aggregate for the country being 1,000,000,000 tons, having a value of $20,000,000,000. For its distribution from merchant to consumer, the provision of instruments, the issues of banks and bankers, exceeded $3,000,000,000, this sum not including the currency in its various forms issued by the United States. As may well be supposed the free and orderly movement of such a vast mass in quality and value had come to be the matter of chiefest concern. To arrest it for a single day was to arrest the movement of 3,000,000 tons, having a value of $60,000,000. In view of the momentous consequences at stake, the consternation created by the seizure by a mob of the railways and the arrest of their traffic at the great point of concentration, Chicago, can be better imagined than described. To the free and orderly movement of their vast tonnage there must not only be no disturbance, but no apprehension of disturbance at home; or abroad, as the relations of nations are now so interwoven that antagonism or collisions between any two affect to a greater or less degree the industries of all. It is from the disturbances, almost certain to be created, that all in affairs throughout the country view, always with apprehension and often with profound alarm, the ordinary meetings of Congress, as a great many of its members, having little idea of their consequences, are constantly bringing forward propositions the tendency of which is to disturb the even flow of affairs, production and distribution being arrested in ratio to the degree of apprehension created. Of this the experience of the last four years has furnished striking examples. Without any change in principle in our protective system the menace of it had the effect almost of its complete overthrow. Without a foreign war, the threat of it, which any member of the Government can make, has had very nearly the effect of an actual outbreak. The terrible disasters that have been suffered in the arrest of industries is a lesson that is not to be forgotten. So far as domestic matters are concerned it has taught us the necessity of a National Government of paramount authority throughout the length and breadth of the land which, to all in affairs, has with us come to have one purpose, and only one, the protection of property wherever it may be; its owners to have citizenship wherever they may be. It is this sense, not the Constitution, that has made us a nation. Without it, following the guidance of General Jackson, South Carolina, with no industries worthy of the name, has throughout been a free-booter in our system, as untamed to-day as she was in 1832, when she passed her first act of secession, the levying of protective duties being then the occasion; and in 1860, when she passed her second act on losing, with her associates, the control of the National Government. Now that the practical rules in affairs she is to be taught her proper place in our system, and that a very subordinate one. Social order is secured in ratio as the theoretical is subordinated to the practical. With the supremacy of the practical the widest diversities of soil, climate, production and race — elements otherwise too discordant to be reconciled — are compatible with the highest degree of social order. With adequate means of distribution, the greater the diversity of natural conditions the greater the dependence of one section upon another and the stronger the tie that holds them together. General

Jackson carried the country with him, for the reason that at the time the people, North and South, had so little at stake that the maintenance of social order threatened to cost more than it would come to.   With the means of a people, colossal in amount, and scattered far and wide, social order must be maintained at any cost.   The importance of its maintenance is greatly increased by the tendency, with ample means of distribution, of every section of the country to devote itself to that kind of industry to which by nature it is specially fitted, producing only a few articles entering into general consumption ; all others to be reached in exchange for those of its own.   The consequence is that in case of interruption of industries, carried on on a large scale workmen, trained to one specialty by means of which the best results in quality and quantity are secured, cannot, when thrown out of employment, readily engage in any other.   Interruption in the distribution of the products of their industries may suddenly bring them face to face with want.   It is far more acutely felt in commercial and manufacturing than agricultural districts, as in the latter producers may have the means of subsistence, even if they have no market for their products.   When, therefore, the revolutionary elements made their appeal to the country, the conscious community between labor and capital, for the first time fully demonstrated, rendered the recent Presidential election the event of our history.   With industrial conditions similar to those which existed in 1832 the revolutionary elements of the country combined at Chicago would have certainly carried the day.   The result showed that we had as a nation become a Timocracy, the end of which is secure possession as well as freedom of action, workingmen being intelligently massed in its support.   In republics covering a wide extent of territory, the function of their rulers prescribed by a law higher than their own being purely administrative, the only guarantee of order is a supreme and personal sense on the part of the people of its value.   Of such governments neither moralists nor jurists are necessary to proclaim the attributes.   The kind is instinctive with any one who has anything to lose.   The moral and social welfare of every people is necessarily based upon their material welfare.   Whatever increases their material well-being increases their moral well-being, and is consequently an additional guarantee of social order.   The inventor by whose processes the cost of steel was reduced from $150 to $20 the ton, the productive capacity of labor being increased somewhat in ratio to the degree of the fall in price, the gain or advantage being largely its own, made a greater contribution to good government than all the sages or jurists that ever breathed. There will be no end to political theories, but the wildest license may be safely tolerated so long as the people have enough at stake to prefer a certain present to an uncertain future. The impotence of great lawyers on the right side was strikingly illustrated in the famous debate in 1830 on what were termed the "Foot Resolutions." In it Mr. Webster won great fame and the title of the "Defender of the Constitution," giving it, as was claimed, its true scope and meaning. His speeches, eloquent and able as they were, had no more influence over the great question at issue, the supremacy of the Government of the United States in reference to those of the States, than if they had been recitations of "Mother Goose" to a band of Choctaws. His audience, the people of the North, were at the time the most incongruous, distracted and unpatriotic crew that ever breathed, having not the faintest conception of the conditions upon which, on a large scale, Government and social order must rest. A multitude of insults at last taught them that one condition at least of social order was the sword. Mr. Hayne, the great champion of the supremacy of the States in relation to the United States, and his audience were in perfect accord. He meant the destruction of the National Government unless his State could have its own way. His audience applauded to the echo. Under such teaching within two years the State of South Carolina passed her first act of secession, the occasion being the protective tariff of 1832. The North, having little compared with the enormous amount now at stake, made all haste to call back the recalcitrant member, by allowing her to dictate the terms of her return, establishing a precedent justifying to the letter the second act of secession in 1860. The War of the Rebellion after an infinite waste of life and property overthrew one of General Jackson's great assumptions that every man was to be a law for himself. Time unfortunately has only served to aggravate the evils resulting from the second measure that distinguished his administration, — the overthrow of the best monetary system ever created. After infinite waste and suffering through a period of more than two generations the currency of the Fathers still remains to be restored. Fortunately, the great task can now be entered upon with perfect assurance that social order is at last secure.

In 1830, according to Mr. Gallatin, 330 banks, including that of the United States, were in operation. Their share capital equalled $145,192,268 ; their loans and discounts $200,451,214 ; their note circulation $61,323,928 ; their deposits $55,559,928, the amount of the two, notes and deposits, equalling $116,886,856. As the veto was regarded as decisive of the fate of the bank the State banks began to increase largely their issues to fill the vacuum about to be created in the currency. Great numbers of the latter were created for the same purpose. With a large increase of issues they could still find means of making good any balances arising in favor of the National Bank. So long as this was done no note of warning was heeded.

The first returns published by Government of the operation of the banks, including that of the United States, were for the year ending December 31, 1833. The number at that date was 506 ; their share capital $200,005,944 ; their loans and discounts $325,119,499 ; their note circulation $94,834,970 ; their deposits $75,666,986. The aggregate of their notes and deposits was $170,501,956.

On the first day of January, 1837, 788 banks were in operation. Their share capital equalled $290,772,091 ; their loans and discounts $525,115,702 ; their note circulation $149,185,890 ; their deposits $127,397,185 ; their notes and deposits $276,583,075, the increase of the latter over the issues of 1834 being $106,071,119 ; over 1830, $159,646,219, the rate of increase being about 140 per cent. At a normal rate of increase the notes and deposits in the banks January 1, 1837, would have been about $160,000,-000, a sum $100,000,000 less than the actual amount. The inflation was largely in the south and south-western divisions, as shown in the following statement :

Statement showing, by divisions, the number, share capital, loans and discounts, and the notes and deposits and the aggregate of the same, for each year, of all the banks in the United States, January 1, 1830 and 1837, and the totals for each year:

DIVISIONS.	1830. No. of Banks.	1837. No. of Banks.	1830. Share Capital.	1837. Share Capital.	1830. Notes in Circulation.	1830. Deposits.	1830. Total Notes and Deposits.
Eastern......	171	314	$35,297,869	$62,172,720	$9,554,026	$4,991,339	$14,545,365
Middle	116	231	82,979,784	113,454,949	38,127,457	41,860,928	79,988,385
Southern	22	82	18,500,129	31,444,448	10,683,860	5,377,890	16,061,750
Southwestern	8	83	6,775,900	62,307,111	3,738,136	2,746,860	6,484,996
Western	13	78	1,639,386	21,392,863	1,000,000	583,610	1,583,610
Totals	330	788	$145,192,268	$290,772,091	$61,323,898	$55,559,928	$116,883,826

DIVISIONS.	1837. Notes in Circulation.	1837. Deposits.	1837. Total Notes and Deposits.	1830. Loans and Discounts.	1837. Loans and Discounts.	1837. Increase of Loans and Discounts.
Eastern........	$22,513,292	$15,505,933	$39,019,225	$40,480,651	$98,651,703	$51,571,086
Middle	56,524,339	55,342,290	111,866,629	116,836,910	211,440,794	95,203,804
Southern	28,483,170	15,182,406	43,665,576	24,978,694	62,035,190	37,356,496
Southwestern..	24,346,667	22,137,627	46,404,294	10,954,891	112,554,311	101,969,029
Western	17,318,422	19,228,928	36,547,350	1,865,678	40,438,704	38,573,026
Totals	$149,185,890	$127,397,185	$276,583,075	$200,451,214	$525,115,702	$324,564,338

The eastern division included Maine, New Hampshire, Vermont, Massachusetts, Rhode Island, and Connecticut.

The middle included New York, Pennsylvania, New Jersey, Delaware, Maryland, and the District of Columbia.

The southern included Virginia, North Carolina, South Carolina, Georgia, and Florida.

The south-western included Alabama, Louisiana, Mississippi, Arkansas, and Tennessee.

The western included Kentucky, Missouri, Illinois, Indiana, Ohio, Michigan, and Wisconsin.

The wild delirium of speculation and waste due to the vast increase of the currency, rivalled that which followed the winding up of the first bank; the cause, in both instances, being the same, — the entire withdrawal of superintendence by the National Government. It will be readily understood by those who were witnesses of the scenes which in the war of the Rebellion followed the issue of the legal tender notes of the Government.

A striking illustration of the spirit of speculation that was created was the increased purchase of the public lands. The following statement will show the number of acres sold, and the amounts received therefor, each year, from 1832 to 1838 inclusive:

Years.	Acres Sold.	Amount Received.	Years.	Acres Sold.	Amount Received.
1832	2,462,342	$3,115,376	1836	20,074,870	$25,167,833
1833	3,856,227	4,972,284	1837	5,601,103	7,007,523
1834	4,658,218	6,099,981	1838	3,414,907	4,305,564
1835	12,364,478	15,999,804			

For the years 1835 and 1836 the sum received equalled $41,167,-637, the average amount for the two years being nearly sevenfold greater than for 1832, a year of extraordinary activity in affairs. The moneys received therefor were the notes of the State banks, largely in the West. In 1836 an act was passed by Congress for the deposit of $37,267,618, the proceeds of the sales, with the States in ratio to their representation in Congress. The deposits were to be made quarterly, in four equal sums, the first to be made January 1, 1837. The withdrawal of such a vast sum from the banks, to be paid in specie or its equivalent, was one of the causes that precipitated the suspension of specie payment.

Another striking illustration of the effect of the withdrawal of the United States from all supervision of the currency was the vast increase of banks in western and south-western States. In this the State of Mississippi was conspicuous. The following statement will show the number of banks, their share capital, loans and discounts, note circulation and deposits, of the State, from January 1, 1834, to January 1, 1840, inclusive:

Years.	No. of Banks.	Share of Capital.	Loans and Discounts.	Note Circulation.	Deposits.	Specie.
1834......	1	$2,666,805	$5,461,464	$1,510,426	$545,353	$113,220
1835......	10	5,890,162	10,379,651	2,418,475	1,888,762	359,302
1836......	13	8,764,550	19,124,977	4,490,521	6,401,518	659,470
1837......	18	12,872,815	24,351,414	5,073,425	5,345,384	1,369,457
1838......	26	19,231,123	28,999,984	7,472,334	4,638,669	766,360
1839......	26	30,379,403	48,333,728	15,171,639	8,691,601	867,977

The following statement will show the extent of the banking operations in Mississippi on Jan. 1, 1840, compared with those of the States of New York, Massachusetts, and Pennsylvania:

States.	Free Population.	No. of Banks.	Share Capital.	Loans and Discounts.	Note Circulation.	Deposits.	Specie.
Mississippi ...	170,000	26	$30,379,403	$48,333,728	$15,171,639	$8,691,601	$867,977
New York ...	2,400,000	98	37,101,460	79,313,188	24,198,000	30,883,179	6,857,020
Massachusetts,	730,000	117	34,478,110	56,643,172	10,892,249	8,784,516	1,455,230
Pennsylvania,	1,700,000	49	23,750,338	44,601,930	13,749,014	12,902,250	3,113,990

The amount of loans and discounts of the banks of Mississippi equalled $285 per head of free population; their circulation, including deposits, $140 per head. Those of the banks of the State of New York equalled $30 per head; their circulation, including deposits, equalled $23 per head.

For two banks the State, by an issue of its bonds, supplied capital to the amount of $7,000,000: for the Planters, $2,000,000; for the Union, $5,000,000. In 1840 the whole system exploded; passed entirely out of existence. No trace of them thereafter is to be found in the reports of the Government. Their share capital, whatever the amount provided, was wholly wasted. Their loans were never paid. Their notes and deposits were wholly repudiated. The whole system fell a huge and rotten mass to the ground. With the failure of the Planters and Union Banks the interest on the bonds issued to provide the capital therefor ceased. The bonds were sold abroad at their full value. Failing to receive any returns, the holders naturally became importunate. They could, however, do little but remonstrate, as "Mississippi was a sovereign State." The payment of the bonds issued on account of the Union Bank was sought to be avoided on the ground of some informality in their issue. The State, however, graciously allowed the legality of the bonds to be determined by its highest judicial tribunal. That tribunal decided that the bonds were well issued, and were obligations binding on the State. But as no process could issue against a "Sovereign State," all the bondholders took in this case was a bootless decision in their favor.

The holders of the bonds issued by the Planters Bank, the regularity of the issue of which was never questioned, were equally persistent in their efforts for redress. So late as 1853 they obtained from the Legislature of the State, twelve years after default in payment of interest, an act referring the question of their payment to the people. These "rose in their majesty," to quote the language which reported their great achievement, and voted that the bonds should not be paid! Having exhausted all remedies open to them in the Legislature of the State, as well as in the courts of conscience and law, the unlucky holders of both classes of bonds, seeing nothing in store for them but continued losses and insults, slowly and sullenly retired from the contest.

From the explosion in 1840 of the banking system of Mississippi no trace of a bank appeared in that State for nearly twenty years. The people were too poor to provide the means and too dishonest to be entrusted with other people's money. In the Constitution of the State, adopted January 1, 1890, a clause was inserted providing that "No future Legislature shall assume, secure, or pay any indebtedness or pretended indebtedness alleged to be due by the State of Mississippi to any person, association, or corporation whatever, claiming the same as owner, holder or assignee of any bond or bonds now generally known as the Union Bank and Planters Bank bonds," — the first instance in history of a people emblazoning their infamy in their organic law.

The State of Ohio afforded another pertinent illustration of what was going on in nearly all the States. At the close of 1833 there were in it twenty-four banks, the share capital of which equalled $5,819,692; their circulation, $5,221,520; their deposits, $2,090,065; their loans and discounts, $9,751,973. In 1837 the number of banks had increased to thirty-two; their share capital to $9,247,-246; their circulation to $8,326,974; their deposits to $7,590,933; their loans and discounts to $18,178,699.   In 1844, the year after specie payments were fully resumed, the number of banks was reduced to eight; their share capital to $2,167,628; their note circulation to $2,246,999; their deposits to $505,430; their loans and discounts to $2,968,441.

In the want of some controlling power every western State was hatching some new system of paper money.   So late as 1852 an act was passed by the State of Indiana providing for an issue by banks upon the deposit by them of the bonds of the United States or of the several States.   The law did not require either the stockholders or directors of banks to reside within the State.   The manner in which banks were gotten up and utilized is well told by the following extract from the message, in 1853, of the Governor to the Legislature of the State :

> The speculator comes to Indianapolis with a bundle of bank-notes in one hand and the stock in the other; in twenty-four hours he is on the way to some distant point of the Union, to circulate what he denominates a legal currency authorized by the Legislature of Indiana.   He has nominally located his bank in some remote part of the State, difficult of access, where he knows no banking facilities are required, and intends that his notes shall go into the hands of persons who have no means of demanding their redemption.

As a matter of course the State bonds deposited had often little value.   In 1854, under the above Act, eighty-six banks had been established.   The returns from sixty-seven of these for that year showed a share capital of $32,900,000; a note circulation of $7,425,000.   In 1856, by the failure of banks, the share capital of those that remained equalled $4,045,325 ; their notes, which were selling all the way from 25 to 75 cents on the dollar, were reduced to $4,516,422.   In a year or two following not a trace of the new " Safety Fund System," as it was called, remained.   The history of many other States was the same in kind.

In his farewell address, of March 3, 1837, the " Banks " were, throughout, General Jackson's great theme :

> It is one of the serious evils of our present system of banking, that it enables one class of society — and that by no means a numerous one — by its control

over the currency, to act injuriously upon the interests of all the others, and to exercise more than its just proportion of influence in political affairs. . . . . .

The planter, the farmer, the mechanic, and the laborer, all know that their success depends upon their own industry and economy, and that they must not expect to become suddenly rich by the fruits of their toil. Yet these classes of society form the great body of the people of the United States ; they are the bone and sinew of the country ; men who love liberty, and desire nothing but equal rights and equal laws, and who, moreover, hold the great mass of our national wealth, although it is distributed in moderate amounts among the millions of freemen who possess it. But with overwhelming numbers and wealth on their side they are in constant danger of losing their fair influence in the government, and with difficulty maintain their just rights against the incessant efforts daily made to encroach upon them.

The mischief springs from the power which the moneyed interest derives from a paper currency which they are able to control, from the multitude of corporations with exclusive privileges, which they have succeeded in obtaining from the different States, and which are employed altogether for their benefit ; and unless you become more watchful in your States, and check this spirit of monopoly and thirst for exclusive privileges, you will, in the end, find that the most important powers of government have been given or bartered away, and the control of your dearest interests has passed into the hands of these corporations.

The paper-money system, and its natural associates, monopoly and exclusive privileges, have already struck their roots deep in the soil ; and it will require all your efforts to check its further growth, and to eradicate the evil. The men who profit by the abuses, and desire to perpetuate them, will continue to besiege the halls of legislation in the general government as well as in the States, and will seek, by every artifice, to mislead and deceive the public servants. It is to yourselves that you must look for safety, and the means of guarding and perpetuating your free institutions. In your hands is rightfully placed the sovereignty of the country, and to you every one placed in authority is ultimately responsible. It is always in your power to see that the wishes of the people are carried into faithful execution, and their will, when once made known, must sooner or later be obeyed. And while the people remain, as I trust they ever will, uncorrupted and incorruptible, and continue watchful and jealous of their rights, the government is safe, and the cause of freedom will continue to triumph over all its enemies.

But it will require steady and persevering exertions on your part to rid yourself of the iniquities and mischiefs of the paper system, and to check the spirit of monopoly and other abuses which have sprung up with it, and of which it is the main support. So many interests have united to resist all reform on this subject, that you must not hope the conflict will be a short one, nor success easy. My humble efforts have not been spared, during my administration of the government, *to restore the constitutional currency of gold and silver ; and something, I trust, has been done toward the accomplishment of this most desirable object.* But enough yet remains to require all your energy and perseverance. The power, however, is in your hands, and the remedy must and will be applied, if you determine upon it.

The preceding extracts are given not so much to be replied to as by way of illustration of the manner in which our people have been swayed by demagogues, of whom General Jackson was the conspicuous example. One form of currency was bills serving in the place of metallic money for the transfer of merchandise, *in gross*. To these certainly no objections could be raised. The notes and credits of banks issued in their discount served for its transfer from merchant to consumer. The two forms of credit discharging capital from the exchanges were precisely the same in kind. None other will ever be used in commercial countries like the United States as the ordinary instruments of exchange unless it be an imposed one of government notes, but in such case the issues of banks and bankers will equal in nominal amount the value of the subjects of consumption, the imposed one being wholly superfluous. When a bill is drawn the first step of the holder is to apply to the banks, not to the government, to turn it into money. Government is never present in such transactions as these. Its issues are made for the acquisition of capital for consumption, not primarily as instruments of distribution. There could, at the time, have been no monopoly of issue, as charters for banks were always to be had for the asking. That there was no monopoly was well shown by the fact that from 1830 to 1837 the number of banks increased from three hundred and twenty-nine to seven hundred and eighty-eight; their share capital, from $145,192,268 to $290,772,-091 ; their loans and discounts from $200,451,214 to $525,115,702 ; their notes and deposits from $116,883,826 to $276,583,075. As the veto of 1832 was conclusive of the fate of the bank its interest for the maintenance of a sound currency was of course greatly weakened. Up to 1834 the State banks were able to provide for the balances found against them. From the removal of the deposits in that year, the revenues being paid into and held by the "Pet Banks," all control over the currency from any quarter was at an end, all the banks vying with each other in the amount of their loans and issues.[1]

---

[1] "That the reader," says Parton, "may see the movements of this gentleman (Isaac Hill) as they appeared to General Jackson, and that he may fully understand the process by which the administration was brought into collision with the parent bank, I will present here a brief condensation of the papers and letters relating to the Portsmouth affair, in the order in which they were produced.

The great mission, in his own words, of General Jackson was the "restoration of the money, gold and silver, of the Constitution." The necessary effect of every step he took in his work of restoration was to drive gold and silver out of circulation and to substitute in their place vast issues of the rottenest monetary system ever created. Having accomplished the great work of his life he prayed that, "broken with the cares of the State which he had so long and faithfully served, he might at last be allowed to depart in peace."

Hardly were the words of his " Farewell Address " out of his mouth when, early in May, 1837, came the inevitable and terrible explosion, — the suspension of specie payments by all the banks, to be followed by a process of liquidation so severe that six years elapsed before the country was again fairly on its feet. The process went on until in 1843 the notes of the banks were reduced from $149,185,890 in 1837 to $58,563,608 ; their deposits from $127,397,185 to $56,116,623 ; the aggregate of the two in 1843 being $114,680,231, a sum $161,902,844 less than the aggregate for 1837, and $2,203,495 less than that for 1830. At the rate of increase, forty-five per cent., from 1820 to 1830 the amount of notes and credits of the banks

---

The correspondence began in June and ended in October. I believe myself warranted in the positive assertion, that this correspondence relating to the desired removal of Jeremiah Mason was the direct and real cause of the destruction of the bank. If the bank had been complaisant enough to remove a faithful servant, General Jackson, I am convinced, would never have opposed the rechartering of the institution." — *Life of General Jackson, by James Parton. Vol. III., page 260.*

- An earlier affront, undoubtedly, still rankled in General Jackson's bosom. " An incident," to quote further from Parton, " occurred during the stay of General Jackson at New Orleans, which was afterwards supposed to have made a lasting impression upon his mind, and to have been a remote cause of important events. He came into collision with the Bank of the United States. Desiring to take with him to Florida a sum of money, with which to defray the first expenses of organizing his government, he sent an aide-de-camp to the branch of the United States Bank at New Orleans to learn whether the bank would advance ten or fifteen thousand dollars on a draft to be drawn by General Jackson upon the Department of State. The messenger returned with the reply that the branch bank had no authority to advance money upon drafts. The mother bank, said the cashier, had expressly forbidden him to negotiate drafts. The aide-de-camp remonstrated, and pointed out the inconvenience that might result from the refusal; but the cashier was immovable, as he was bound to be." — *Ibid. Vol. II., p. 596.*

in 1837 would have equalled $152,000,000, a sum $124,000,000 less the amount of that year.[1] At the same rate of increase their notes and credits would, in 1840, have equalled $169,443,826, and in

[1] *Statement showing the Number, Amount of Share Capital, Loans and Discounts, Note Circulation, and Deposits of the Banks and Branches of the same, and the Value of Imports and Exports of the United States, from 1830 to 1845, inclusive.*

YEARS.	Number of Banks.	Share Capital.	Loans and Discounts.	Note Circulation.	Deposits.	Imports.	Exports.
1830..	330	$145,192,268	$200,451,214	$61,323,928	$55,559,928	$70,876,920	$73,849,508
1833..	506	200,005,044	365,163,834	103,692,445	83,081,365	126,521,332	104,336,973
1834..	699	231,250,337	457,506,080	140,301,038	115,104,440	140,897,742	121,693,577
1835..	713	251,875,298	525,115,702	149,185,890	127,397,185	189,980,035	128,063,046
1836..	788	290,772,091	485,631,687	116,338,910	84,691,184	140,989,217	117,419,376
1837..	829	317,635,778	492,278,015	135,170,995	90,240,146	113,717,404	108,486,616
1838..	840	327,132,512	462,896,523	106,968,572	75,696,857	162,092,132	121,028,416
1839..	860	363,629,227	386,487,662	107,290,214	64,890,101	107,141,519	132,085,946
1840..	861	313,608,959	323,957,569	83,734,011	62,408,870	127,946,177	121,851,803
1841..	784	260,171,797	254,544,937	58,563,608	56,168,628	100,162,087	104,691,534
1842..	692	228,861,948	264,905,814	75,167,646	84,550,785	86,338,398	112,461,973
1843..	691	210,872,056	288,617,131	89,608,711	88,020,646	108,435,035	111,200,146
1844..	696	206,045,969	312,114,404	105,552,427	96,913,070	117,254,564	114,654,606
1845..	707	196,894,309	311,282,945	105,519,766	91,792,533	121,691,797	113,648,622

1843, $194,944,826, a sum $80,000,000 greater than the amount then outstanding. It was not until 1851, eighteen years after the tide turned in 1843, that the notes and credits of the banks exceeded the aggregate for 1837, the amount for 1851 being $284,122,883, of which $155,165,281 were notes, and $128,-957,602 were deposits. The country was in a far worse condition in 1843 than in 1830. For thirteen years instead of progress there was a steady retrocession, not only in its material but in its moral welfare, a strange spectacle for the "Model Republic." The disasters from the occupation and ravage of every section of the country by a foreign foe could not have exceeded those which resulted from Jackson's experiment for the "restoration of the money of the Constitution." Strange to say, the author of the disasters described has always remained the idol of the nation to the undoing of which, as far as was possible, he was the chief instrument, for the War of the Rebellion, as well as the worst currency possible, of debt instead of capital, with all the terrible calamities which followed, were the direct result of the overthrow by him of the authority of the Supreme Court, which, instead of a loose confederacy, dissolvable upon the motion of any member, had declared us to be a nation, competent to deal with all matters that concerned its existence, as well as the common welfare.

The preceding statements, so far as the bank is concerned, are compiled from the reports of the department of the Treasury, entitled "State Banks of the United States." After 1837 returns appear to have been made by great numbers of banks which had discontinued business, years being required to wind up their affairs. The great disaster of 1837 by no means put an end, as has been shown, to the creation of new banks, mostly of small capital, in the rural districts.

In 1841 a bill passed both houses of Congress for the creation of a third National Bank. It was vetoed by Mr. Tyler, a pronounced "States' rights" man, whom the Whigs, for the purpose of uniting all elements in opposition to Mr. Van Buren, had nominated for the vice-presidency, and who became president upon the death of General Harrison. From its defeat no other proposition for any National Bank was ever made.

Mr. Van Buren, who, March 4, 1837, succeeded General Jackson in the presidency, pledged to walk in his footsteps, was, up to the great explosion, as unconscious as his illustrious predecessor of the volcano beneath his feet. He woke up one morning, to use the language of Mr. Benton, "with large balances on its books in favor of the Government, but without the means of paying a day's wages to the meanest official in its service," except in the notes of the broken State Banks. An issue of treasury notes to tide over the immediate necessities of the government was made with all speed. The next and obvious step would have been the restoration, following the example of 1816, of the currency by the creation of a third National Bank. That it was not taken was due to the fact that in the period which had elapsed from the creation of the Second Bank the South had learned a new lesson, that she was being rapidly outstripped by the North in numbers and wealth from the exercise by Congress of implied powers, the most obvious example being legislation for the encouragement of domestic industries in which, from the ignorance and poverty of her people, she could not engage. The North cheerfully paid protective duties, domestic markets being thereby created for her products. To the South, which had no industries to protect, the duties levied were taxes imposed upon one section of the country for the benefit of another, and, consequently, unconstitutional, there being no direct warrant therefor. By a necessary inference an act, being the exercise of implicit powers, for the creation of the bank was unconstitutional. Every exercise of implied powers was unconstitutional, as it inured to the benefit of one section at the expense of another. If a state or political body was competent to declare the meaning of the Constitution it was competent to enforce its meaning. Such was the objection to implied powers, their exercise being unconstitutional, to be resisted by force by those assumed to be injured by them. But where were the North and East when a construction of the Constitution, so destructive to their welfare, was established as the law of the land? — Sold out to South Carolina and her sister States, immunity for their peculiar institution being the consideration on one side, and official stations and public plunder to the contingent of northern mercenaries ever ready to assail the Government and social order for a mess of pottage, on the other. The very elements and conditions upon which a government worthy the name must rest for support were overthrown, our own being reduced to a condition of complete imbecility.

Jackson taught the doctrine that each individual was to determine for himself the meaning of the Constitution. As was inevitable his construction speedily became the publicly pronounced creed of the party, the first regular National Democratic Convention ever held, which nominated Mr. Van Buren for his second term, resolving that :

> Congress has no power to charter a United States Bank; that we believe such an institution one of deadly hostility to the best interests of the country, dangerous to our Republican institutions and the liberties of the people, and calculated to place the business of the country within the control of a *concentrated* money power, and above the laws and the will of the people.

This resolution was followed by another, directed against the exercise of implied powers :

> The Federal Government is one of "*limited powers*," derived solely from the Constitution, and the grants of power shown therein ought to be strictly construed by all the departments and agents of the Government, and that it is inexpedient and dangerous to exercise doubtful constitutional powers.

Mr. Van Buren, in his reply to the communication informing him of his nomination, accepted unreservedly every resolution in the platform, adding that :

> Thomas Jefferson has taught us, that to preserve that common sympathy between the States, *out of which the Union sprang*, and which constitutes its surest foundation, we should exercise the powers which of right belong to the general government in a spirit of moderation and brotherly love, and religiously abstain from such as have not been delegated by the Constitution.

The Constitution provided that " the Supreme Court of the United States shall have jurisdiction in all matters of law and equity arising under it." That august tribunal, in 1819, declared, in the celebrated case of McCullough, against the State of Maryland, that the National Government sprang from the people, not from the States, and that it was one of unlimited powers as to everything that came within its scope, the creation of a bank by the exercise of implied powers being an illustration.[1] In both of these assumptions, that tribunal

---

[1] The decision of the Supreme Court to which General Jackson referred was that of McCulloch against the State of Maryland. In 1818 that State passed an act for taxing the assets and operations of the Baltimore branch of the bank. In a suit in her behalf in her own courts judgment was rendered in her favor. The position taken was that the State, being sovereign, could levy

was overruled by a political party, by declarations repeated thereafter by every national gathering down to and including the nomination of Mr. Buchanan for the presidency.

---

taxes on all persons and property in its domain.   By a writ of error taken out by James W. McCulloch, cashier of the bank, the case was taken to the Supreme Court of the United States, which reversed the decision of the State courts, and ordered judgment therein to be entered for the bank.   In his argument Chief-Justice Marshall, who delivered that opinion, in which all the judiciary concurred, said:

" In the case now to be determined, the defendant, a sovereign State, denies the obligation of a law enacted by the Legislature of the Union, and the plaintiff, on his part, contests the validity of an act which has been passed by the Legislature of that State.   The Constitution of our country, in its most interesting and vital part, is to be considered; the conflicting powers of the Government of the Union and of its members, as marked by that Constitution, are to be discussed, and an opinion given which may essentially influence the great operations of the Government.   No tribunal can approach such a question without a deep sense of its importance, and of the awful responsibility involved in its decision.   But it must be decided peacefully, or remain a source of hostile legislation, perhaps of hostility of a still more serious nature; and if it is to be so decided, by this tribunal alone can the decision be made.   On the Supreme Court of the United States has the Constitution of our country devolved this important duty.

" The first question made in the cause is — Has Congress power to incorporate a bank?

" It has been truly said that this can scarcely be considered as an open question, entirely unprejudiced by the former proceedings of the nation respecting it.   The principle now contested was introduced at a very early period of our history, has been recognized by many successive Legislatures, and has been acted upon by the Judicial Department, in cases of peculiar delicacy, *as a law of undoubted obligation.   .   .   .*

" The power now contested was exercised by the first Congress elected under the present Constitution.   The bill for incorporating the Bank of the United States did not steal upon an unsuspecting Legislature, and pass unobserved.   Its principle was completely understood, and was opposed with equal zeal and ability. After being resisted, first in the fair and open field of debate, and afterwards in the executive Cabinet, with as much persevering talent as any measure has ever experienced, and being supported by arguments which convinced minds as pure and as intelligent as this country can boast, it became a law.   The original act was permitted to expire ; but a short experience of the embarrassments to which the refusal to revive it exposed the Government convinced those who were most prejudiced against the measure of its necessity, and induced the passage of the present law.   It would require no ordinary share of intrepidity to assert that a measure adopted under these circumstances was a bold and plain usurpation to which the Constitution gave no countenance.   .   .   .

" In discussing this question, the counsel for the State of Maryland have deemed

The preceding resolutions were followed at subsequent conventions by others, in order to make their meaning more explicit and

---

it of some importance, in the construction of the Constitution, to consider that instrument *not as emanating from the people, but as the act of the Sovereign and Independent States. The powers of the General Government, it has been said, are delegated by the States, who alone are truly sovereign ; and must be exercised in subordination to the States, who alone possess supreme dominion.*

" It would be difficult to sustain this proposition. The Convention which framed the Constitution was indeed elected by the State Legislatures. But the instrument, when it came from their hands, was a mere proposal, without obligation, or pretensions to it. It was reported to the then existing Congress of the United States, with a request that it might ' be submitted to a Convention of delegates, chosen in each State by the people thereof, under the recommendation of its Legislatures, for their assent and ratification.' This mode of proceeding was adopted ; and by the Convention, by Congress, and by the State Legislatures, the instrument was submitted to the people. They acted upon it in the only manner in which they can act safely, effectively, and wisely on such a subject — by assembling in convention. It is true they assembled in their several States — and where else could they have assembled ? No political dreamer was ever wild enough to think of breaking down the lines which separate the States, and of compounding the American people into one common mass. Of consequence, when they act, they act in their States. But the measures they adopt do not, on that account, cease to be the measures of the people themselves, or become the measures of the State Governments. From these conventions the Constitution derives its whole authority. *The Government proceeds directly from the people ;* is ordained and established in the name of the people ; and is declared to be ordained ' in order to form a more perfect union, establish justice, ensure domestic tranquillity, and secure the blessings of liberty to themselves and their posterity.' The assent of the States in their sovereign capacity is implied in calling a Convention, and thus submitting that instrument to the people. But the people were at perfect liberty to accept or reject it; and their act was final. It required not the affirmance, and could not be negatived by the State Governments. The Constitution, when thus adopted, was of complete obligation, *and bound the State Sovereignties.*"

The judgment of the Court was as follows :

This cause came on to be heard on the transcript of the record of the Court of Appeals of the State of Maryland, and was argued by counsel. On consideration whereof, it is the opinion of this Court that the act of the Legislature of Maryland is contrary to the Constitution of the United States, and void ; and, therefore, that the said Court of Appeals of the State of Maryland erred in affirming the judgment of the Baltimore County Court, in which judgment was rendered against James W. M'Culloch; but that the said Court of Appeals of Maryland ought to have reversed the said judgment of the said Baltimore County Court, and ought to have given judgment for the said appellant, M'Culloch. It is plain. The climax was reached in 1852, when Franklin Pierce was nominated for the presidency, by one which declared that :

> The Democratic party will faithfully abide by and uphold the principles laid down in the Kentucky and Virginia resolutions of 1798 and 1799, and in the report of Mr. Madison to the Virginia Legislature in 1799, that it adopts those principles as *constituting one of the main foundations of its political creed, and is resolved to carry them out in their obvious meaning and import.*

The Virginia and Kentucky resolutions, drawn by Mr. Jefferson, among other things, recited that :

> The several States who formed the Constitution, being sovereign and independent, have an unquestionable right to judge of the infraction; and that a *nullification* by these sovereignties of all unauthorized acts done under color of that instrument is the rightful remedy.

---

therefore adjudged and ordered that the said judgment of the said Court of Appeals of the State of Maryland, in this case, be, and the same hereby is, reversed and annulled. And this Court, proceeding to render such judgment as the said Court of Appeals should have rendered, it is hereby adjudged and ordered that the judgment of the Baltimore County Court be reversed and annulled, and that judgment be entered in the said Baltimore County Court for the said James W. M'Culloch.

Power is sublime when without lictors or bayonets it executes its decrees. That displayed by the Supreme Court of the United States in bidding a proud State to humbly register its commands has but one example in history, that related by Montaigne in his Essay, " Of the Roman Grandeur " : " Antiochus possessed all Egypt and was about conquering Cyprus and other appendages of the Empire. Being upon the progress of his victories, C. Popilius, almost unattended, came to him from the Senate, and at their first meeting refused to take him by the hand till he had first read the letters he brought him. The king having read them told him he would consider of them, but Popilius made a circumference about him with the wand he had in his hand, saying, ' Return me an answer, that I may carry back to the Senate, before thou stirrest out of this circle.' Antiochus, astonished at the roughness of so positive a command, after a little pause replied, ' I will obey the Senate's command,' renouncing so great a monarchy, and such a torrent of successful fortune, upon three scratches of the pen."

The logical sequence was the secession of the South in 1860; an act perfectly legal and proper according to all the precedents and doctrines of the Democracy.

The situation stated, Mr. Van Buren, in his message to Congress, September 4, 1837, made the astounding announcement that the people had long called for a separation of the fiscal operations of the Government from those of the people, demanding the creation of an "Independent Treasury," into which, for the use of the Government, nothing but gold and silver was to enter, — the people as a class lower and distinct from their officials being left to take care of themselves.   The suggestion came from the dilemma in which the Government found itself.   The National Bank was destroyed.   Jackson's substitute for it, — the State Banks, — which he declared had discharged the duties assigned to them in a manner far more satisfactory than similar ones had been discharged by the national one, — had proved themselves to be utterly incompetent to serve as the fiscal agents of the Government.   The people were wholly committed to the use of paper money, good or bad, no matter which.   The Government, cut off from the bank which had supplied all its wants, had to draw metallic money, — the only kind that could go into the "Independent Treasury," — directly from the people.   So far as it alone was concerned the change by it from a paper to a metallic currency did not seem to work great inconvenience; its operations being then on a scale so small that a few million dollars, which could be readily provided, sufficed.   When from $100,000, the expenses of the Government in the great rebellion rose to $2,500,000 daily, the return by it to a paper currency, from the impossibility of procuring specie, was inevitable; and as no return was to be made to a symbolic currency, — that is to one of banks over which it could constitutionally exercise control, one of its own notes was the only alternative.   The necessary result was that the cost of the war from the depreciation of the Government notes, all its obligations being finally made payable in gold, was more than doubled; the war itself being greatly prolonged from the demoralization necessarily resulting from the floods of paper money which, costing nothing, was poured out almost for the asking. The precedent established, we committed, in a period of profound peace, the incredible folly of increasing an issue of Government notes, until the amount is now much greater than that reached at any time during the war; some 500,000,000 having been issued since the Government, in 1878, undertook the resumption of specie payments. A Government may well issue notes, not legal tender, in anticipation of the revenues and payable in them, the amount not to exceed the demand for such purpose, such currency being symbolic, the incoming dues being its constituent. Such notes, like "Exchequer Bills," usually bearing a low rate of interest, have not unfrequently been resorted to by our own Government, and are very proper expedients, as a corresponding amount of specie, or the money of banks, are discharged from its operations. It is probable that an issue of, say, $50,000,000, the incoming revenues equalling $1,500,000 daily, would, to those indebted to the Government, have a value equal, or nearly equal, to that of coin. Such notes are not money in any sense, as they are not in terms, or in fact, payable in the universal equivalent, the necessary attribute of all kinds of paper money properly issued. Notes issued in the anticipation of the revenues have no tendency to inflate the currency, as they have a specific function, do not enter into general circulation, and are retired by their use. No greater wrong can be committed by a Government than an issue by it of its notes, forms of debt to serve as money. The temptation is always great as the notes are welcomed by all classes, every one seeming to be enriched in ratio to their amount, no distrust at the outset being felt, as the whole means of the people is assumed to be pledged therefor. As their issue sets everything in motion, their retirement involves a contraction of all the operations of society in ratio to the amount of their issue. When issued in vast amounts relative to the means of a people the penalty exacted for their retirement is often too great to be paid, and they are usually repudiated, or retired only with a very meagre provision for their discharge.

In 1840 the "Independent Treasury" was established, the act being repealed the following year, the "Whigs" having achieved a momentary triumph. It was finally established in 1846 under the administration of Mr. Polk. At the time the abandonment by the Government of the money of banks — of commerce, for coin, did not work great inconvenience. The danger was to come when, from its enormously increased expenditures, metallic money would not suffice for its wants, the alternative being an issue of its own notes to reserve as money, precisely that adopted in the War of the Rebellion.

CHANGE OF STANDARDS.   ACTS OF 1834 AND 1837.

By the act of June 28, 1834, the weight of the gold eagle, no provision having been yet made for the coinage of the gold dollar, was changed from 270 to 258 grains, its fineness from 916⅔ to 899.225.   By the Act of January 18, 1837, the fineness was changed to 900.   The value of the gold dollar authorized by the Act of March 3, 1849, corresponded to that of the eagle.   By the reduction in the value of the gold coins, no change being made in those of silver, the coin ratio between the two metals was changed from 15 to 16 to 1.   The purpose of the acts was the substitution of gold as the standard money of the country in the place of silver which had previously been the standard in use serving as the reserves of banks.   The change was called for by the increased transactions of the country, gold, from its higher relative value, having become the more convenient money.   By the change gold was undervalued about 3 per cent.   The substitution of gold for silver as the money of the country was one of the most important measures of General Jackson's administration, and received his earnest support as well as that of the public, not a voice being raised in opposition.   It had the approval which every improved method or process in affairs is certain to receive.

DEBASEMENT OF THE SILVER CURRENCY.   ACT OF 1853.

By the ratio established in 1837, the bullion value of silver coins for a series of years exceeded their coin value, the excess at times equalling 4½ per cent.   In consequence silver coins of all denominations were taken for export to such an extent as to be a source of very great inconvenience.   For the purpose of remedying the evil Mr. Corwin, Secretary of the Treasury, in his annual report for 1852, called the attention of Congress to the matter.   He said :

So soon as the state of our foreign commerce, as is now the case, requires the exportation of specie, it is obvious that our silver coin must be exported so long as it can be had.   There seems to be but one immediate and direct remedy for this evil, and that is the one that has already been adopted in Great Britain, of changing the relative value of gold and silver coin by reducing the intrinsic value of the latter.   This could be advantageously done by making the silver dollar weigh 384, in the place of 412½ standard grains, and the smaller coins in proportion.   If such a scale of weights were adopted, the relation of silver in such pieces to gold would be as 14.884 to 1.   This plan, if adopted by Congress, will, of course, involve the necessity of making silver coin a legal tender only for debts of small amounts, not, say, exceeding ten dollars, which is about the same limit, forty shillings, which has been established in England.

Pursuant to this suggestion, Congress, by an Act of February 21, 1853, reduced the weight of silver in the half-dollar from 206.25 to 192 standard grains, and in the smaller coins in like ratio, such coins to be legal tender in the payment of debts not exceeding five dollars. No reduction was made at the time in the weight of the silver dollar, for the reason, to use the words of Mr. Hunter of Virginia, Chairman of the Committee on Finance of the Senate, "that the great measure of adjusting the legal tender ratio between gold and silver as *legal tender* in unlimited amounts cannot be safely attempted until some permanent relation in the value of the two metals shall be established," the discovery of gold in California a few years previous having disturbed largely the commercial ratio which had prevailed between the two metals. The excess in 1852 in value of a dollar in silver over one in gold was 2.57 per cent.; in 1853, 4.26 per cent. Congress could well postpone action upon the matter of the silver dollar as there was none in circulation, nor had any been in circulation from the foundation of the Government. The total coinage up to 1806, when it was stopped by order of the President as involving a needless outlay of the public money, all such coins being exported as fast as they came from the mint, equalled $1,439,517. In reporting the bill to the House, Mr. Dunham, of Indiana, a Western man, Chairman of the Committee of Ways and Means, among other things, said :

An objection to this proposed change (*i.e.*, the reduction of the weight of the minor coins) is that it gives us a standard of currency of gold only. What advantage is to be obtained by a standard of the two metals, which is not as well, if not much better, attained by a single standard, I am unable to perceive. . . . Wherever the experiment of a standard of a single metal has been tried, it has proved eminently successful. *Indeed, it is utterly impossible that you should long at a time maintain a double standard.* . . . Gentlemen talk about a double standard of gold and silver as a thing that exists, and that we propose to change. That has been, and now is, gold. We propose to let it remain so, and to adapt silver to it, to regulate it by it.

Up to and including 1853 the total coinage of silver dollars equalled $2,506,890; of subsidiary silver, $66,716,481; of gold,

$276,169,529. By the Act of 1853 the country was put wholly upon a gold basis, the coinage of silver dollars having been practically abandoned, the minor coins being too debased in value for export.

CONSEQUENCES RESULTING FROM THE ABANDONMENT BY THE GOVERNMENT OF OVERSIGHT OF THE CURRENCY.

In the long period from 1829 to 1860 there were but two apparent breaks in the tule of the Democracy, the first made by the election of General Harrison in 1841, to the presidency, which was without result, as his death almost immediately followed his inauguration. Mr. Tyler, of Virginia, a prominent advocate of States' rights, and of a strict constructionist, became president. The Democracy was defeated in 1848 in the contest for the presidency, but held both branches of the national Legislature, so that its control may be said to have been unbroken through a period of thirty years. The result of its rule, during this long period, was drawn in striking colors by Mr. Buchanan in his annual message for 1857:

We have possessed all the elements of material wealth in rich abundance, and yet, notwithstanding all these advantages, our country, in its monetary interests, is at the present moment in a deplorable condition. In the midst of unsurpassed plenty in all the productions of agriculture, and in all the elements of national wealth, we find our manufactures suspended, our public works retarded, our private enterprises of different kinds abandoned, and thousands of useful laborers thrown out of employment and reduced to want. The revenue of the Government, which is chiefly derived from duties on imports from abroad, has been greatly reduced, whilst the appropriations made by Congress at its last session for the current fiscal year are very large in amount.

Under these circumstances a loan may be required before the close of your present session; but this, although deeply to be regretted, would prove to be only a slight misfortune *when compared with the suffering and distress prevailing among the people*. With this the Government cannot fail deeply to sympathize, *though it may be without the power to extend relief*.

It is our duty to inquire what has produced such unfortunate results, and whether their recurrence can be prevented. In all former revulsions the blame might have been fairly attributed to a variety of coöperating causes; but not so upon the present occasion. It is apparent that our existing misfortunes have proceeded solely from our extravagant and vicious system of paper currency and bank credits, exciting the people to wild speculations and gambling in stocks. These revulsions must continue to recur at successive intervals so long as the amount of the paper currency and bank loans and discounts of the country shall be left to the discretion of *fourteen hundred irresponsible banking institutions*, which, from the very law of their nature, will consult the interest of their stock-holders rather than the public welfare.

The framers of the Constitution, when they gave to Congress the power to coin money and regulate the value thereof, and prohibited the States from coining money, emitting bills of credit, or making anything but gold and silver coin a tender in payment of debts, supposed they had protected the people against the evils of an excessive and irredeemable paper currency. They are not responsible for the existing anomaly that a government endowed with the sovereign attribute of coining money and regulating the value thereof *should have no power to prevent others from driving this coin out of the country and filling up the channels of circulation with paper which does not represent gold and silver*

It is one of the highest and most responsible duties of government to insure to the people a sound circulating medium, the amount of which ought to be adapted with the utmost possible wisdom and skill to the wants of internal trade and foreign exchanges. If this be either greatly above or greatly below the proper standard, the marketable value of every man's property is increased or diminished in the same proportion, and injustice to individuals as well as incalculable evils to the community are the consequence.

Unfortunately, under the construction of the Federal Constitution, which has now prevailed too long to be changed, this important and delicate duty has been dissevered from the coining power, and virtually transferred to more than fourteen hundred State banks, acting independently of each other, and regulating their paper issues almost exclusively by a regard to the present interest of their stockholders. Exercising the sovereign power of providing a paper currency instead of coin for the country, the first duty which these banks owe to the public is to keep in their vaults a sufficient amount of gold and silver to insure the convertibility of their notes into coin at all times and under all circumstances. . . . In a recent report made by the Treasury Department, on the condition of the banks throughout the different States, according to returns dated nearest to January, 1857, the aggregate amount of actual specie in their vaults is $58,349,838, of their circulation $214,778,822, and of their deposits $230,351,352. Thus it appears that these banks, in the aggregate, have considerably less than one dollar in seven of gold and silver, compared with their circulation and deposits. It was palpable, therefore, that the very first pressure must drive them to suspension, and deprive the people of a convertible currency, with all its disastrous consequences.

From this statement it is easy to account for our financial history for the last forty years. It has been a history of *extravagant expansions in the business of the country, followed by ruinous contractions.* At successive intervals the best and most enterprising men have been tempted to their ruin by excessive bank loans of mere paper credit, exciting them to extravagant importations of foreign goods, wild speculations, and ruinous and demoralizing stock gambling. When the crisis arrives, as arrive it must, the banks can extend no relief to the people. In a vain struggle to redeem their liabilities in specie, they are compelled to contract their loans and their issues; and, at last, in the hour of distress, when their assistance is most needed, they and their debtors together sink into insolvency.

It is this paper system of extravagant expansion, raising the nominal price of every article far beyond its real value, when compared with the cost of similar articles in countries whose circulation is wisely regulated, which has prevented us from competing in our own markets with foreign manufacturers, has produced extravagant importations, and has counteracted the effect of the large incidental protection afforded to our domestic manufactures by the present *revenue* tariff.

In the meantime, it is the duty of the Government, by all proper means within its power, to aid in alleviating the sufferings of the people occasioned by the suspension of the banks, and to provide against a recurrence of the same calamity. *Unfortunately, in either aspect of the case, it can do but little.* . . . Long experience has deeply convinced me that a strict construction of the powers granted Congress is the only true, as well as only safe, theory of the Constitution.

Here is a graphic picture of the condition of the country from the advent, with Jackson, of the Democracy, to its overthrow in 1860. It was the picture of a people wholly incapable of applying the most obvious remedy to the greatest of evils — a disordered currency. "In the midst of unsurpassed plenty in all the productions of agriculture and all the elements of national wealth, we find," said Mr. Buchannan, "our manufactures suspended, our public works retarded, our private enterprises abandoned, thousands of useful laborers thrown out of employment and reduced to want; the revenues of the Government greatly reduced, to be made good only by a loan before the close of the present session; such loan being only a slight misfortune compared with the suffering and distress prevailing among the people. With this distress the Government cannot fail to sympathize, though it may not be in its power to afford relief."

Why, in the midst of boundless elements of wealth and in a period of profound peace, was it possible that such a terrible picture could be drawn? For the reason that "the currency was left to the discretion of 1,400 banking institutions. . . . The framers of the Constitutions are not responsible for the anomaly that a Government, endowed with sovereign attributes for coining money and regulating the value thereof, should have no power to prevent others from driving this money out of the channels of circulation with paper that does not represent gold and silver." Of course not. They addressed themselves, like men of sense, not as the servile tools of an exacting and relentless slave-holding oligarchy, to a practical matter, to be determined upon its own merits, not upon abstract considerations of government. From their experience of the past, one of the first measures of the "framers of the Constitution," who dominated wholly the first Congress, was the provision of a system under which, no matter the amount, paper money, whether issued by State or National Banks, could not only have no tendency to drive silver and gold out of the country, but, on the contrary, had a direct tendency to attract them from other countries to supply the reserves of the issuers of paper money to be increased in ratio to the increased transactions and prosperity of our people. Had a picture been drawn of the condition of our country for twenty years following the foundation of our Government it would havē been ǫne of unsurpassed prosperity and contentment, the people turning to the best account their boundless resources ; the chief instruments therefor being a currency which, under the supervision of the Government, not only discharged coin from the exchanges, but which was always at the value of coin. For the brief period between the two banks the picture drawn by Mr. Buchanan would have been true to the letter, the currency being wholly committed to a vast number of banks over which the Government had no control. Of the condition of the country following the creation of the second bank, after the situation was restored, the picture, drawn by Gallatin, and by Committees of both Houses of Congress, one of universal contentment and prosperity, has been given. The moment that the National Government discharged itself of one of the most important duties of sovereignty the supervision of the currency all was changed. "Congress was clothed," said Mr. Buchanan, "with the attribute of coining money and regulating the value thereof ; " but it was a power which could be defeated by issuers of currency responsible only to themselves. An attribute that cannot be enforced is not sovereign. In the matter of the currency the banks alone were clothed with sovereign power.

Under the rule of Mr. Buchanan, not only was Government discharged of all power over the currency, by which the purpose of the attribute of " coining money and regulating the value thereof " was wholly defeated, but it was discharged of every attribute necessary to its own existence. From the nomination of Jackson for a second term, by the adoption, always repeated, by the nominating conventions of the " Two-thirds rule," no Democrat could hope to reach the presidency unless he personally pledged himself to oppose no obstacle to the withdrawal of any State from the " Confederacy," the term applied by the States' rights party to the National Government. General Jackson declared that the meaning of the Constitution was a matter for every one one living under it. By the National Conventions which followed his doctrines were definitely formulated.

The result was that, at the close of Mr. Buchanan's administration, the National Government existed by sufferance alone. To attacks from within it could oppose no resistance whatever. All life, or purpose, or power of self-defence was at an end. When near its close the Southern States were seceding in a body, he declared that, while they had no right to go, no force could be opposed to their going. It will be always so with a party that draws its inspiration from the lowest elements of which it is composed. The Democracy, under General Jackson, came into possession of a vast and goodly estate, which was wholly wasted at the end of thirty years. But for the new life that came with the great uprising of the North, our boasted Republic would have come to an end. From the experience of the past no wonder the terror that seized the nation when it seemed possible that at the recent election, the Democracy, in which for the moment were combined all the revolutionary elements of the country, might again carry the day.

If it be objected that politics have no place in a treatise on money, it may be replied that the construction of the Constitution under General Jackson turned wholly upon the question whether the Government of the United States was competent to exercise supervision over the money of the country in ordinary use. He denied that it possessed such power in the face of its exercise for forty years by the establishment of two banks, sustained by the authority of Jefferson and Madison, and of the Supreme Court of the United States, the tribunal created by the Constitution to determine the validity of all matters in law and equity arising under it. It was the turning point in the history of the country, leading directly to the secession of the Southern States and the war of the Rebellion. For nearly seventy years the currency has been the great political question of the country, and never more so than at the present moment. There have since the war of Independence been but two great subjects of history in the United States — the Currency and the war of the Rebellion. The former is by far the most important, as it shows how the war arose, the events of the latter being of little consequence except in their bearing upon the restoration of the supremacy of the National Government in its relation to that of the States. To regain the ground occupied by the Fathers we must learn how we have wandered so far, and restore the system they established by showing how foully it was overthrown.

UNITED STATES NOTES.

No sooner was it seen that the war of the Rebellion was to be a life and death struggle between the two sections of the country than the chief care of the Government, now for the first time for thirty years wholly in the hands of the North, was provision of the means for its prosecution. For this purpose Mr. S. P. Chase, Secretary of the Treasury, on the 9th of August, 1861, met in conference a large number of citizens of New York, at the house of the Assistant Treasurer, J. J. Cisco, in that city. Of that meeting and the results that followed, Mr. George S. Coe, then President of the American Exchange Bank in New York, gave the following account :

After the disastrous battle of Bull Run, and when Washington was closely beleaguered, and the avenue thence to New York through Baltimore was intercepted by the enemy, Mr. Chase, then Secretary of the Treasury, came to this city *via* Annapolis, and immediately invited all persons in this community who were supposed to possess or control capital to meet him on the evening of August 9th, at the house of John J. Cisco, Esq., then Assistant Treasurer of the United States in New York. This invitation drew together a large number of gentlemen of various occupations and circumstances. During the discussion which ensued I suggested the practicability of uniting the Banks of the North by some organization that would combine them into an efficient and inseparable body, for the purpose of advancing the capital of the country upon government bonds in large amounts ; and, through their clearing-house facilities and other well-known expedients, to distribute them in smaller sums among the people in a manner that would secure active co-operation among the members in this special work, while in all other respects each Bank could pursue its independent business. This suggestion met the hearty approbation of the assembled company, and arrested the earnest attention of the Secretary. At his request, it was presented to the consideration of the Banks, at a meeting called for that purpose at the American Exchange Bank on the following day ; and was so far entertained as to secure the appointment of a Committee of ten bank officers, to give it form and coherence. The Committee convened at the Bank of Commerce, whose officers zealously united in the effort, and a plan was reported unanimously. Their report was cordially accepted and adopted by the Banks in New York ; those in Boston and Philadelphia being represented at the meeting, and as zealously and cordially united in the organization. . . .

It was at once unanimously agreed that the Associated Banks of the three cities would take fifty millions of 7-3 notes at par, with the privilege of an additional fifty millions in sixty days, and a further amount of fifty millions in sixty days more, making one hundred and fifty millions in all, and offer them for sale to the people of the country at the same price, without charge. In this great undertaking, the Banks of New York assumed more than their relative proportion. To insure full co-operation and success, the expedient of issuing clearing-house certificates, and of appropriating and averaging all the coin in.the various Banks as a common fund, which had been invented but the year before, was applied to this special object with good effect. . . .

The capitals of the Banks thus associated made an aggregate of one hundred and twenty millions, — an amount greater than the Bank of England and the Bank of France combined, each of which institutions had been found sufficient for the gigantic struggles of those great nations, from time to time, in conflict with all Europe. . . .

The following figures also show that the financial condition of the Banks at the time was one of great strength:

| | Liabilities. | | Assets in Coin. |
	Deposits.	Circulation.	
Banks in New York .	$92,046,308 . . .	$8,521,426 . . .	. $49,733,990
" Boston . .	18,235,061 . . .	6,366,466 . . .	. 6,665,929
" Philadelphia .	15,335,838 . . .	2,076,857 . . .	. 6,765,120
	$125,617,207	$16,964,749	
		125,617,207	

Total . . . . $142,581,956, against $63,165,039

coin on hand, equal to 45 per cent. of all liabilities. Surely, such conditions as these, with judicious administration, were adequate to the work which the country required. A great merit of this bank combination at that critical moment, when the life of the nation hung in the balance, consisted in the fact that it fully committed the hitherto hesitating moneyed capital of the North and East to the support of the government. The bank officers and directors who thus counselled and consented were deeply sensible of the momentous responsibility which they assumed ; but all doubt and hesitation were instantly removed, and perfect unanimity was secured by the question, " *What if we do not unite ?* " And acting as guardians of a great trust exposed to imminent danger, they fearlessly elected the alternative best calculated to protect it.

The problem to be practically resolved by the Banks was this : How can the available capital be best drawn from the people, and devoted to the support of government, with the least disturbance to the country? and by what means can arms, clothing, and subsistence for the army be best secured in exchange for government credit? These were simple questions of domestic exchange, and most naturally suggested the use of the ordinary methods of bank-checks, deposits, and transfers, that the experience of all civilized nations had found most efficient for the purpose ; and that this should be accomplished by the Associated Banks, in a manner best calculated to prolong their useful agency and to preserve the specie standard, *it was indispensable that their coin reserves remain with the least possible change.* Accordingly, it was at once proposed to the Secretary that he should suspend the operations of the Sub-Treasury Act in respect to these transactions, and, following the course of commercial business, that he should draw checks upon some one Bank in each city representing the Association, in small sums as required, in disbursing the money thus advanced. By this means his checks would serve the purpose of a circulating medium, continually redeemed, and the exchanges of capital and industry would be best promoted. This was the more important in a period of public agitation, when the disbursement of these large sums exclusively in coin rendered the reserves of the Banks all the more liable to be wasted by hoarding. To the astonishment of the Committee, Mr. Chase refused ; notwithstanding the Act of Congress of August 5th, which it seemed to us was passed for the very object then presented. This issue was discussed from time to time with much zeal ; but always with the same result. It was seen by the most experienced bank officers to be vital to the success of their undertaking. To draw from the Banks in coin the large sums involved in these loans, and to transfer them to the Treasury, thence to be widely scattered over the country at a moment when war had excited fear and distrust, *was to be pulling out continually the foundations upon which the whole structure rested*. And inasmuch as this money was loaned to the government, and was in no sense a trust reposed in the Banks, there appeared to them no reason why it should not be drawn by checks in favor of government contractors and creditors, who would require to exchange them for other values in commerce and trade, through the process of the clearing-house. And this consideration was greatly strengthened by the fact, that these advances were made, and the money publicly disbursed, a long time before the treasury notes were ready for delivery to the Banks which had paid for them. In the light which has since been shed upon the Act of Congress referred to, it is evident that undue weight was given to the views of the Secretary, and that the Banks would have conferred an incalculable benefit upon the country, had they adhered inflexibly to their own opinions. . . . It soon became manifest that, in consenting to have their hands tied and their most efficient powers restricted, while engaged in these great operations, and in allowing their coin reserves to be wasted by pouring them out upon the community in a manner so unnecessary and exceptional, the Banks deprived themselves and the government of the ability of long continuing, as they otherwise could have done, to negotiate the National loans upon a specie standard.

This first great error, if it did not create a necessity for the legal-tender notes, certainly precipitated the adoption of that most unhappy expedient, and thereby committed the nation at an earlier day to the most expensive of all methods of financiering.

One other subject of discussion between the Secretary and the Associated Banks at the same time arose, which led in the same direction. Congress by its Act of 17th July had authorized loans to the amount of two hundred and fifty millions. This could be issued either in bonds running twenty years at not over seven per cent. interest — 7-3 notes running three years, or fifty millions of the amount could, at the discretion of the Secretary, be made *in currency notes payable on demand without interest*. As the undertaking of the Associated Banks covered one hundred and fifty millions of this sum, and it was desired that they continue the work thus auspiciously begun, a question of the expediency of putting out the circulating notes was immediately raised by one of its members. A very small amount had been emitted. The Treasury was empty of coin to redeem them, and could only be replenished by the proceeds of the bank loans. *It was*

evident to the bank officers that they could not sustain coin payments, if the trans-
fers from their vaults to that of the Treasury were subject to be intercepted and
absorbed by these notes of government.   Nor could the Banks receive them upon
deposit from the public as money, while they were responding to the government
and to their own dealers in coin. *It was an inflation of the currency in the form*
most embarrassing to the enterprise they had commenced.   Accordingly, the Secretary was urgently solicited to refrain from exercising the discretionary powers
given him of creating the Treasury currency, until all other means were exhausted.
In response to a resolution to that effect, the Secretary assured the bank officers
of his acquiescence in their suggestion ; but at the same time insisted that it was
improper for a public officer *to openly pledge himself not to exercise a power con-*
ferred by the law.   With this understanding the Banks began their work ; paying
into the Treasury, in coin, one hundred and fifty millions, in sums at the rate of
about five millions, at intervals of six days.   Even with all these unfavorable circumstances surrounding them, it was an encouraging fact, observed by those who
were anxiously watching the practical operation of this great and novel experiment, that, while the circulating notes in the country were restricted, the dis-
bursements of the government for the war were so rapid, and the consequent
internal trade movement was so intense, that the coin paid out upon each instal-
ment of the loan came back to the Banks, through the community, in about one
week ; the natural effect of this general commercial activity upon the circulating
medium being simply to quicken its flow.

After taking the third amount of fifty millions by the Associated Banks, those
in New York, who had at that time paid in of their proportion over eighty millions in all, found themselves in this position :

Their aggregate coin, which on the 17th August, before the first pay-
    ment into the Treasury, was $49,733,990
Was on December 7th 42,318,610
                                                                  ————————
A reduction of only $7,415,380

and the other two cities in like proportion.

In the meantime the 7-3 notes taken by the Banks had been purchased by
the people to the extent of some fifty millions, notwithstanding a prolonged and
vexatious delay in issuing them by the Treasury Department.   The popular feel-
ing was all that could have been desired for continuing that method of distribution.   It may be confidently affirmed, that, had the Banks been permitted to
exercise their own methods of exchanging the bonds for the varied products of
industry required by the government, they could have continued their advances
in sums of fifty millions for an indefinite period, and until the available resources
of the people had been all gathered in.   It is to be borne in mind that these
resources were all existing at home, and that the increased industry which the
war excited was daily increasing new means for investment. . · .

But at this time the demand notes were paid out freely by the Treasury, and
began to appear as a cause of embarrassment among the Banks which were
pressed to receive them upon deposit ; and while they could not decline them
without diminishing public confidence in the government credit, they could not

give them currency without impairing their own specie strength. *In fact, the notes became at once a substitute for coin withdrawn from circulation, and their emission expressed a purpose of resorting to government paper issues to carry on the war.* So soon as these notes thus appeared, the reflux of coin to the Banks at once sensibly diminished. During three weeks from the 7th December, the reserves of the Banks in New York fell to $29,357,712, — a loss of $13,000,000 within that short period ; and on the 28th December, after conference with the Secretary, in which he still adhered to the views before expressed, it was decided as expedient for the Banks to suspend specie payments.

At that moment the Associated Banks yet held over forty millions in coin, and it was still possible for them to continue their advances to the government but for the two obstacles thus interposed. Before entering into this last conference with the Associated Banks, some of the members expressed to the Secretary the importance of continuing his relation to an organization which combined so much of experience, capital, and financial resource, and which was yet capable of rendering the government invaluable service ; and that if an irredeemable paper currency was the inevitable resort, it would be more expedient and economical for the government not to become involved in its dangers, but to impose the duty and responsibility of issuing the notes upon the Banks, which would naturally be compelled to keep the day of redemption continually in view. Thus, as a suspension of coin payment was about to be declared, it was practicable to preserve from distribution and set aside the forty millions of coin then owned by the Banks, together with one hundred and fifty or sixty millions of government bonds, which could be taken by them as a special security for two hundred millions of notes, which could then be immediately issued by the Associated Banks, from their own plates, and be verified and made National by the stamp and signature of a government officer. It was claimed that such an issue, so supported by coin and bonds, at once simple and expeditious, would serve the temporary purpose required, with little if any deterioration below coin value ; and that it would be then practicable for the Banks to continue, without further agitation, their advances. But the Secretary declined to entertain this suggestion ; preferring the system of National Banks, which he had already conceived.

Looking back over events that have since transpired, it must be admitted that this suggestion possessed true merit. It would have preserved a coin basis for the currency, prevented the destructive expansion, relieved the government from its almost inextricable entanglement with the circulating notes, and compelled an early restoration of coin payments. And with a proper use of the expedients and machinery of Banks, by utilizing their power of effecting exchanges, which was substantially applied by the Secretary in the National Banking system without reserve, this amount would have been found sufficient. When we review the excessive cost of the war, the vast increase of the National debt, and the public and private evils which a profuse currency has entailed upon the country, it must appear evident that, in failing early to use and to exhaust all those means and appliances of commerce and banking that the experience of other civilized nations has proved most effective, a great and irreparable mistake was made. . . .

This forcible entry of the government into the private affairs of the people, so utterly at variance with the fundamental principles of our system, so great an abridgment of personal liberty, and operating as a tax so unequal in its effects, was a rigorous measure of war, and as such was vindicated only as a temporary act of dire necessity. In enforcing this unequal burden, Congress did not leave the holders of the notes without some measure of relief; but it gave to all the option of converting them at pleasure into a six per cent. gold-interest-bearing bond, payable in twenty years. By this means, the notes became equal in value to the bonds for which they were made exchangeable ; and while during the war, the payments of gold interests continually operated to produce a curtailment of the volume of the notes in circulation, the return of peace opened a market abroad for the bonds, which would have insured the early and entire absorption of the war currency, and thus clear the way for specie payments.

But, in an evil hour for the country, other counsel obtained possession of the good judgment of the Secretary ; and, yielding to it, he consented and urged Congress to withdraw this privilege of converting the notes. so that thenceforth all issues were made without it. All notes emitted consequently became an un-mitigated burden upon commerce, of indefinite duration, from which there was no escape. A new currency was created, utterly at variance with all economic laws, and in conflict with all recognized rules of commerce and exchange. It did not, like all sound currency, naturally spring out of industry, production, and trade ; but it was an enforced result of exhaustion and necessity. It did not come and go, following the beneficent courses of commerce, expanding and contracting with the times and seasons that required it ; but it remained an unyielding, inflexible mass, subject only to the chances and vicissitudes of war. As the war progressed and the country became poorer, this currency increased, giving new instruments and facilities to expend just in proportion as the means of payment were consumed. With a compulsory currency thus made the measure of prices, and daily deteriorat-ing yet still increasing, is it strange that all other property was eagerly sought for in preference to this, and that prodigal expenditure became the law of the land? [1]

Here is a picture by a most competent hand, a leading actor in the scenes described, of the events which led to the suspension of specie payment by the banks, and to the issue by the United States of legal tender notes which still remain the great disturbing element in affairs. It is to be read and re-read by every one who would understand the situation at the time, and the levity or wanton-ness with which all past experience was thrown aside, and the coun-sel of those perfectly competent to guide spurned by the weak, vain, ignorant, and perverse character holding, next to the President, the most important place in the Government. For the issue at the time of notes to serve as money not the slightest necessity existed, as through the banks of the loyal States every dollar of the issues of their people, at the value of coin, could have been reached for the

---

[1] "Financial History of the War," by George S. Coe, President of the American Ex-change Bank. See "Banker's Magazine," January, 1876.

prosecution of the war, and far more effectually by their issues than by those of the Government. At the time the only currency in ordinary use, and by all classes preferred to coin, was that of banks. It would, in the spirit of patriotism that was aroused, have been accepted by the people in their military as readily as in their ordinary operations. It cannot be too often repeated that the people will never use any other than paper money as their ordinary instrument of exchange. Their currency will always be that of banks or bankers, or of Government. Why were not recommendations so wise, so reasonable, and so earnestly pressed upon the Secretary, heeded, that in the emergency the money of commerce, representing as it did at the value of coin precisely the kind of merchandise required by it in all its operations; which was of the value of coin and could be had in unlimited amounts, or in amounts equal to the means of the people; means as the result showed fully adequate to the demands to be made upon them, should be that of the Government? For the reasons set forth in the following extract from the report of the Secretary, made under date December 10, 1861:

The circulation of the banks of the United States on the 1st day of January, 1861, was computed to be $202,000,767. Of this circulation, $150,-000,000, in round numbers, was in the States now loyal, including Western Virginia, and $50,000,000 in the rebellious States. *The whole of this circulation constitutes a loan without interest from the people to the banks, costing them nothing except the expense of issue and redemption and the interest on the specie kept on hand for the latter purpose;* and it deserves consideration whether sound policy does not require that the advantages of this loan be transferred, in part at least, from the banks representing only the interests of the stockholders, to the Government representing the aggregate interests of the whole people.

Here is the old story inherited from Jackson that the issues of banks were forms of credit costing nothing, but for the use of which interest was charged; the necessary inference on the part of the Secretary, to repeat his own words, being, "that the advantages of such loans should be transferred, in part at least, from the banks representing the interests of the stockholders, to the Government representing the aggregate interests of the whole people." To escape the exactions of the banks, lenders of money of their own creation, why should not the Government, when a borrower on an enormous scale, create by an act of sovereignty money for itself, saving thereby a sum equal to the interest on the amount created?

If the currency of banks by a small provision of means circulated readily at the value of coin, why should not that of the Government having behind it, as was assumed, the entire means of the people? The reply is as obvious as it is conclusive. The legal tender notes, greenbacks, now outstanding of the Government were, at first, forms of credit payable at its pleasure. For the time, in the estimation of those receiving them, that was to elapse before the Government would be able or disposed to redeem them in coin, interest, or its equivalent in the reduced rates at which they were accepted, or in the increased price of what was delivered in exchange therefor, was charged. Forbearance of payment at the instance of the debtor is always to be purchased in one form or another. In the darkest days of the rebellion the amount charged for such forbearance was nearly three times greater than the nominal value of the notes. When these are payable presently they circulate at their par value so long as confidence in the issue remains unimpaired. The notes of the Continental Congress, with nothing behind them but the credit of that body, and although for their redemption no provision was made, circulated for nearly two years at the par of coin. It may be laid down as a rule that the public, so long as confidence is unshaken, will never, from the convenience of their use, present notes to the Government for payment. They will be presented only when coin is wanted for the discharge of balances arising in the foreign or domestic trade of the country, and then only by those against whom such balances arise. The evil of Government notes results from their being instruments in excess of the means of consumption, not arising naturally out of the industrial operations of society, being always instruments of forced loans. They are always in excess for no other reason than that in countries like the United States the issues of banks, whether payable presently or at a future day, always equal in their nominal amount the means of consumption. They are precisely in the nature of issues made by banks in the discount of "accommodation paper" to supply the lack of means of borrowers. Every one understands that as a rule issues so made will be improvidently expended, to be taken in consequently by the issuers by paying out a corresponding amount of their reserves. No matter the amount issued in the discount of merchants' bills no distrust or apprehension can be created, for the reason that they measure the value of the subjects of consumption. They are never in excess, for the reason that they cannot be diverted from their proper function, the distribution of their constituent, being retired by the process. Issues made in the discount of bills not representing merchandise for distribution, having no appropriate function, speedily find their way into the hands of those who present them as creditors, not debtors, for redemption, the issuers usually making a loss equal to their amount. The disasters which overtake the issuers of currency arise almost wholly from the discount of fictitious paper. The loss is the same whether it falls upon the banks, or, in their inability to make good their issues, upon the public. In either case the currency must be contracted in ratio to the waste or loss that has been sustained. The notes of the United States, now that it assumes to be upon a specie basis, have precisely the same effect in the waste that results as the notes of banks issued in the discount of "accommodation paper." Provision for their retirement is to be made *after* instead of *before* their issue. They are wholly superfluous as instruments of distribution, as the necessary amount of currency therefor is always supplied by the banks. The effect of their retirement is the same as the retirement of an equal amount of the issues of banks made in the discount of "accommodation paper," a contraction of all the operations of society. Ordinarily the retirement of currency issued by banks is not felt, as new issues take the place of the old, the volume in prosperous communities always steadily increasing to represent new creations of merchandise. The issues, well made, of banks can create no waste, as their constituent cannot be reached unless a proper equivalent is rendered in exchange. The effect of the discount of "accommodation paper" is now so well understood that were it believed that the amount outstanding by banks equalled that of the Government notes, $830,000,000, an instant rush would be made for the reserves of the issuers, to be followed, from the inadequacy of means immediately at their command, by a suspension of specie payments. That a corresponding rush is not made for the conversion of the "accommodation paper" of the Government into coin, forcing it to suspend specie payments, is due to the fact that so far no considerable apprehension has yet been felt by the great mass as to the ability or disposition of the Government to make good its issues, the means of the whole people, through its taxing power, being assumed to be pledged therefor. So long as this is the case the notes of the Government, from the convenience of their use, will be preferred to coin as money. But great apprehension of the solvency of Government in case of a run upon it is now felt in commercial circles, and to such an extent that within a comparatively short period it has been forced into the market to raise some $300,000,000 in gold for the redemption of its notes, without any considerable diminution in their amount, as, in the want of adequate revenues, they are presently re-issued. No matter the amount of the issues of banks properly made there can be no run upon them for gold, as they will as a rule be used to reach their constituent. The distrust once confined to narrow circles is spreading rapidly, arresting all the industrial operations of the country. Every one is beginning to feel that something is wrong, — what, he cannot distinctly see. All are limiting their expenditures to their absolute wants, holding with a tight grip whatever they have, wearing out old possessions before new ones are acquired. Such a state of distrust cannot long continue without taking shape in some form. Unless a way out is soon shown, the people will take the remedy into their own hands, driving the Government out of the field as an issuer of currency by demanding the immediate conversion of every dollar of its issues into gold.

The manner in which the suspension of specie payments was precipitated well illustrates the delicacy of the machinery of distribution, and how easily it may be thrown out of gear. The loan taken by the banks, authorized by the act of July 17, 1861, provided that $50,000,000 of the $250,000,000 might be in the form of notes, not legal tender, payable on demand in coin. No sooner did the banks begin their payments, averaging about $1,000,000 daily of the great loan, than a small amount of the demand notes of the Government began to make their appearance. No sooner was this seen than the Committee of the Banks immediately and earnestly remonstrated against their issue, urging that if continued they would be offered in payment of bills discounted, or for deposit, reducing to the extent so received the return of the gold they were paying out; that if persisted in the worst consequences were to be feared. "The Secretary assured the committee of his acquiescence in their suggestion, but at the same time he insisted that it would be improper for a public officer openly to pledge himself not to exercise a power openly conferred upon him by law." Upon such assurances the banks proceeded with their work. The result far exceeded their expectations. The greater part of the gold paid out speedily returned to them on deposit or in the payment of their bills. It would naturally return to them as its proper custodians so long as confidence was undisturbed. When the banks of the city of New York had paid out something over $80,000,000, their share of the two first instalments of the loans, they held $42,318,610, against $49,733,990 when they began their payments, the loss being only $7,415,380. The result may seem remarkable, as the gold paid out was scattered broadcast over the length and breadth of the land. Time given and confidence preserved, every dollar would have necessarily returned so as to be largely available for future loans. When the banks entered upon the payment of the third instalment, the Secretary, in violation of his express assurances, began the issue on a large scale of Treasury Notes to serve as money, the amount reaching in a comparatively short period the sum of $33,460,000. As soon as it was seen that very large issues were being made the Committee of the Banks again urged their remonstrances, reminding the Secretary of the assurances that had been given them, to all of which he now turned a deaf ear. The result of the largely increased issue of Government notes was that the specie in the New York banks fell from $42,318,610, December 7, 1861, to $29,357,-712, December 27, the loss equalling $13,000,000 in a period of about three weeks. Within another month, their payments continued, the banks might find themselves without a dollar of specie in their vaults, leaving them no reserves for liabilities to the public to the amount of $100,000,000. In view of the situation, on the 28th of December, they decided to suspend specie payments, to be followed by the Government as well as by all the banks of the country.

But even with the suspension of specie payments it was urged by the representatives of the banks of the city of New York "that if an irredeemable currency was the inevitable resort, it would be more expedient and economical for Government not to become involved in its danger, but to impose the duty and responsibility of issuing notes upon the banks, which would naturally be compelled to keep the day of redemption constantly in view," — the proposition being to set apart the gold still held by them, with $150,000,000 bonds to be issued by the Government, the whole to be made a basis of the issue of $200,000,000 of notes by the banks, to be verified and made national by the stamp of the Government. With such provision it was held that the notes to be issued would circulate very nearly if not quite at the value of coin, their redemption being thrown wholly upon the banks. But this suggestion was rejected by the Secretary in order to make way for an issue of Government notes. To speed their issue he addressed, on the 3d of February, 1862, a communication to the Hon. E. G. Spaulding, member of the Committee of Ways and Means of the House, in which, among other things, he said :

> It is true that I came with reluctance to the conclusion that the legal tender clause is a necessity, but I came to it decidedly, and I support it earnestly. I do not hesitate when I have made up my mind, however much regret I may feel over the necessity of the conclusion to which I come.
>
> Immediate action is of great importance. The Treasury is nearly empty. I have been obliged to draw for the last instalment of the November loan ; *so soon as it is paid I fear the banks generally will refuse to receive the United States notes.* You will see the necessity of urging the bill through without more delay.

Permission given, the Government notes were poured out like water until, in various forms, they reached the enormous sum of $684,138,959, of which $433,160,569 were in the form of plain notes, — greenbacks ; $217,024,160 of compound interest legal tender notes ; and $33,954,203 of five per cent. notes. The amount of plain notes outstanding each fiscal year from 1862 to 1878, inclusive, was as follows :

Statement showing the circulation of legal tender notes in the United States, from 1862 to 1878, inclusive.

Years.	Legal tender notes.	Years.	Legal tender notes.	Years.	Legal tender notes.
1862	$96,620,000	1868	$356,000,000	1874	$382,000,000
1863	297,767,114	1869	356,000,000	1875	375,771,580
1864	431,178,670	1870	356,000,000	1876	369,772,284
1865	432,687,966	1871	356,000,000	1877	359,764,332
1866	400,619,206	1872	357,500,000	1878	346,681,016
1867	371,783,599	1873	356,000,000		

The interest bearing legal tender notes never entered into general circulation, and were at the close of the war speedily converted into long bonds of the Government.

In his annual report for 1865 Mr. McCullough, who followed Mr. Chase as the Secretary of the Treasury, warmly urged upon Congress that, as the issue of the notes was a " war measure," the first care of Government, the war ended, should be their retirement.   In response the House of Representatives, by a vote of 144 to 6, adopted a resolution " cordially approving the views of the Secretary of the Treasury in relation to the necessity of contracting the currency with a view to the early resumption of specie payments." This resolution was followed by an act of Congress of March 12, 1866, authorizing cancellation of legal tender notes not exceeding the amount of $10,000,000 within six months from the passage of the act, and thereafter at the rate of $4,000,000 per month.   Under this act the amount of the notes, December 31, 1867, was reduced to $356,000,000.   On the fourth of February, 1868, an act was passed forbidding a further reduction of the notes.   Their amount was increased in the period from October 1, 1872, to January 15, 1874, to $382,979,815.   By the act of June 20, 1874, the maximum of the notes was fixed at $382,000,000.   By the act of January 14, 1875, authorizing the increase of circulation of the notes of the National Banks, the Secretary was required to retire legal tender notes to an amount equalling 80 per cent. of the notes issued to them, till the legal tender notes were reduced to $300,000,000.   Under the operation of the last preceding act notes to the amount of $35,-318,984 were cancelled, the total amount being reduced to $346,-610,016, the amount now outstanding.   On the thirty-first of May, 1878, an act was passed that " when any of said notes be redeemed or received into the Treasury they shall not be retired, cancelled, or discharged, but they shall be reissued and paid out again and kept in circulation."

Mr. Coe dwelt with almost mournful emphasis upon the withdrawal by Congress of the rights of the holders of the notes to convert them at pleasure into the bonds of the government.   If the right had not been withdrawn it is certain, but for restrictions imposed upon the issues of bank notes, that the whole amount of the government notes would have been retired without the intervention of a dollar in gold.   With the end of the war, the great " war measure," the issue of legal tender notes, as it was termed, without any further action on the part of the Government, would have silently disappeared, debt of the Government bearing interest being always preferable to debt bearing no interest.   Of this withdrawal Mr.

Spaulding, in his " Financial History of the War," gave the following account:

The first legal tender notes were issued bearing date March 10, 1862, and on the back of them was printed these words:

" This note is a legal tender for all debts, public and private, except duties on imports and interest on the public debt, *and is exchangeable for United States six per cent. bonds, redeemable at the pleasure of the United States after five years.*"

The right to exchange these notes at par for *six* per cent. bonds was distinctly authorized by the second section of the legal tender act, *and was in the nature of a contract* made by the Government with the holders of the notes. It was inserted as a just and equitable provision for the benefit of those persons who should be compelled, by the legal tender clause, to take the notes, by giving them, at any time, the privilege of converting them into a six per cent. bond. It was, in effect, a forced loan, but the right of immediately returning them to the Government for gold bonds divested the forced character of the transaction of any material hardship. It also had a tendency to prevent any great inflation, for the reason that as soon as this currency became redundant in the hands of the people, and not bearing interest, they would invest it in the six per cent. bonds to prevent any loss of interest.

This right to exchange the notes for bonds was, at the request of Secretary Chase, taken away by the third section of the above act after July 1, 1863. It is true that the Secretary had still the *discretionary* power to receive the notes at par for bonds, but it never seemed to be quite right to change the law while any of the legal tender notes were outstanding with the above endorsement upon them.

The act forbidding the further cancellation of the United States notes was undoubtedly due to the influence of Mr. Sherman, at the time Secretary of the Treasury, now Secretary of State of the United States. In his annual report for 1877 he considered at great length the financial policy of the Government, and the various forms of money in use. The occasion was one of supreme importance, as the Government, by the Act of January 14, 1875, was to resume specie payment on the first of January, 1879. The question of the kind of money for the future was to be determined, — whether greenbacks should be continued as the money of the country, or whether a return should be made to the money of banks — of commerce — springing naturally out of the business operations of the country. Of that discussion Mr. Sherman, in his " Forty Years in the House, Senate, and Cabinet," published in 1895, gave the following synopsis:

I expressed in my report the opinion that the notes of the Government, when redeemed after the 1st of January, 1879, if the amount outstanding was not in excess of $300,000,000, might be reissued as the exigencies of the public service required. . . . These notes were of great public convenience — they circulated readily; were of universal credit; were a debt of the people without interest; were protected by every possible safeguard against counterfeiting; and, when redeemable in coin at the demand of the holder, formed a paper currency as good as had yet been devised. . . . It was conceded, I said, that a certain amount could, with the aid of an ample reserve in coin, be always maintained in circulation. Should not the benefit of this circulation inure to the people, rather than to corporations, either State or national? The Government had ample facility for the collection, custody, and care of the coin reserves of the country. . . . I said that the legal tender quality given to United States notes was intended to maintain them in forced circulation at a time when their depreciation was inevitable. When they were redeemable in coin this quality might either be withdrawn or retained, without affecting their use as currency in ordinary times. But all experience has shown that there were periods when, under any system of paper money, however carefully guarded, it was impracticable to maintain actual coin redemption. Usually contracts would be based upon current paper money, and it was just that, during a sudden panic, or an unreasonable demand for coin, the creditor should not be allowed to demand payment in other than the currency upon which the debt was contracted. To meet this contingency, it would seem to be right to maintain the legal tender quality of the United States notes. If they were not at par with coin it was the fault of the Government and not of the debtor, or, rather, it was the result of unforeseen stringency not contemplated by the contracting parties.

In establishing a system of paper money, designed to be permanent, I said it should be remembered that theretofore no expedient had been devised, either in this or other countries, that in times of panic or adverse trade had prevented the drain and exhaustion of coin reserves, however large or carefully guarded. Every such system must provide for a suspension of specie payment. Laws might forbid or ignore such a contingency, but it would come; and when it came it could not be resisted, but had to be acknowledged and declared, to prevent unnecessary sacrifice and ruin. In our free Government the power to make this declaration would not be willingly intrusted to individuals, but should be determined by events and conditions known to all. It would be far better to fix the maximum of legal tender notes at $300,000,000, supported by a minimum reserve of $100,000,000, of coin, only to be used for the redemption of notes, not to be reissued until the reserve was restored. A demand for coin to exhaust such a reserve might not occur, but, if events should force it, the fact would be known and could be declared, and would justify a temporary suspension of specie payments. Some such expedient could, no doubt, be provided by Congress for an exceptional emergency. In other times the general confidence in these notes would maintain them at par in coin, and justify their use as reserves of banks and for the redemption of bank notes.

There can be no doubt that the notes of the United States *seemed* to be a great public convenience. All forms of money are alike convenient so long as circulation is to be had for them, as to their holders they have the potency of capital. That which seems at the outset to be good money may in the end prove to be the worst kind of money, even if finally taken in at its nominal value. No money seems more convenient than the issues of banks made in the discount of "accommodation paper," yet no kind is worse, as the waste and loss are usually in ratio to the amount issued. A long time may elapse before the kind is disclosed. So the notes of the United States, instead of being as "good money as has been devised," were the very worst kind, no adequate provision being made previous to their issue for their redemption, there being no limit to their issue but the caprice or necessity of the issuer. For such money the appropriate penalty will always be exacted. It has in our case been already exacted in the apprehension that has been created, arresting to a greater or less extent all the operations of our people. The penalty already paid exceeds fifty-fold any assumed advantage of "debt without interest." After all that has been suffered a more terrible penalty still may have to be paid, — suspension of specie payments by the Government, to be followed by all issuers throughout the country.

With the Secretary, money, whatever the kind, derives its value from the necessity of a *medium* of exchange, the greater part of it to remain in circulation. It is only the excess of issue that will ordinarily be presented for coin. As it is the rule with banks to provide reserves equalling twenty-five per cent. of their issues, our Government, when it determined to remain in the field, assumed to provide reserves in similar ratio to its immediate liabilities. It wholly overlooked the fact that in addition to their reserves the banks have the undertaking of the customers to return to them every dollar of their issues without interposition on their part. While with the Secretary the excess only was ordinarily to be provided for, it might happen that all the issues might be suddenly presented for coin. "All experience," he said, "has shown that there were periods when under any system of paper money, however carefully guarded, it was impossible to maintain actual coin redemption." Nothing is easier than to maintain coin redemption of paper money which symbolizes the subjects of consumption, as such money cannot be diverted from its use to reach its constituent; and as the makers of bills discounted, into whose hands, as the holders of merchandise, the issues of banks necessarily flow, instead of presenting them for coin, will hold them for the payment of their bills. When a currency is symbolic the merchandise it represents will ordinarily be taken for consumption within the time in which the bills have to run. Consumption goes on as steadily after suspension of specie payments by banks as before. To reach their constituents the issues of those in suspension are as valuable as before. In the event of a panic, as issuers naturally stop discounting, sixty days will ordinarily suffice for the return to them of all their issues without the paying out of a dollar of coin. The laws of trade speedily place them in position to resume business, as the gold with which they may have parted returns in the payment of their bills, or, confidence restored, for deposit. Panics arise and runs are made upon issuers solely from the violation of the proper rules of issue. So long as these are observed, no disturbance calling for coin can arise, either in the foreign or domestic trade of the country. But the issues of governments will never be made in the discount of bills the payment of which necessarily retires the issues made in their discount. Their reserves, consequently, — the only means provided to meet their immediate liabilities, — will bear only a very small ratio to the amount of the latter, in order that the greatest advantage may be secured from a money of "debt without interest." No other provision for the retirement of the notes of governments will ever be made than their reserves. If full provision were to be made for the redemption of their notes their issue would never suggest itself. If provided by creating debt in another form, they would lose a sum equal to the interest on the amount, no charge being made for their issues, necessarily "debt without interest," or if the amount equal to the issues were provided by taxation the public would be without interest on a corresponding sum.

As panics under a Government currency will necessarily arise, the only alternative is a suspension of specie payment to be proclaimed as soon as it is seen that the run upon it is to be a formidable one. It is here that, according to the Secretary, the value and importance of the legal tender attribute comes in, in order that "the creditor may not be allowed to demand payment in any other currency than that in which the debt was contracted;" and further, "as every system of paper money must provide for suspension of specie payment it would have to be acknowledged and declared to prevent unnecessary sacrifice and ruin. . . . In our free Government the power to make such declaration would not be willingly intrusted to individuals, but should be determined by conditions known to all," — that is, first known to the Government, which would be the first called upon for coin, its notes serving as the reserves of all other issuers of currency. "In case of a suspension the fault would be that of the Government, not of the debtor; or, rather, it would be the result of an unforeseen stringency not contemplated by the contracting parties." But with a Government currency all contracts are entered into at the value of coin. The Government notes are assumed to be the equivalents of coin. If, upon suspension, they fall greatly in value, the creditor must suffer in like ratio. The Continental currency, at the outset legal tender, and a very "convenient form of money," circulated for a considerable period at its nominal value. Those accepting it in exchange for property or merchandise, and holding it, made a loss equal to the nominal amount received. The history of the times is full of pictures of the terrible suffering that resulted. In the war of the Rebellion vast losses were suffered from the fall of value of the notes, at one time to about one-third of their nominal value. Fortunately, as was the case of the war of Independence, they have not been repudiated, still remaining the pest and menace of the nation. But where does this function or right of the Government to declare suspension of specie payments leave the commercial, industrial, and monetary interests of the country, — with weak, ignorant, vain, or unscrupulous politicians in the Department of the Treasury, a prey to their caprices or fears; or posing as the particular champions of "the people"? Is it not better to leave the currency to the guidance of national laws than to such guardians as these?

UNITED STATES SAFETY—FUND BANKING SYSTEM.

The second measure that distinguished Mr. Chase's administration of the finances was the establishment of our present National Safety Fund Banking System. The first act therefor, greatly amended by that of June 3, 1864, was passed February 25, 1863. Its most important feature was the provision made for the conversion of the notes of issuers into coin by deposits of securities over which they had no control. No more absurd and ill-timed measure could have been devised. The Government derived no considerable advantage therefrom, either in the sale of bonds or in the increase of the currency. There was never any difficulty in selling bonds, while it could readily create for itself all the currency that was wanted.

No National Bank currency, said Mr. Spaulding in his " Financial History of the War," was issued until about the first of January, 1864. After that time it was gradually issued. On the first of July, 1864, the sum of $25,825,695 had been issued ; and on the 22d of April, 1865, shortly after the surrender of General Lee, the whole amount of National Bank circulation issued to that time was only $146,927,975. It will therefore be seen that comparatively little direct aid was realized from this currency until after the close of the war. *All the channels of circulation were well filled up with the greenback notes, compound interest notes, and certificates of indebtedness to the amount of over $700,000,000, before the National Bank act got fairly into operation. This bank issue was in fact an additional inflation of the currency.*

It has already been sufficiently shown that the conversion of notes of banks into coin can be amply secured by restrictions imposed upon issuers to the discount of merchants' bills. So long as such rule is observed the issues made will be employed as instruments to reach their constituents, for which they serve equally well with coin. With it the notes returning for coin will never as a rule exceed the amount of the reserves of the issuers. For a period of forty years under the two banks, the currency, whether issued by the State or National Banks, although in terms payable in coin, was almost wholly retired by its use in reaching its constituents. By such use it came directly into the hands of holders of merchandise, to be returned by them to the issuers in the payment of their bills. During the existence of the two banks the suggestion never occurred to the holder of a note, whether of National or State Banks, that it was not adequately secured ; that it needed any other guarantee for its payment than its constituent, supplemented by the reserves of the issuers. The result was secured by restrictions imposed by law upon a single institution, the National Bank, which, from its commanding position as the holder of the public revenues, was able to compel all other issuers to make good daily all balances arising against them. As the charters of State Banks allowed them to make loans, no matter the kind of security, upon whatever promised the greatest return, no sooner was the National Bank out of the way and all restrictions removed, than the picture so graphically drawn by Mr. Buchanan became possible. As no other than paper money was to be that of the people, their instinct naturally turned to the improvement of that in use.

One of the first measures of the kind adopted was the Suffolk Bank system, by which all the banks of the New England States entered into an agreement to redeem daily in Boston, their business metropolis, at the Suffolk Bank, all balances found against them. It was a Clearing House which included the banks of six States. A bank which did not belong to it could obtain no circulation for its notes. It was the " Suffolk " system which suggested the establishment of Clearing Houses for banks of the same city, and which are now to be found in every considerable place of business in the United States. When Mr. Buchanan's picture was drawn the New England States had a currency perfectly sound and perfectly suited to the wants of the people, as had New York and other cities in which Clearing Houses had been established. With such establishments without the intervention of positive law, a perfect currency, through the operation of natural laws, would have been secured to every part of the country. A currency will always be relative to the condition of a people. In needy communities the temptation, too strong to be resisted, will lead to the issue of bank-notes without any proper constituent. Among other remedies adopted by many States following the overthrow of the Bank of the United States was the establishment of Safety Fund Systems upon which the present Safety Fund System was modelled, except in the kind of securities to be deposited. Those accepted under the State systems might be real property, or bonds, often largely depreciated, of State or municipal bodies. The weakness of every Safety Fund System is that, with provision of adequate security for their notes, the issuers part with the means necessary to carry on their operations. The first step in the direction of reform is the total abolition of the existing system, and in the place of securities, restrictions of issues to bills of exchange, by means of which a perfect currency will be created, always adequate and always flexible in representing the subjects of consumption.

But the burdens imposed by our present system and the obstacles it presents to all remedial measures are by no means the only wrongs committed by its establishment. State Banks as the issuers of notes existed at the foundation of the Government. The right was unchallenged for a period of seventy-two years. For the whole period of our existence as a nation the greater part of the currency has been supplied by them ; for nearly seventy years the whole of it. The exercise of such right unchallenged for so long a period was equivalent to a provision in the Constitution in its favor. It would have been such an equivalent with any other people than our own. We have a dual government with a vast number of powers reserved to the States. The creation of corporations was certainly a right which they might exercise. The National Government may levy taxes for the purpose of revenue, but it cannot, by the mode of their levy, purposely destroy rights or powers reserved to the States. All taxes must be uniform in their application. Now the tax of 10 per cent. on the circulation of States Banks was not levied for revenue ; none was expected from it. It was equivalent to a declaration that the banks should not exercise one of the functions alike necessary and proper to their welfare. It was levied, not for revenue, but for the purpose of creating a market for bonds. If, under the pretext of taxation, the National Government can destroy the banks of the States, it could, under the same pretext, destroy or render valueless all corporations, — insurance, manufacturing, railroad companies and the like, reducing the States to the position of mere creatures of its will.

In the denial to the State Banks of the right to issue notes, the National Banks, from the burdens imposed, restricting themselves to the minimum amount of issues, we seem to have exhausted human ingenuity in the creation of the worst possible monetary system that could be devised. If the State Banks had been left free we should have had long ago a currency perfect in its kind from the application of the methods that have been described. Left free, the inevitable antagonism that would have arisen between their issues and those of the National Government would have long ago driven the latter out of the field.

The climax of this strange episode in our history was the elevation of Mr. Chase from the office of Secretary of the Treasury to the Chief Justiceship of the Supreme Court of the United States. In that exalted position the question of the constitutionality of the issue, of which he was the chief instrument, of the legal tender notes, came up for adjudication and was declared by him to exceed the constitutional powers of the Government.[1]

---

[1] In describing Mr. Chase, Mr. James Russell Lowell, in a letter from Washington, November, 1868, to Leslie Stephen, said : "As for Mr. Chase, he is a weak man with an imposing presence, a most unhappy combination of which the world has not wanted examples from Saul and Pompey down. Such men as infallibly make mischief as they defraud expectation." — *Life of James Russell Lowell, Vol. II., page 7.*

Statement showing the amount of notes issued to the National Banks from 1864 to 1896 inclusive.

Years.		Years.		Years.	
1864	$31,235,270	1875	$354,408,009	1886	$311,694,454
1865	146,137,860	1876	332,998,386	1887	279,217,788
1866	281,479,908	1877	317,048,872	1888	252,368,321
1867	298,625,379	1878	324,514,284	1889	211,378,963
1868	290,762,855	1879	329,691,697	1890	185,970,775
1869	299,742,475	1880	344,505,427	1891	167,927,974
1870	299,766,984	1881	355,042,675	1892	172,683,850
1871	318,261,241	1882	358,742,034	1893	178,713,872
1872	237,664,795	1883	356,073,281	1894	203,110,023
1873	347,267,061	1884	339,499,883	1895	213,887,630
1874	351,981,032	1885	318,576,711	1896	233,639,357

GOLD CERTIFICATES.

On the 3d of March, 1863, an act was passed authorizing the issue of certificates on deposits of gold in the Treasury to the amount of $20 and upwards. For several years the amount of deposits was comparatively small. On the 1st of July, 1883, they reached the sum of $74,428,580. July 1, 1891, they reached the sum of $157,-562,979. The Government derived no advantage whatever from these transactions, while the act served as an example for two of the most disastrous measures ever adopted in this country, — the issue of the certificates under the act of 1878, and the issue of notes under the act of 1890.

DEMONETIZATION OF THE SILVER DOLLAR. ACT OF 1873.

Up to the close of the fiscal year 1869, 4,709,590 silver dollars had been coined, the rate averaging about 60,000 dollars annually. Up to that time $444,904,787 of gold had been coined. Not one of the silver dollars remained in circulation, having been taken up for export or for use in the arts as fast as they came from the mint. From 1834 to 1853 they had, at the mint ratio, a value averaging about 3.50 per cent. greater than that of gold. Minor coins of silver had the same relative value as the silver dollar. To prevent their exportation was the purpose of the act of 1853. Up to 1873, eighty-one years having elapsed from the establishment of the mint, there had been no revision of the coinage laws, although we had as a nation become the great producer of precious metals, and had established numerous local mints. In consequence, on the 25th of April, 1870, Mr. Boutwell, Secretary of the Treasury, transmitted to Mr. Sherman, Chairman of the Committee on Finance of the Senate, a bill for the revision of the coinage, and for the codification of the laws relating thereto. The bill, prepared by Mr. J. J. Knox, Deputy Comptroller of the Currency, was accompanied by a communication from him as to the method and purpose of its preparation, in which he said :

The method adopted in the preparation of the bill was, first, to arrange in as concise a form as possible the laws now in existence upon these subjects (mint, assay offices, and coinage), with such additional sections and suggestions as seemed valuable. Having accomplished this, the bill, as thus prepared, was printed upon paper with wide margin, and in this form transmitted to the different mints and assay offices; to the first comptroller, the treasurer, the solicitor, the first auditor, and to such other gentlemen as are known to be intelligent upon metallurgical and numismatical subjects, with the request that the printed bill should be returned, with such notes and suggestions as experience and education should dictate. In this way the views of more than thirty gentlemen who were conversant with the manipulation of metals, the manufacture of coinage, the execution of the present laws relative thereto, the method of keeping accounts and of making returns to the department, have been obtained. Having received these suggestions, the present bill has been framed, and is believed to comprise within the compass of eight or ten pages of the Revised Statutes every important provision contained in more than sixty different enactments upon the mint, assay offices, and coinage of the United States, which are the result of nearly eighty years of legislation upon these subjects.

. . . .

The coinage of the silver dollar piece is discontinued in the proposed bill. It is by law the dollar unit, and, assuming the value of gold to be fifteen and one-half times that of silver, being about the mean ratio for the past six years, is worth in gold a premium of about 3 per cent. (its value being $1.0312), and intrinsically more than 7 per cent. premium in other silver coins, its value thus being $1.0742. The present laws consequently authorize both a gold dollar unit and a silver dollar unit, differing from each other in intrinsic value. The present gold dollar piece is made the dollar unit in the proposed bill, and the silver dollar piece is discontinued. If, however, such coin is authorized, it should be issued only as a commercial dollar, not as a standard unit of account, and of the exact value of the Mexican dollar, which is the favorite for circulation in China and Japan, and other Oriental countries. (Sen. Mis. Doc. No. 132, second session, 41st Congress, 11.)

The bill drawn by Mr. Knox, which suspended altogether the coinage of the silver dollar as a unit of value, became the basis of all action of Congress upon the subject. On the 28th of April, 1870, it was, with the information which had been collected, referred to the Committee on Finance of the Senate. On the 2d of May 500 copies of the bill were ordered to be printed. On the 19th of December, 1870, it was reported back to the Senate, amended, and ordered to be printed.   On the 9th and 10th of January, 1871, it was taken up and debated at great length, and passed by a vote of 36 to 14.   The section in reference to silver, identical with that in the bill transmitted to the Senate by the Department of the Treasury, was as follows :

> That of the silver coins the weight of the half-dollar, or piece of fifty cents, shall be 192 grains, and that of the quarter-dollar and dime shall be respectively one-half and one-fifth of the weight of said half-dollar; that the silver coins issued in conformity with the above section shall be legal tender in any one payment of debts for all sums not exceeding $5.

This section was followed by another providing that " No coins, either of gold or silver or minor coinage, shall hereafter be issued from the mint other than those of the denominations, standards, and weights herein described."

A similar section was contained in all the different bills that were reported in either House, and in the coinage act of 1873.

On the 25th of June, 1870, the bill as drawn by Mr. Knox was introduced into the House and the printing of 500 copies ordered. On the 10th of January, 1871, the bill, as it had passed the Senate, came to the House.   On the 11th it was referred to the Committee on Coinage, Weights, and Measures.   On the 13th of January the printing of the bill was again ordered.   On the 25th of February the bill was reported to the House with a substitute, ordered to be printed, and recommitted.   On the 3d of March, 1871, the Forty-first Congress expired by limitation, all unfinished business inaugurated by it falling to the ground.

On the 9th of March, 1871, the original bill was revived in the House of the Forty-second Congress, and ordered to be printed.   No further action was taken at this session, which was a short one.   On the 9th of January, 1872, the bill was again reported to the House by Mr. Kelley, Chairman of the Committee on Coinage, and debated at great length, the debate occupying nearly two full days.   In reporting the bill, with a recommendation that it pass, Mr. Kelley said :

> This is a measure originated by the Treasury Department, and growing out of the necessities of the case.   The mint law of this country has never been revised.   It was originally framed for a single institution at Philadelphia, and it involves many crudities necessarily arising from the fact that we have established

several mints and quite a number of assay offices in different parts of our very much more widely extended country than the law was originally intended to cover. We were not then a bullion producing people, while we are to-day the greatest producers of gold and silver in the world. Our mints are situated on the Atlantic and Pacific coasts, and in the heart of what was but a few years ago regarded as the inaccessible desert of America.

The Secretary of the Treasury, discovering the difficulty of administering the affairs of so many mints and assay offices, gave the subject his personal consideration, and then invited to his aid some of the most experienced gentlemen of the country in the matters of coinage and the management of mints, and directed one of the officers of the Treasury, in connection with those gentlemen, to codify the mint laws.

That was done, and the codification, with such suggestions as those commissioners, as I may call them, made, were submitted to the two Houses of Congress. The Senate took up the bill and acted upon it during the last Congress, and sent it to this House. It was referred to the Committee on Coinage, Weights, and Measures, and received as careful attention as I have ever known a committee to bestow on any measure. The committee, before proceeding to consider it, sent copies of it, not to the director of the mint alone, but to the offices of all the mints and to those gentlemen who within the last fifteen or twenty years have been connected with the mints, and made reputations which justified the committee in attaching importance to their opinions and the results of their experience; and thus enlightened from sources to which the Secretary had not applied, the committee proceeded with great deliberation to go over the bill, not only section by section, but line by line, and word by word.

We omitted, so far as I know, no gentleman in the country who has had protracted official connection with the mints or assay offices, or any gentleman whose scientific attainments in connection with the system of coinage or mint usages was sufficient to bring him to our notice. The committee having no special views, regarding themselves as charged with a very important function, that of providing for the integrity of the coinage and an economical administration of the mints of the country, sought information from all recognized authorities, whether official or unofficial, American or foreign.

I would like to follow the example of England and make a wide difference between our gold and silver coins . . . and make the gold dollar uniform with the French system of weights, taking the gram as the unit. (Congressional Globe, second session, 42d Congress, page 322.)

The section in the bill reported by Mr. Kelley in reference to the coinage of silver was identical with that in the bill passed by the Senate.

On the 9th of February, 1872, the bill was again reported to the House, with amendments, one of which provided for the coinage of a base dollar of 384 grains, and ordered to be printed. On the 13th of February it was reported back to the House by Mr. Hooper, a member of the Committee on Coinage and made the special order for March 18 following. On April 9 the bill came up for consideration in that body. In bringing it to the attention of the House, Mr. Hooper gave abstracts of each one of the sixty-nine sections of which it was composed, his remarks filling ten closely printed columns of the Congressional Globe. In reference to the coinage of silver, he said :

> Section 16 reënacts the provisions of the existing laws defining the silver coins and their weights, respectively, except in relation to the silver dollar, which is reduced in weight from 412½ to 384 grains, thus making it a subsidiary coin in harmony with the silver coins of less denomination to secure its concurrent circulation with them.
>
> The silver dollar of 412½ grains, by reason of its bullion or intrinsic value being greater than its nominal value, long since ceased to be a coin of circulation, and is melted by manufacturers of silver ware. It does not circulate now in commercial transactions with any country, and the convenience of these manufacturers in this respect can better be met by supplying small stamped bars of the same standard, avoiding the useless expense of coining the dollar for that purpose. (Congressional Globe, 2d session, 42d Congress, page 2304.)

Mr. Hooper was followed by Mr. Stoughton, a member of the committee, who said :

> The silver coins provided for are the dollar (384 grains troy), the half-dollar, quarter-dollar, and dime, of the value and weight of one-half, one-quarter, and one-tenth of the dollar, respectively ; and they are made a legal tender for all sums not exceeding $5 at any one payment. The silver dollar, as now issued, is worth for bullion 3¼ cents more than the gold dollar and 7¼ cents more than the two half-dollars ; having a greater intrinsic than nominal value, it is certain to be withdrawn from circulation whenever we return to specie payment, and to be used only for manufacture and exportation as bullion.

To the leading features of the bill there was no opposition. To the proposition for dropping the dollar from the coinage, except in a debased form, not a word of objection was raised. The opposition, such as it was, was led by Mr. Potter, a member from New York, who, in commenting upon the bill, said :

> This is a bill of importance. When it was before the House in the early part of this session, I took some objections to it, which I am now inclined to think, in view of all the circumstances, were not entirely well founded ; but after further reflection I am still convinced that it is a measure which it is hardly worth while for us to adopt at this time. .   .   .

This bill provides for the making of changes in the legal tender coin of the country, and for substituting as legal tender coin of only one metal, instead, as heretofore, of two. I think myself this would be a wise provision, and that legal tender coins, except subsidiary coins, should be of gold alone; but why should we legislate on this now, when we are not using either of those metals as a circulating medium? The bill provides also for a change in respect to the weight and value of the silver dollar, which I think is a subject which, when we come to require legislation about it at all, will demand at our hands very serious consideration, and which, as we are not using such coins for circulation now, seems at this time an unnecessary subject about which to legislate.

In reply to Mr. Potter, Mr. Kelley said :

I wish to ask the gentleman who has just spoken if he knows of any government in the world which makes its subsidiary coinage of full value. The silver coin of England is ten per cent. below the value of gold coin, and, acting under the advice of experts of this country and of England and France, Japan has made her silver coinage within the last year twelve per cent. below the value of gold coin, and for the reason that it is impossible to retain the double standard. The values of gold and silver continually fluctuate. *You cannot determine this year what will be the relative value of gold and silver next year. They were 15 to 1 a short time ago; they are 16 to 1 now. Hence all experience has shown that you must have one standard coin which shall be a legal tender for all others*, and then you may promote your domestic convenience by having a subsidiary coinage of silver, which shall circulate in all parts of your country as legal tender for a limited amount and be redeemable at its face value by your government. *But, sir, I again call the attention of the House to the fact that the gentlemen who oppose this bill insist upon maintaining a silver dollar worth 3½ cents more than the gold dollar and worth 7 cents more than two half-dollars, and that so long as those provisions remain, you cannot keep silver coin in the country.*

The bill now before the House, as amended, differed from that prepared at the Department of the Treasury and which passed the Senate in retaining the dollar as a subsidiary coin, the value of the same being reduced from 412½ to 384 standard grains, it being made competent for the payment of debts not exceeding $5.

On the 27th of May, 1872, the bill was again brought to the consideration of the House by Mr. Hooper, who offered an amendment in the nature of a substitute, which was read. The section in the substitute in relation to silver was precisely the same as in the bill that was superseded, the two differing only in matters of detail. The subject at this time had ceased to attract attention, as it had for more than two years been before Congress, which had been plied with every suggestion and argument that ingenuity could invent, and had been debated *ad nauseam* in both Houses. The bill passed in the House by a standing vote of 106 to 16, the yeas and nays not being demanded. The debate immediately previous to the passage of the bill was of the nature of a colloquy rather than an argument. Among the members who interposed was Mr. Holman, from Indiana, who said :

> Before the question is taken upon the question of the rules and passing the bill, I hope that the gentleman from Massachusetts will explain the leading changes made by this bill in the existing law, especially in reference to the coinage. It would seem that all the small coinage of the country is intended to be recoined.
>
> MR. HOOPER. — This bill makes no changes in the existing law in that regard. It does not require the coinage of the small coins.

The question related wholly to the matter of the minor coinage, as did the reply.

The bill that passed the House was, on the 29th of May, 1872, taken up by the Senate, ordered to be printed, and referred to the Committee on Finance. On the 16th of December, 1872, Mr. Sherman, chairman of the committee, in reporting the bill back to the Senate, said :

> This bill has in substance passed both Houses. It was passed by the Senate at the session of the last Congress, went to the House, and now, somewhat modified, has passed the House at this Congress, so that the bill has practically passed both Houses of Congress. The Senate Committee on Finance propose the modification of only a single section for a "trade dollar" of 420 grains. As this is not the same Congress that passed the bill in the Senate, I suppose we shall have to go through the form of a full reading.

The bill was thereupon ordered to be printed with the amendments. On the 7th of January, 1873, it was again reported with the amendments and printed for the information of the Senate. On the 17th of January, after a protracted debate, the report of which filled nineteen closely printed columns of the Globe, the bill was passed without division. In the course of the debate Mr. Sherman said :

> This bill proposes a silver coinage exactly the same as the French and what are called the associated nations of Europe, who have adopted the international standard of silver coinage; that is, the dollar (two half-dollars) provided for in this bill is the precise equivalent of a five-franc piece. It contains the same number

of grams of silver, and we have adopted the international gram instead of the grain for the standard of our silver coinage. The "trade dollar" has been adopted mainly for the benefit of the people of California and others engaged in trade with China.

That is the only coin measured by the grain instead of by the gram. The intrinsic value of each is to be stamped upon the coin. The Chamber of Commerce of New York recommended this change, and it has been adopted, I believe, by all the learned societies who have given attention to coinage, and has been recommended to us, I believe, as the general desire. That is embodied in these three or four sections of amendment to make our silver coinage correspond in exact form and dimensions and shape and stamp with the coinage of the associated nations of Europe, who have adopted an international silver coinage. (Congressional Globe, 3d session, 42d Congress, page 668.)

On the 21st January, 1873, the Senate bill reached the House, and on the motion of Mr. Hooper was printed with amendments. The House adhered to its bill, and appointed a committee of conference. The Senate insisting, a conference committee was created. In the committee the House surrendered its proposition for a base dollar of 384 grains to be legal tender in payments not exceeding $5, accepting therefor the "trade dollar," and on the 12th of February, 1873, the report of the conference committee being accepted by both branches, by the approval of the President, the bill became a law. Section 15 in relation to the coinage was as follows:

That the silver coinage of the United States shall be a trade dollar, a half-dollar or 50-cent piece, a quarter-dollar or 25-cent piece, a dime or 10-cent piece; and the weight of the trade dollar shall be 420 (standard) grains troy; the weight of the half-dollar shall be 12 grams (grammes) and one-half of a gram (gramme); the quarter-dollar and the dime shall be, respectively, one-half and one-fifth of the weight of said half-dollar; and said coins shall be a legal tender at their nominal value for any amount not exceeding $5 in any one payment.

Section 17 provided that

No coins, either of gold, silver, or minor coinage, shall hereafter be issued from the mint other than those denominations, standards, and weights herein set forth.

Such is the history of the famous Act of 1873. The bill for this act came from the Secretary of the Treasury early in 1870 with a communication recommending its passage. In addition it was pressed upon the attention of Congress in his annual reports for 1870, 1871, and 1872. It was before Congress for five successive sessions of that body and for a period of nearly three years. It was printed by its order thirteen times.

The reports of the debates in the Senate upon the measure fill 66 closely printed columns of the Globe ; in the House, 78.   In every bill reported, printed, or debated, the silver dollar, except as a subsidiary coinage, was forbidden in express terms.   The dollar proposed for home circulation was a base one of 384 standard grains, the legal competency of which was not to exceed $5 in any one sum. The " trade " dollar for exportation to the Orient had a value at the time 10 per cent. greater than the gold dollar, its legal competency being no greater than the proposed debased one.

During the whole period in which this matter was under consideration the records of Congress contain no suggestion that the old dollar of 412½ grains be retained.   For 1870, the year in which the bill was received from the Department of the Treasury, the excess in value of the silver over the gold dollar was 2.67 per cent. ; in 1872, the measure becoming a law early in 1873, the excess equalled 2.25 per cent.   No bill that ever passed Congress received greater consideration measured by the time spent upon it and in the efforts made to bring it to the notice of the public and members of Congress, and no public measure was ever better received.

In answer to the charge that the Act of 1873 was surreptitiously passed, the following extracts from Mr. Knox's work, entitled " United States Notes," are given, he having had more to do with the measure than any other person :

During the debate on the bill of 1878 the charge was repeatedly made, in and out of Congress, that the Act of 1873, discontinuing the free coinage of the silver dollar, was passed surreptitiously.   This statement has no foundation in fact.   The report of the writer, who was then deputy comptroller of the currency, transmitted to Congress in 1870 by the Secretary, three times distinctly stated that the bill accompanying it proposed to discontinue the issue of the silver dollar piece.   Various experts, to whom it had been submitted, approved this feature of the bill, and their opinions were printed by order of Congress. The House was informed by its members of this provision, and the bill was printed thirteen times by order of Congress, and once by the commissioners revising the statutes, and was considered during five successive sessions.

It is not probable that any act passed by any Congress ever received more care in its preparation, or was ever submitted to the criticism of a greater number of practical and scientific experts than was this coinage act of 1873.   The statement in reference to the surreptitious or inadvertent passage of the bill was subsequently repeated in the city of Paris by a member of the silver commission.

From 1853 to 1873 the coinage of silver dollars equalled $5,538,948; of minor coins of silver in value $51,598,562. The coinage of gold was $540,736,349. The total coinage of silver dollars up to 1873 was $8,045,938; of minor silver coins $137,096,046. The total coinage of gold up to 1873 was $816,905,874.[1]

[1] Statement showing the number of silver dollars coined from the establishment of the Mint to 1873, inclusive:

YEARS.	Dollars.	YEARS.	Dollars.	YEARS.	Dollars.
1795	$204,791	1822	. . . .	1849	$62,600
1796	72,920	1823	. . . .	1850	47,500
1797	7,776	1824	. . . .	1851	1,300
1798	327,536	1825	. . . .	1852	1,100
1799	423,515	1826	. . . .	1853	46,110
1800	220,920	1827	. . . .	1854	33,140
1801	54,454	1828	. . . .	1855	26,000
1802	41,650	1829	. . . .	1856	63,500
1803	66,064	1830	. . . .	1857	94,000
1804	19,570	1831	. . . .	1858	. . . .
1805	321	1832	. . . .	1859	288,500
1806	. . . .	1833	. . . .	1860	600,530
1807	. . . .	1834	. . . .	1861	559,900
1808	. . . .	1835	. . . .	1862	1,750
1809	. . . .	1836	$1,000	1863	31,400
1810	. . . .	1837	. . . .	1864	23,170
1811	. . . .	1838	. . . .	1865	32,900
1812	. . . .	1839	300	1866	58,550
1813	. . . .	1840	61,005	1867	57,000
1814	. . . .	1841	173,000	1868	54,800
1815	. . . .	1842	184,618	1869	231,350
1816	. . . .	1843	165,100	1870	588,308
1817	. . . .	1844	20,000	1871	657,929
1818	. . . .	1845	24,500	1872	1,112,961
1819	. . . .	1846	169,600	1873	977,150
1820	. . . .	1847	140,750		
1821	. . . .	1848	15,000	Total	$8,045,838

Statement showing the yearly average value, in cents, of the silver dollar, compared with gold, for twenty years, ending with 1872:

YEARS.	Value in Cents.	YEARS.	Value in Cents.	YEARS.	Value in Cents.
1853	104.26	1860	104.58	1867	102.67
1854	104.26	1861	103.10	1868	102.57
1855	103.95	1862	104.60	1869	102.47
1856	103.95	1863	104.06	1870	102.67
1857	104.69	1864	104.06	1871	102.57
1858	103.95	1865	103.52	1872	102.25
1859	105.22	1866	103.63		

The average value of the silver dollar for the whole period was 103.63 cents.

From the establishment of the Mint down to and including the Act of 1873, a period of eighty-three years, whenever the subject of the coinage was considered it was always from a business point of view, precisely as the subject of weights and measures had been considered that the same standards might be provided for all, high and low, rich and poor. In the matter of the standard of value the changes in the metals used always suggested themselves. A thousand years ago copper was good money. Sixty years ago silver was good money. Silver is no longer good money except in the form of subsidiary coins. It was disused precisely as have been great numbers of methods, good in their day, but good for nothing now. The changes that have taken place in the standards of value form an interesting chapter in the progress of society. In his report in 1792 upon the Mint, Mr. Hamilton assumed that of the two metals gold was the more uniform in value and for this reason was entitled to the preference as the standard of value. He believed, however, that a ratio could be established corresponding so nearly to the commercial value of the two metals as to render indifferent the choice between them, each at the time being equally well fitted to serve as money; silver, perhaps from its long use, having the preference. He assumed that the difference in the value of the coins of the two, not exceeding the cost of exportation estimated at one-half of one per cent., would not disturb the relation between them. Both metals were consequently adopted as money under the idea that the amount might thereby be increased; a very natural conclusion at the time. He was mistaken; a difference equalling one-quarter of one per cent. being enough to disturb the equilibrium sought to be secured, either kind being equally convenient in use. As by the ratio established gold was undervalued, although provision was made for two kinds, silver alone remained as money. But its establishment as such had no effect to bring it into use as the ordinary instrument of exchange. It was the sole money of the country in 1831 when the Select Committee of the House of Representatives recommended the discontinuance of its coinage, except in inconsiderable sums in the form of small coins, the total amount in the hands of the people at the time not exceeding $5,000,000, or 30 cents per head, the population equalling 13,000,000. The transactions of the people at the time in ratio to their numbers did not equal one-tenth their present amount. The old earth roads served, or seemed to serve, at the time very well for the movement of their persons and property. In 1834 came the first change, the great increase in transactions calling for a money having a higher relative value than silver. But the establishment of gold as the money of the country had no effect to bring it into use as the ordinary instrument of exchange. It had the effect, however, at the ratio at which it was coined, of driving silver, the undervalued metal, out of the country for the discharge of balances arising in foreign trade, and to such an extent as to be the source of great inconvenience, an evil remedied by the Act of 1853, whereby the minor coins of silver were so debased that they could be exported only at a loss. The purpose of the Act of 1873 was to give systematic or codified form to the numerous acts on the statute book, and a legal sanction to the disuse of the silver dollar which from the foundation of the Government had, as money, existed only in name. Never was there a public measure in the history of the nation more appropriate, more thoroughly considered, better understood, or more cordially accepted at the time of its enactment, than the Act of 1873.

REMONETIZATION OF SILVER.

By the Act of February 28, 1878, provision was made for the coinage of the silver dollar at the old ratio of 16 to 1, although at the time the commercial ratio between the two metals was about 18 to 1, the fall, from its greatly increased production, in the price of silver from 1873 having been about 12 per cent. The act, called the " Bland Act," from the name of the member of the House who had the measure chiefly in charge in that body, provided for the purchase at its commercial value for coinage by the Secretary of the Treasury of not less than 2,000,000, nor more than, 4,000,000 ounces per month of silver bullion, any gain or seigniorage arising to be conveyed into the Treasury, the coins to be legal tender at their nominal value for all debts, public and private. The act further provided that any holder of the dollars might deposit the same with the Treasurer, or any Assistant Treasurer, of the United States, in sums not less than ten dollars, and receive therefor " certificates " receivable in the payment of all public dues. The bill first introduced into the House provided for the unlimited coinage of silver at the ratio of 16 to 1. It passed that body November 5, 1877, by a vote of 163 to 34. The bill was amended in the Senate, taking very nearly the form in which it finally became a law, passing that body by a vote of 48 to 21. As amended, it passed the House by a vote of 203 to 72. The bill was vetoed by the President, Mr. Hayes, for the following reasons :

> If it is now proposed, for the purpose of taking advantage of the depreciation of silver in the payment of debts, to coin and make a legal tender a silver dollar of less commercial value than any dollar, whether of gold or paper, which is now lawful money in this country, such a measure, it will be hardly questioned, will, in the judgment of mankind, be an act of bad faith as to all debts heretofore contracted. The silver dollar should be made a legal tender only at its market value. The standard of value should not be changed without the consent of both parties to the contract. National promises should be kept with unflinching fidelity. There is no power to compel a nation to pay its just debts. Its credit depends on its honor. The nation owes what it has led or allowed its creditors to expect. I cannot approve a bill which, in my judgment, authorizes the violation of sacred obligations. The obligation of the public faith transcends all questions of profit or public advantage. Its unquestionable maintenance is the dictate as well of the highest expediency as of the most necessary duty, and should ever be carefully guarded by the Executive, by Congress, and by the people. It is my firm conviction that if the country is to be benefited by a silver coinage, it can be done only by the issue of silver dollars of full value which will defraud no man. A currency worth less than it purports to be worth will in the end defraud not only creditors, but all who are engaged in legitimate business, and none more surely than those who are dependent on their daily labor for their daily bread.

The bill passed the House over the veto by a vote of 196 to 63 ; and the Senate by a vote of 46 to 19.

In 1870, when proceedings for the demonetization of the silver dollar were first taken, its value compared with gold was 102.67 cents. In 1878, when it was remonetized at the old ratio of 16 to 1, its value had fallen to 89 ; the fall in value equalling 13.67 cents, the percentage of the fall being 15 per cent. After the fall had taken place the great crime of 1873 was for the first time discovered. To undo it was the purpose of the Bland Act. In the debates which took place a great many pictures of the fraud were drawn, one of the most graphic being that of Mr. Voorhees, then member of the House, subsequently a member of the Senate from the State of Indiana :

> There is, he said, a numerous and powerful class in our midst who believe, as Alexander Hamilton declared, that the British Government, on this as well as on other points, is the best ever devised by the wisdom of man. Those enter-

taining this opinion have thus far triumphed in the financial legislation of the United States, and the time has now arrived when their victories must be reversed or soon this Government will cease to be republican and the people no longer free. . . .

Sir, this theme becomes humiliating to every honest American mind. It fills with shame every honest patriotic heart. The naked fact confronts us at every step that no pledge, however high, solemn, or binding in law and morals, has been strong enough to compel the authors of our financial legislation to obey it. No sense of national honor or good faith has restrained for a single moment the unbridled avarice of idle interest-bearing capital whenever it has been tempted, like some hungry marauding animal, to break over the barriers erected between it and new fields of spoilage that lie beyond. The silver dollar came to us with the birth of our Government. It was devised as a unit of value by Thomas Jefferson. It stood as honored as gold through every storm that beat upon this Government. It is associated with all our development, our strength, our growth, and our glory. With it as a currency, more than any other, the picket lines of civilization have pushed westward. The pioneer in the shadow of the great forests or on the wide prairies toiled to lay it by, one by one, until the coveted sum of one hundred lay before him. Then tightening the girths of his saddle, he rode with speed to the distant land office, where the Government took his one hundred silver dollars for eighty acres of land, which thenceforward became that most blessed spot on earth, a home ; a home where trees were planted, where children were born and grew to be men and women, and they in turn went forth into the great world, still to the west, there to live over again in labor and privation the lives of the father and mother left behind.

The silver dollar is peculiarly the laboring man's dollar, as far as he may desrie specie. When specie payments were authorized before the war it was the favorite currency with the people. Throughout all the financial panics that have assailed this country no man has been bold enough to raise his hand to strike it down ; no man has ever dared to whisper of a contemplated attack upon it ; and when the hour of its danger and destruction drew nigh, when the 12th day of February, 1873, approached, the day of doom to the American dollar, the dollar of our fathers, how silent was the work of the enemy ! Not a sound, not a word, no note of warning to the American people that their favorite coin was to be destroyed as money ; that the greatest financial revolution of modern times was in contemplation and about to be accomplished against their highest and dearest rights ! The tax-payers of the United States were no more notified or consulted on this momentous measure than the slaves on a Southern plantation before the war, when their master made up his mind to increase their task or to change them from a corn to a cotton field. Never since the foundation of the Government has a law of such vital and tremendous import, or indeed of any importance at all, crawled into our statute books so furtively and so noiselessly as this. Its enactment there was as completely unknown to the people, and indeed to four-fifths of Congress itself, as the presence of a burglar in a house at midnight is to its sleeping inmates. This was rendered possible partly because the clandestine movement was so utterly unexpected, and partly from the nature of the bill in which it occurred.

Sir, in the entire catalogue of crimes against human society, not one can be found so awful in all its consequences, both immediate and remote, as a Government commits when it deliberately destroys the money of its own citizens. Wherever in all the regions of time such measures have been accomplished the horrors of history have taken place. No shrinkage in the amount of money, no contraction of the currency in the hands of the people was ever enforced by law to any considerable extent, except amid broken lives, ruined hopes, despair, lost honor, and all the vices springing from the lowest depths of poverty and human misery. The worst ingredients of war, pestilence, and famine all flow from the act of a government violently tearing from the hands of the laboring masses the money they so much need. Murder, theft, robbery, prostitution, forgery, embezzlement, and fraud of every hue and mien curse the land that is deprived of a full and sufficient circulating medium on which to give employment to its toiling men and women.

But what is the duty of the Government in this regard ? Is it true that the people are not dependent on the policy of their Government for money on which to do business ? Is it true, as often asserted, that in some way or other those who are willing to work, or have something to sell, can always obtain money regardless of all financial legislation ? No greater fallacy than this was ever put forward in defence of wrong and injustice. Money is the creature of government both as to quality and quantity. It exists merely by the assertion of law, and in no other way. Article 1, Section 8, of the Constitution of the United States provides that "The Congress shall have power . . . to coin money, regulate the value thereof, and of foreign coin, and fix the standard of weights and measures," and Section 10 of the same article denies all such powers to the States, thus making Congress the exclusive creator of money for the American people. Without the action of Congress not one dollar can exist in the United States. If the article called money, whether of gold, silver, or paper, is necessary at all in the transactions of life, here alone is the fountain from which it emanates. How, then, shall this high power be exercised ? Shall only enough lawful money be created, in proportion to the labor and other commodities which it is designed to pay for, to give ten cents a day to the laborer, and ten dollars for a horse ; or shall it be furnished in sufficient amount to afford a just equivalent for labor and for every other thing of value? On the answer to this question has depended the prosperity or the adversity of the American people in all the past ; on it their present deplorable condition can alone be explained, and their future fate foretold. A circulating medium being a recognized necessity of civilized nations, and its existence depending solely on national authority, that government which, for any reason, fails to make a supply adequate to the business prosperity of its citizens, violates that fundamental compact of duty which must prevail in every free political commonwealth.

Not only, however, has this Government failed in this great duty, but the manner it has adopted to furnish the people with their limited and insufficient supply of currency was conceived and perfected by the owners of retired inactive capital. The system of national banking now in use is the most elaborate and complete scheme for making the people pay tribute to wealth, in order to obtain a circulating medium, ever known in the financial history of the world. There is not a dollar to-day in the hands of the people on which they have not paid a tax for the privilege of having it put in circulation by the Government. The national bank is the middle man between the Government and the people, and is enormously paid for what the Government ought directly to do itself. According to the report of the Comptroller of the Currency there were two thousand and eighty national banks Oct. 1, 1877, and they owned in even numbers $336,-000,000 of government bonds as the basis of a bank note circulation of $291,000,000. The interest paid by the people on the bonds thus used to secure a currency on which to transact their business amounts to not less than $16,000,000 per annum. This is the tax paid for the bank-note circulation. The bondholder has been made the banker of the country, and he is banking on the interest-bearing debt of the people. For every $100 of currency they pay him nearly six dollars interest on the bonds which secure that hundred. His advantages, however, only begin with this bonus of sixteen millions.

The report of the Comptroller shows that, Oct. 1, 1877, the national banks had loans outstanding to the amount of eight hundred and ninety-one millions. No one will pretend that these loans are made on an average interest of less than ten per cent. This makes an interest amount of eighty-nine millions per annum, and this is an under rather than an over estimate. Of other bonds, stocks, debts, real estate, specie, currency, clearing-house exchanges, United States certificates of deposit, and all other sources, the property of the national banks, at the above date, amounted to something over five hundred and fourteen millions, which, at the rate of five per cent., makes an additional interest income of twenty-five millions. The following statement will therefore correctly represent the facts:

Oct. 1, 1887:

National banks	2,080
Resources	$1,741,000,000
Interest on resources paid by the people per annum . .	130,000,000

In return for the establishment of this stupendous money power it simply acts as an agent in transmitting the currency of the United States from the Treasury to the people. Will any one pretend that a cheaper and more equitable mode of supplying the country with a circulating medium cannot be framed by our legislative wisdom?

The power of money in the midst of times like these is very great, but I am much deceived in the people if they have not turned at last in defiance and bold warning upon their oppressors. They demand that certain specific wrongs shall be redressed.

First, those for whom I speak demand the restoration of the silver dollar exactly as it stood before it was touched by the act of February, 1873. They desire that it shall have unlimited coinage, not fearing that it will become too plenty for their wants ; and that it be made a full legal tender, believing that it is as good now with which to pay all debts, public and private, as it was during eighty-one years of American history.

Second, they demand the repeal, unconditionally, of the act of Jan. 14, 1875, compelling a resumption of specie payments in January, 1879, holding that the question of a return to a specie basis for our currency should be controlled entirely by the business interests of the country.   They do not believe that the country should be dragged through the depths of ruin, wretchedness, and degradation in order to reach a gold standard for the benefit alone of the income classes.

Third, they demand that the national banking system be removed and a circulating medium provided by the Government for the people, without taxing them for the privilege of obtaining it.   And they ask that the amount thus placed in circulation shall bear a reasonable and judicious proportion to the business transactions and the population of the United States.

Fourth, they demand that the currency circulated on the authority of the Government shall be made a legal tender in payment of all debts, public and private, including all dues to the Government, well knowing that it will then be at par with gold, or more likely at a premium over it.

And fifth, they demand that hereafter the financial policy of the country shall be framed permanently in their interest ; that they shall not be discriminated against in future legislation as in the past, and that their prosperity, and not mere growth of incomes to retired capitalists, shall be the primary duty of the Government.   (Congressional Record, 45th Congress, Vol. I., 330.)

The language of Mr. Voorhees is so direct and his meaning so clearly expressed as hardly to require comment.   He was a member of the House for the whole period pending the demonetization of the silver dollar, having been elected in 1869.   From an examination of the Journals he appears to have been constant in his attendance at its sittings.   Upon his table were laid all the reports of the committees of the House and all the bills in their various forms relating to the coinage.   No member of the House outside the committee was probably more familiar with the progress of the measure in its various stages.   In the face of all this his statement that there was " Not a sound, not a word of warning to the American people that their favorite coin was to be destroyed ; that never from the foundation of the Government did a law of such tremendous import, or of any importance at all, crawl so furtively into our statute books as this ; its enactment being as completely unknown to four-fifths of Congress as the presence of a burglar in a house at night to its sleeping inmates," was a piece of mendacity unmatched in legislative history.   The most painful part of the whole businesss is that it has been accepted by the country as solemn truth.

" The silver dollar," said Mr. Voorhees, " was devised as a unit of value by Thomas Jefferson, and was associated with all our development, our strength, our growth and our glory.   It was always the money of the picket line of our civilization. No sooner was the coveted hundred dollars secured than the possessor rode to a distant land office to exchange them for eighty acres of land to become his future home." The same process, he declared, was repeated by children and grandchildren till the mighty wave of civilization was carried to the Pacific Ocean. Of the $8,000,000 coined up to 1878 not a dollar ever entered into general circulation; not a dollar ever crossed the Alleghanies! As for Jefferson he had no more to do with devising the mint ratio of the silver dollar as the unit of value than Adam. When in this country lying is to be done on a colossal scale Jefferson and Jackson are always summoned as vouchers.

"In the entire catalogue of crimes against human society not one can be found so awful in its consequences as when Government deliberately destroys the money of its own citizens." But not a dollar of money was destroyed by the Act of 1873. By it the obsolete provision for the coinage of the silver dollar, never in circulation, was dropped from the statute book. The few that were coined, having a greater commercial than coin value, were taken for use in the arts, or for export, as fast as they came from the mint. In a country like the United States metallic money will take care of itself. It may as well consist of the coinage of other mints as of its own. Symbolic money under free conditions will also take care of itself, its nominal value equalling that of the subjects of consumption; so that the terrible pictures of "war, pestilence, famine, murder, theft, robbery, prostitution, forgery, embezzlement, and fraud of every hue" due to the want of money were of Mr. Voorhees' own creation, or rather examples of lying with a circumstance.

And what was the remedy? The creation by Government of money, the quantity and quality dependent upon its will, but enough, so that instead of 10 cents a day to labor and $10 for a horse there should be enough to secure ample reward for labor, and a remunerative price for all the products of labor. "When a Government fails to supply an adequate amount of money to the people, it violates," Mr. Voorhees declared, "the fundamental compact of duties which must prevail in every free commonwealth." The Government, he said, had wholly neglected this great duty, leaving the supply of currency to the banks, in consequence of which they realized

$130,000,000 annually, "simply for acting as agents in transferring the currency of the United States from the Treasury to the people."

The remedy was first, the repeal of the Act of 1873 and the unlimited coinage of silver; second, the repeal, unconditionally, of the acts for the resumption of specie payments, "that the country be no longer dragged through the depths of ruin, wretchedness and degradation in order to reach a gold standard for the benefit alone of the income classes; third, that the National Banking system be abolished; fourth, that the money of the country, created and issued by the Government, be legal tender in the payment of all debts, public and private, including all dues to Government, "well knowing that such money will be at the par of gold or more likely at a premium over it;" and finally, "that the financial policy of the country shall be framed permanently in the interests of the people, and that their prosperity, not the mere growth of income to retired capitalists, should be the primary duty of the Government."

In 1877 Mr. Voorhees was elected to the Senate, in which he served for eighteen years consecutively. In that long period he never omitted an opportunity to repeat the doctrines of his great speech of 1878. In 1893, by regular gradation, being the oldest member of his party in service in the Senate, he was advanced to the chairmanship of the Committee on Finance, a place of influence, dignity, and honor, second only to that of the President of the United States. In 1893, when chairman of that committee, he made a speech in his place in which, among other things, he said:

Silver is the money of the Constitution, and so specified in that great instrument, and should be coined on the same terms that gold is coined, "without discrimination against either metal, and without charge for mintage." This has been the doctrine of the Democratic party from the days of Jefferson to the Chicago Convention of 1892, and it is the doctrine of the laboring masses to-day, irrespective of party, throughout the United States. In fact, the American people, the plain working people, have been benefited in the last one hundred years far more by silver money than by gold money, and the whining cant of sordid avarice which we now hear, that " gold is sound money " and silver is not, has the profound contempt of every man familiar with the history and the developments of his country.

As to the *parity* of the two metals when coined, even the small children of finance know that the purchasing power of a dollar is not fixed by the quality or the quantity of the material which composes it, but by the law which makes it a legal-tender in the payment of debts. Much vapid nonsense has been spoken and written in regard to what is styled " fiat money." The fiat of the government

simply means "thus saith the law," and there was never, in this or any government on earth, and never will be, a dollar, whether of gold, silver, or paper,
other than absolutely and entirely the creature of the law. When silver is coined,
therefore, at the ratio of 16 to 1 in gold, or any other ratio, and clothed with the
authority of law, it has never failed to be on a par with gold in its purchasing and
debt-paying power. I am ready at any auspicious time to fight for the fair and
honorable restoration of silver coinage to its old place alongside of gold. I care
but little for the attitude of foreign nations on this subject. We are not subject
to their dictation, and for their disapproval we may compensate ourselves with
the approval of our own people.

Extracts from the speeches of Mr. Voorhees are given at considerable length, but they should be read and reread by every citizen who would get an adequate idea of political life in America, in
which the highest offices are within easy reach of the most ignorant,
malevolent, and revolutionary characters, and of the dangers to
which our institutions are consequently exposed.

Among the members of the House who voted for the bill of 1878
was the Hon. John G. Carlisle, of Kentucky, afterwards Speaker of
the House of the 48th, 49th, and 50th Congresses, and Secretary of
the Treasury for the whole period of Mr. Cleveland's second term.
From his speech the following extracts are given :

I know that the world's stock of precious metals is none too large. Mankind
will be fortunate, indeed, if the annual production of gold and silver coin shall keep
pace with the annual increase of population, commerce, and industries. According to my view of the subject, the *conspiracy* which seems to have been formed
here and in Europe to destroy by legislation or otherwise from three-sevenths to
one-half of the metallic money of the world *is the most gigantic crime of this
or any other age*. The consummation of such a scheme [the disuse of silver] would
ultimately entail more misery upon the human race than all the wars, pestilences,
and famines that have ever occurred in the history of the world. The absolute and
instantaneous destruction of half the entire movable property of the world, including houses, ships, railroads, and all other appliances for carrying on commerce,
while it would be felt more sensibly at the moment, would not produce anything
like the prolonged distress and disorganization of society that must inevitably
result from the permanent annihilation of one-half the metallic money of the
world. With an ample currency an industrious and frugal people will speedily
rebuild the works of internal improvement and repair losses of property, but no
amount of industry or economy on the part of the people can create money.
*When a government creates it or authorizes it the citizen may acquire it, but
he can do nothing more.*

I am in favor of every practical and constitutional measure that will have a
tendency to defeat or retard the perpetration of *this great crime*, and I am also in

favor of every practical and constitutional measure that will aid us in devising a just and permanent ratio of value between the two metals, so that they may circulate side by side, and not alternately drive each other into exile from one country to another. I desire to add only, in conclusion, that while the measure in its present form is not what the country had a right to expect, it is infinitely better than anything the people have been able ever to obtain at the hands of Congress *during the last fifteen years.* It is the *first victory* won by the people during many weary years of warfare with the *consolidated wealth* of this and other countries, and although it is not by any means a complete triumph, it marks the beginning of a new and more popular era in national legislation; it attests a mighty revolution in public sentiment as represented at the capitol. It places the great industrial and producing masses of the people in the front and the non-producers in the rear. For fifteen years the people have been on the defensive, and although fortified by the plainest provisions of law and the clearest principles of equity, *they have been completely driven from one position to another until they have stood at last upon the very verge of financial ruin.* Gathering up all their energies for this struggle, they have advanced, not very far, it is true, but they have advanced far enough to recover part of the ground lost in the previous conflict.

Our power of legislation on this subject will not be exhausted by the passage of this measure, and we ought not to halt for a single moment in our efforts to complete the work only inaugurated by it. The struggle now going on cannot cease and ought not to cease until all the industrial interests of the country are fully and finally emancipated from the *heartless domination of syndicates, stock exchanges, and other great combinations of money-grabbers in this country and in Europe.* (Appendix, Congressional Record, 2d Session, 45th Congress, page 41.)

Although Mr. Carlisle voted for the bill, he declared himself, in a speech delivered on the occasion, to be in favor of unlimited as against the free coinage of silver, in order that the Government might have the benefit of the large gain or seigniorage that would result, the subsidiary coinage which took the place of the fractional currency issued during the war being an example. For this purpose 31,897,371 ounces of silver bullion were purchased at a cost of $34,118,203, and converted into coins having a nominal value of $39,685,618, the gain or seigniorage resulting being $5,567,415. The same policy, he declared, should be pursued in the coinage of the silver dollars, unlimited in amount, but on account of the Government. Free coinage might be limited; that is, a certain amount authorized for any given period. He was for the unlimited coinage of silver precisely on the same terms as the coinage of gold. If the coinage of silver was not on account of the Government, the miners of it, bankers, and the governments of the Old World intent upon getting rid of their stocks of it would reap the whole benefit of the coinage, as the dollars were to circulate at their nominal value. With him, as with Mr. Voorhees, money was "Thus saith the law" — or, to use his own words, "when a government creates money or authorizes it the citizen may acquire it, but he can do nothing more." But cannot the citizen create money by digging the metal out of the ground; can he not lay the foundation of symbolic money by the creation of merchandise — functions which governments cannot or will not exercise? The coinage of the silver dollars proceeded according to his plan. The seigniorage on the same from 1878 to the close of 1895 equalled $75,219,137 conveyed as profit into the Treasury. The trouble with Mr. Carlisle was that the coinage did not proceed with sufficient rapidity. The purchase of $2,000,000 per month was a small affair, but it was great in being the first victory won by the people in their warfare of fifteen years with the "consolidated capital of this and other countries." The value of the victory was the possibility of the future. But for ten of these fifteen years of weary warfare the coinage of silver was wholly free. When it was free no one presented it for coinage, its bullion being three per cent. greater than its coin value.

"The fifteen years of weary warfare in which the people were driven from one position to another until they stood on the very verge of financial ruin" must therefore have had a purpose other than the coinage. What was it? Who drove the people from one position to another until they stood at last upon the very verge of financial ruin? What was the object of this terrible crusade? How was it that the people could oppose no resistance? In this country the people are the Government and the Government the people. The popular branch of the National Legislature is chosen once in two years. Were its members for fifteen years regularly bribed that the people might be driven to the very verge of financial ruin? For capital to push them to such terrible extremes would be to destroy its own value by destroying the ability of the people to use and pay for it. But in place of the terrible scenes described the period of fifteen years at the end of which, according to Mr. Carlisle, the people stood upon the very verge of financial ruin was one full of activity and hope, one of the most progressive and prosperous in our history. It was the most honorable in our history, this repairing in a manly way the waste and confusion of war, paying off and funding the great variety of obligations that had been created, a steady advance being made towards the resumption of specie payments by the retirement of the legal tender notes. The fifteen years were the most creditable period in our history. In them the genius of our people showed at its best. It was an easy thing to put down the rebellion. It was a work of destruction. To lay deep the foundations of social order so that every man was the same before the law, to create a prosperity without example, were far greater achievements. The party that accomplished such results seemed too firmly entrenched to be overthrown except by appeals to the passions of the people. Hence the terrible pictures drawn of the "oppressions of consolidated capital" — all pure inventions. In drawing them Mr. Carlisle was only Lucio in the play. "He spoke but according to the trick." People like to be told that the reason why they have so little is that they have been robbed, and who would be so likely to rob them as "consolidated capital"? What is "consolidated capital" but the fruits of robbery? Possession was conclusive of the fact. How could capital be consolidated except by robbery? The changes that Mr. Carlisle rung on "consolidated capital" were all the stock in trade that demagogues required to sway vast masses of people to their will. No man could handle these words with more dexterity and effect than Mr. Carlisle. Everything was sure to go on well so long as they remained mere declamation. For a long time they were nothing but declamation. But it was inevitable that in time invectives so constantly and fiercely uttered should become convictions on the part of the hearers no longer to be held in control. They did become convictions, and the platform of the late National Democratic convention was the result. The little knot of "consolidated capitalists," including Mr. Cleveland, who so long controlled the Democracy, and capitalists, up to a certain point, are always the obvious and natural leaders of it, suddenly found themselves completely unhorsed. Their mouths, if opened by way of remonstrance, were crammed with their own utterances. Never before in the history of this or any other country was there such a spectacle of men high in office "hoist by their own petard." When hoist they had nothing whatever to oppose to the intense conviction they had created. Not a single conservative influence was left to check the headlong career of the rank and file of the party so long docile in their hands, but which now proposed to carry out to the letter the revolutionary doctrines which had been so long and so persistently taught. Fortunately for the moment, from the apprehension created, a terrible catastrophe was averted. Was the escape an accident, or will the foes of "consolidated capital," from the teachings of their old leaders, gather up their forces and finally carry the day? Whatever the event, we have well learned that utterances like those of Mr. Carlisle, to which great emphasis was given by the exalted position which he subsequently held, have already exacted a terrible but appropriate penalty. Whether as a people we can profit by the lesson we have received remains to be seen.

Few things in history are more remarkable than the manner in which the advocates of cheap money became their own dupes. They demanded that Government create money, so that, to use the graphic language of Mr. Voorhees, "more than 10 cents should be paid for a day's labor, and more than $10 for a horse." With Mr. Carlisle, as with Mr. Voorhees, money was "thus saith the law!" Now a "thousand millions" is as easily placed on the statute-book as a "hundred millions." The small victory of two million ounces per month became in twelve years one of transcendent importance in the purchase for coinage of 291,272,018 ounces, at the cost of $308,279,260, the equivalent of about 400,000,000 dollars. In 1890 a still greater victory was achieved in the purchase for coinage of 4,500,000 ounces per month. Under this act 168,674,682 ounces, at the cost of $155,931,002, were purchased. Under the two acts 459,946,701 ounces, the equivalent of about 550,000,000 dollars, were purchased, at the cost of $464,210,262. At the remonetization of silver in 1878 Mr. Carlisle would undoubtedly have been glad to compromise upon one-half such sum. From 1878 to the present time the value of silver has steadily declined, so that the dollar is worth only 50 cents in the place of 89 cents when the first victory of the people was achieved, which with Mr. Carlisle was a matter of the greatest exultation. At the close of his official career as the Secretary of the Treasury he proclaimed to the world that not a dollar of their rightful and proper money was to go into the hands of the down-trodden people but at the value of gold! He was at last compelled to obey a law higher than his own — to join "the great conspiracy of syndicates, stock-jobbers, and other great combinations of capital in this country and in Europe" for the robbery and oppression of the poor! He started as their champion to lead

them into the promised land. He led them into the wilderness,
there to leave them a prey to their ignorance and fears, without a
single hint from him of any way of escape. As for the people whom
he long championed they are still not only without their promised
money, but the process by which it was to be reached, the debasement of the currency, has created such apprehension and disturbance
that the employment as well as the wages of labor have been greatly
reduced, so that widespread actual has taken the place of the alleged
suffering that led to the crusade for cheap money. This is not all.
But for the acts of 1878 and 1890 the vast accumulations of silver
now piled up, an idle mass, in the Treasury would, as capital, have
been made the basis of production, giving greatly increased employment and higher wages to labor, while the amount of money in circulation would have been much greater than its present volume,
measuring the value of the increased subjects of distribution, symbolic money being in ratio to their amount or value.   Under normal
conditions, from the improvements coming constantly into use, the
increase in the productive capacity of our people has been in a ratio
threefold greater than that of their numbers.   For a long time past,
from the apprehension created by our abnormal monetary system,
the increase of their products has hardly kept pace with that of their
numbers.   Not only has not a single purpose of its advocates ever
been realized, but, left to themselves, they would never establish
silver as their own money.

The most pronounced instinct of the race is for good money, as it
constitutes its reserves, awaiting opportunity or necessity for their
use. When people receive money the thought uppermost in their
minds is not the payment of debts, but its exchangeable value in
the purchase of other kinds of merchandise, that money having the
highest relative and the greatest uniformity of value always having
the preference. In all history, where metallic money has been debased from wear or other causes, the most valued coins will always
be hoarded, the least valuable alone remaining in circulation. It is
not for ordinary use, but for a single purpose — for the payment of
debts — that the coinage of silver is demanded. That purpose
accomplished, debased silver money would never voluntarily be taken
back as money by the parties paying it out, nor by those producing
it, from the danger and inconvenience attending its use ; a far better
metallic money being provided — gold — as the standard of value,

symbolic money being the ordinary instrument of exchange. Silver can no more again become the money of any class than can earthways again become with any the instruments of transportation, on a large scale, of persons or property. In this matter self-interest will always be the imperative rule or guide. Debts paid, gold, as standard money, will be as much insisted upon by day laborers as by the commercial classes. Its superiority as money over silver will be as much understood by the former as by the latter. The aversion against silver will, in fact, be much stronger with the laboring than with the commercial classes, as the latter, constantly dealing in it as merchandise, will have none of the prejudices naturally felt by those wholly rejecting it as money. The laboring classes will accept or lay by, as money, only that kind about which no apprehension can arise. The graphic pictures drawn by the opponents of silver of the disasters that will be inflicted by its coinage upon the laboring classes, their choice left free, exist in imagination alone. In this matter the laboring classes will prove as competent to take care of themselves as capitalists. In contracts to be made no one will agree to pay or accept silver. No law can be made to compel its use or acceptance except for debts already contracted.

It is not the final event that is the matter of chief concern. It is impossible that the nation should ever voluntarily come or long remain upon a silver basis. But we have, say, $500,000,000 of silver, full legal tender, the great mass lying idle in the Treasury. Suppose the Government should find itself unable to take in the silver certificates and notes in gold? Their market value would fall to that of their constituent, which with such fall could be reached at something like its real value, to be used in the payment of debts at its nominal value. The scene that would result would beggar description, every institution, including the Government, and every individual, being involved in the common disaster, — that debts may be paid at one-half the value at which they were contracted.

Mr. Sherman's part in the maintenance in circulation of the notes of the United States has already been shown. In his Report for 1877, summarized in his " Forty Years," he also considered at great length the matter of the coinage :

It had been the careful study of statesmen for many years to secure a bi-metallic currency not subject to the changes of market value, and so adjusted that both kinds could be kept in circulation together, not alternating with each other. The growing tendency had been to adopt, for coins, the principle of "redeemability" applied to different forms of paper money. By limiting tokens, silver and paper money, to the amount needed for business, and promptly receiving or redeeming all that might at any time be in excess, all these forms of money could be kept in circulation, in large amounts, at par with gold. In this way, tokens of inferior intrinsic value were readily circulated, and did not depreciate below the paper money into which they were convertible. The fractional coin then in circulation, though the silver of which it was composed was of less market value than the paper money, passed readily among all classes of people and answered all the purposes for which it was designed. And so the silver dollar, if restored to our coinage, would greatly add to the convenience of the people. . . .

I did not agree with the President in his veto of the bill, for the radical changes made in its terms in the Senate had greatly changed its effect and tenor. The provisions authorizing the Secretary of the Treasury to purchase not less than $2,000,000 worth of silver bullion per month, at market price, and to coin it into dollars, placed the silver dollars upon the same basis as the subsidiary coins, except that the dollar contained a greater number of grains of silver than a dollar of the subsidiary coins, and was a legal tender for all debts, without limit as to amount. The provision that the gain or seigniorage arising from the coinage should be accounted for and paid into the treasury, as under the existing laws relative to subsidiary coinage, seemed to remove all serious objections to the measure.

I believed that all the beneficial results hoped for from a liberal issue of silver coin could be secured by issuing this coin, in pursuance of the general policy of the act of 1853, in exchange for United States notes coined from bullion purchased in the open market by the United States, and by maintaining it by redemption, or otherwise, at par with gold coin. It could be made a legal tender for such sums and on such contracts as would secure to it the most general circulation. It could be easily redeemed in United States notes and gold coin, and only reissued when demanded for public convenience. If the essential quality of redeemability given to the United States notes, bank-bills, tokens, fractional coins, and currency maintained them at par, how much easier it would be to maintain the silver dollar, of intrinsic market value nearly equal to gold, at par with gold coin, by giving to it the like quality of redeemability. ("Forty Years," Vol. II., Chapters I. and II.)

Instead of its having been, as asserted by the Secretary, "the careful study of statesmen for many years to secure a bi-metallic currency so adjusted that both kinds could be kept in circulation together," the study, if the word may be used, for many years has, at least so far as this country is concerned, been in an exactly opposite direction. The exchanges being effected by means of symbolic money, metallic money could be well left to take care of itself, the coins of other nations being as valuable as our own and circulating as freely. The kind of metallic money is relative to the condition of the people. At one time, and within historic periods, copper was good money ; at another silver ; now gold ; one by regular gradation giving place to the other. At the formation of our system silver was alike the money of tradition and convenience. From the limited transactions taking place, it was as well fitted as gold to serve as reserves of the issuers of symbolic money. It necessarily became such because, by the ratio established by Hamilton, gold was under-valued. His was the first and only attempt ever made in this country to reconcile the value of the two metals. He assumed that this was possible and, if so, desirable, that the amount of money might be increased. He had little idea that both kinds were, for ordinary use, to be superceded by symbolic money. So completely did silver become discharged from ordinary use, gold being wholly so, that the amount of the former in the hands of the people, so late as 1831, all in the form of subsidiary coins, did not exceed $5,000,000. In 1834, from the greatly increased transactions taking place, it was for the first time seen that gold had become the more convenient metal to serve as the reserves of the banks. To bring it into use an act was passed whereby it was purposely overvalued to the extent of about three per cent. It consequently became the reserves of the issuers of symbolic money. As there was no complaint that silver, when serving as reserves, was not in sufficient abundance, so there was no complaint that gold was not sufficiently abundant when it became the standard money of the country. It was well understood that when " money was scarce " it was for the reason that merchandise was scarce, and for no other. The second change came by the act of 1853, by which the subsidiary coinage was purposely debased to prevent its exportation. The purpose was a wide distinction between the two metals, not their reconciliation. Nothing was further from the purpose of the act of 1878. The cry then was not for good money, but cheap money. Provision for the reconciliation of the two would have been fatal, as it would have wholly defeated the object aimed at.

The Secretary " did not agree with the President in his veto of the bill " (of 1878), which provided among other things that all debts, public and private, could be paid in silver, and that after, from excess of production and its disuse among the continental nations, it had fallen, in a comparatively short period, 13 cents in value. The causes producing the fall still remained in full force ; a fall which continued until a dollar has now only half the value of one of 1873. He approved the act, " as the existing laws relative to the subsidiary coinage seemed to remove all objections to the measure," — and for the reason "that all the beneficial results that could be hoped for from a liberal use of silver could be secured by issues of this coin in pursuance of the general policy of 1853." That act provided that " such silver coins [issued by virtue of it] shall be paid out at the mint in exchange for gold coins at par." There could be no excess, as the coins, unless the supply was short, would not be demanded in exchange for gold. Their value was supported by being accepted in the payment of the revenues at the par of gold. No other provisions in their support were ever made than those described. No other was required. To make the two cases parallel, the silver coined under the act of 1878 could not have left the mint except in exchange for an equal nominal amount of gold. To make them parallel the coinage under the act of 1853 should have been legal tender for unlimited amounts. It was legal tender only for sums not exceeding five dollars. To render them parallel the holders of silver coin issued under the act of 1853 should have had the right to convert them into the notes of the Government, payable, like those of 1878, in gold. Instead of being parallel the two acts antagonized each other in every particular. If under the act of 1878 silver had been coined at a much lower rate, its value, could it have found adequate use, such as the payment of the revenues, would have been maintained at the par of gold, provided the amount did not exceed, say, $50,000,000, the revenues equalling, say, $1,250,000 daily. Use may give value to silver as to exchequer bills bearing no interest, and receivable only in the payment of the revenues. But silver, from the inconvenience of its use, will never have any other employment than that of subsidiary coin, there being an adequate supply of other and better kinds of money.

" By limiting tokens, silver and paper money, to the amount needed for business, and promptly receiving or redeeming all that might at times be in excess, all these forms of money could," said the Secretary, " be kept in circulation in large amounts at par with gold." How is the excess of such money to be determined? With him by the amount returning for redemption. But a money of Government so long as confidence is maintained will be returned for conversion into gold only to meet balances arising in the foreign or domestic trade of the country, the only purpose for which on any considerable scale gold is now used. It may be laid down as an axiom that in affairs in a country like the United States no other money but paper will be used as the ordinary instrument of exchange. No other can be afforded. Suspension of specie payments, and there have been several in the United States, have not had the slightest effect to bring metallic money into general use. Paper, whatever the kind, still remained the money of the people, its value being measured by the standard of gold. The public from their reduced means, alike the cause and result of suspension of specie payment, can far less afford to use metallic money after than before. They use what they have, whatever the value placed upon it. The kind of money is shown by the results, which, in a country like the United States, may be long deferred. The degree of excess is to be inferred from its quality, not quantity. There can be no excess of metallic money in the form of gold. There can be no excess of paper money symbolizing merchandise at the value of gold. These two are the only kinds of money proper for use. Government money is always in excess, for the reason that no adequate provision will ever be made therefor. The acceptance by a people of the money of Government or banks, or that it remains a long time in circulation, is no evidence that it is properly issued. The old Continental money was eagerly welcomed. It seemed just the kind to fill the channels of circulation. For a time no money seemed more opportune or valuable. It was so opportune and valuable that it circulated for nearly two years at the par of gold. So well was it received that a provision of ten times the amount issued would not have been regarded as excessive. Not a dollar ever issued left the channels of circulation until, after working infinite mischief, every dollar was repudiated. The acceptance of a money, or that it remains in the channels of circulation, is no test whatever of its quality or value. At the outset bad may be as well received as good money.

Continental money had no more right to be when it was issued than when it was repudiated. Its quality should have been as palpable when it was issued as when it was repudiated. Our money of government notes is precisely the same in kind. It has produced precisely the same effect as the Continental currency, but from the greatly increased means of our people it has not yet been repudiated, nor worked their ruin. It is in excess not only from not being a symbol of capital, but for the reason that the money of commerce in countries like the United States measures, as it always will measure, the means of the people.   The addition to this of the money of Government is pure inflation.   The great evil of government money is that it will not be presented for redemption in gold, so habituated have our people become to the use of paper money, except for balances arising, from its use, in the foreign or domestic trade of the country, and then only by those who are connected with such trade, or their representatives.   As our Government is the great issuer of paper money it is first called upon to supply the demand for coin, and distrust naturally arises as to its ability to meet the vast amount of its notes outstanding liable at any moment to be presented for payment.   It is this distrust that shows the nature of a currency of government notes, not the circulation obtained for them.   This distrust when the amount is excessive can be allayed only by the removal of the cause.   In the place of Mr. Sherman's fallacious test of good money, the true test is the degree of provision made previous to its issue for its retirement.   The test of his currency is the mischief it has wrought — a mischief which should have been foreseen and avoided by any one familiar with the history of the country or of the attributes and laws of money.

As debased subsidiary coins, from their use, remain in circulation, the Secretary inferred that debased silver dollars would enter into and remain in circulation at their par value.   But by no process, from the inconvenience of their use, can they be brought into or remain in circulation, better and more convenient kinds of money being provided.

It is a sufficient reply to the Secretary to state that no provision was ever made by law for the maintenance of the value of silver dollars at the par of gold ; that no such order was ever given by him in his official capacity, or by any successor in office, for the reason that no such purpose was ever intended, and that not a cent of money has ever been expended therefor.   The incoherence which characterized him arose from his assumption that value, either intrinsic or representative, is no necessary attribute of money.   It is from such an assumption that all the disasters in the matter of the currency, and they have exceeded almost the power of language to describe, have arisen.

Mr. Sherman's ideas as to coinage of silver were further illustrated in his conference, March 9, 1878, with the Committee on Finance of the Senate. To a question proposed by Mr. Morrell, the Chairman, " What effect has the silver bill [of 1878] had, or is it likely to have, upon resumption of specie payments?" he replied :

I shall have to confess that I have been mistaken myself. Now, as to the silver bill, I have watched its operation very closely. I think the silver bill has had some adverse effects, and it has had some favorable effects, on the question of resumption. It has undoubtedly stopped refunding operations. Since the agitation of the silver question, I have not been able largely to sell bonds, although I have made every effort to do so. . . . Now, another adverse effect the silver bill has had is to stop the accumulation of gold coin. Since the 1st of January we have accumulated no coin, except for coin certificates, and except the balance of revenue over expenditure.

Another effect that the silver bill has had is to cause the return of our bonds from Europe. Although the movement of our bonds in this direction has been pretty steady for more than a year, yet it is latterly largely increased ; how much I am not prepared to say.

On the other hand, I will give the favorable effects. In the first place, the silver bill satisfied a strong public demand for bi-metallic money, and that demand is, no doubt, largely sectional. No doubt there is a difference of opinion between the West and South and the East on this subject, but the desire for remonetization of silver was almost universal. *In a government like ours it is always good to obey the popular current; and that has been done, I think, by the passage of the silver bill.* Resumption can be maintained more easily upon a double standard than upon a single standard. The bulky character of silver would prevent payments in it, while gold, being more portable, would be more freely demanded, and I think resumption can be maintained with a less amount of silver than of gold alone.

SENATOR BAYARD. — You are speaking of resumption upon the basis of silver ? or of silver and gold ?

SECRETARY SHERMAN. — Yes, sir ; I think it can be maintained better upon a bi-metallic or alternative standard than upon a single one, and with less accumulation of gold. In this way remonetization of silver would rather aid resumption.

SENATOR BAYARD. — You speak of resumption upon a bi-metallic basis being easier. Do you make that proposition irrespective of the readjustment of the relative values of the two metals as we have declared them ?

SECRETARY SHERMAN. — I think so. Our mere right to pay in silver would deter a great many people from presenting notes for redemption who would readily do so if they could get the lighter and more portable coin in exchange. Besides, gold coin can be exported, while silver coin could not be exported because its market value is less than its coin value.

SENATOR BAYARD. — I understand that it works practically very well. So long as the silver is less in value than the paper, you will have no trouble in redeeming your paper. When a paper dollar is worth 98 cents, nobody is going to take it to the Treasury and get 92 cents in silver ; but what are you to do as your silver coin is minted ? By the 1st of July next or the 1st of January next you have eighteen or twenty millions of silver dollars which are in circulation and payable for duties, and how long do you suppose this short supply of silver and your control of it by your coinage will keep it equivalent to gold — when one is worth ten cents less than the other ?

SECRETARY SHERMAN. — Just so long as it can be used for anything that gold is used for. It will be worth in this country the par of gold until it becomes so abundant and bulky that people will become tired of carrying it about ; *but in our country that can be avoided by depositing it for coin certificates.*

"Resumption of specie payments," according to the Secretary, "could be maintained better upon an alternate standard than upon a single one, and with less accumulation of gold," for the reason that from the inconvenience of its use from its bulky character, and from the fact that silver could not from its debasement be exported, the holders of the obligations of the Government, knowing that they could be paid in it, would not present them for payment. If an impertinent fellow demanded gold, all that the Secretary had to do was to hurl a junk of silver at his head, displaying a plenty of such missiles in reserve. Such was the Secretary's resumption as provided by the act of 1875, supplemented, according to him, by that of 1878. The act of 1878 created a new form of money, legal tender in the payment of all debts, public and private. It was for him to execute the law. The idea that at the time there was anything behind the silver dollar or the certificates issued therefor never entered his head ; nor that there was anything wrong or out of the way in paying all the obligations of the Government in silver, its value having in a short period fallen 13 per cent. New light came with the apprehension subsequently created in view of the enormous amount of the notes of the Government for which no adequate provision was made. That apprehension was allayed, or sought to be allayed, by a recitation in the act of 1890 "that it is the policy of the United States to maintain the two metals on a parity with each other upon the present legal ratio." "Obeying the popular current," the Secretary assumed, in his discussion of the subject in his "Forty Years," that such was the policy of the Government by the act of 1878 — that to the coinage under it "the general policy of the act of 1853, maintaining silver at the par of gold, by redemption or otherwise, applied." All this was an afterthought to meet the change in the "popular current," now demanding that silver be maintained at the par of gold.

The act of 1853 made no provisions for the maintenance of the coins issued other than those described. The recitation in that of 1890 of a purpose to maintain the parity of the two metals no more gave the Secretary of the Treasury the power to maintain the coinage of 1878 at the par of gold than would a recitation on the part of Congress of the desirability of such a step authorize him to purchase the navies of the world! It is not easy at first sight to get at his meaning. A little patience, however, will suffice. He believed that money circulated from the necessity of a medium of exchange; that silver would circulate at the par of gold if not in excess; if excessive, the objection on the score of inconvenience could be overcome by the ues of notes in its place. As the value of the silver dollars could, by the use of certificates issued against them, be maintained at the par of gold, it was no hardship to creditors to be compelled to accept them at the par of gold. At any rate, in advocating the coinage of silver he was only "obeying the popular current," an obedience that, from the era of Jackson, has been the curse of American political life. We have had ample experience of the disastrous consequences which have resulted from following the "popular current." It was the "popular current" which maintained slavery so long in power; the penalty paid being half a million of lives, the waste of more than five thousand millions of property, and the razing of one-half the country by fire and sword. It was the "popular current" that overthrew the most perfect monetary system ever established, the "popular current" declaring it to be the instrument in the hands of the rich for the impoverishment and enslavement of the poor; the penalty paid, as Mr. Buchanan declared, being "a succession of extravagant inflations and ruinous contractions, so that in the midst of unsurpassed plenty in all the products of agriculture, and in all the elements of national wealth, we find our manufactures suspended, our public works retarded, our private enterprises of different kinds abandoned, and thousands of useful laborers thrown out of employment and reduced to want," — a picture as true to-day as when it was drawn forty years ago, so incapable are our people of correcting any great wrong when once committed to it. It was the "popular current" that enacted the law of 1878, one of the most infamous ever placed upon the statute-book, and one which, if we ever recover our senses as a people, will fix an indelible stain on those enacting or approving it; an act to which, more than to any other, the terrible disasters that have recently been suffered, and what is still worse the doubt and irresolution which prevail, and from which there seems to be no way of escape, are due. The danger of following the "popular current" is that the persistent noise and bluster of a very small faction may be the "popular current," and drown the mild remonstrances of the well-to-do and self-respecting classes, who may make no sign except in cases of supreme emergency; a little knot or faction of turbulent or revolutionary characters, the only "popular current" displaying itself, carrying the day. In the close calculation of political chances great concessions are made to States insignificant in numbers, with industries or interests peculiar to themselves which may decidedly antagonize those of the great mass of the people. It is one of the infelicities of our system that a State like that of Nevada, with 40,000 people, counts as much in one branch of the National Legislature as that of New York, with 6,000,000. From the experience of the past we may count upon one thing as certain — that by following the "popular current" we shall soon witness the end of our "Model Republic."

The mischief of the act of 1878 resulted from the subsequent assumed undertaking by the Government to maintain the value of the coins under it at the par of gold. Unlimited coinage at the time, legal tender for all who consented thereto, would have been most opportune as an example, as the act would have remained a dead letter, the coinage being rejected as it is to-day. But for the notes and certificates, the legal tender clause, which would have been availed of, would, from the iniquity and folly of the act, have led to a speedy repeal.

ACT OF 1890.

The greater the amount of government money, whatever the form, the greater the impoverishment of the people and louder the clamor for more as the only source of relief. To meet it, the act of July 14, 1890, superseding that of 1878, provided for the purchase monthly of 4,500,000 ounces of silver by an issue of notes to serve as money of the Government equal to the cost. The bill was framed in committee of conference of the two Houses, the Senate being largely in favor of unlimited, the House insisting upon a limited, coinage. Mr. Sherman, at the time in the Senate, was a member of the committee, and from his instrumentality in framing it the act has since gone by his name. It recited that " upon the demand of any holder of the treasury notes herein provided for, the Secretary of the Treasury shall, under such regulations as he may prescribe, redeem such notes in gold or silver coin at his discretion, *it being the established policy of the United States to maintain the two metals in parity with each other upon their legal ratio, or upon such ratio as may be provided by law.*" It is by virtue of this recitation alone that the dollars coined under the act of 1878 were held to be exchangeable for gold. From the power conferred upon the Secretary he undoubtedly had the right to take in the notes issued under the act of 1890 by the use of any money in the Treasury not otherwise appropriated, but not by borrowing money as provided by the act of 1875 for the resumption and maintenance of specie payment, that act being restricted to a single purpose. An important and unprecedented feature of the act of 1890 was the provision, in a time of profound peace, that the notes should be legal tender in all payments, public and private, and might be held by the banks as their reserves. Its purpose was set forth by Mr. Sherman in a speech delivered by him in the Senate, June 5, 1890, in which he said :

To know what measures ought to be adopted we should have a clear conception of what we wish to accomplish. I believe a majority of the Senate desire, first, to provide an increase of money to meet the increasing wants of our rapidly growing country and population, and to supply the reduction in our circulation caused by the retiring of National Bank notes ; second, to increase the market value of silver, not only in the United States, but in the world, in the belief that this is essential to the success of any measure proposed, and in the hope that our efforts will advance silver to its legal ratio with gold, and induce the great commercial nations to join with us in maintaining the legal parity of the two metals, or in agreeing with us in a new ratio of their relative value ; and, third, to secure a genuine bi-metallic standard, one that will not demonetize gold, or cause it to be hoarded or exported, but that will establish both gold and silver as standards of value, not only in the United States, but among all the civilized nations of the world.

The first purpose of Mr. Sherman was " to provide an increase of money to meet the increasing wants of our rapidly growing country and population, and to supply the reduction in our circulation caused by the retirement of National Bank notes." How is metallic money provided? — by mining the metal or obtaining

it in exchange for other kinds of merchandise from other countries, methods certainly not functions of Government. Another
kind of money are symbols of merchandise, these serving, in its
purchase, the office of metallic money, having a great advantage
over the former in the convenience of their use, an additional one
resulting from the discharge of capital from the exchanges. The
two are the only kinds of money which have any place in affairs —
one being capital, the other the symbol of capital. Mr. Sherman
proposed a third — debt of Government without interest, and
without any provision for its redemption in gold — alike " to meet the
increasing wants of an increasing population," as well as to fill the
vacuum created by the retirement of the notes of the banks, the
amount of these being reduced from $356,060,348 in 1882 to $179,-
449,958 in 1890. Without further evidence than what has been adduced it is submitted that "government debt without interest," for the
conversion of which into coin no adequate provision is made, is not
the kind of money about which a government should busy itself.
That government money of the kind described was with Mr. Sherman to take the place of the note circulation withdrawn by the
banks, shows that he had no proper conception of the subject which
he assumed so gravely to discuss. The notes of the banks were
secured by the bonds of the Government, having a higher market
value than their nominal amount, and, in addition, by the undertaking of the borrowers to return them to the issuers without any interposition on their part. This statement shows the radical difference
between the two kinds of money, a difference which Mr. Sherman
seemed wholly unable to master.

The great wrong, or crime, rather, of the act of 1890 was the legal
tender attribute with which its notes were clothed, not an additional
dollar being provided for their retirement. As they had in the discharge of contracts the potency of gold, it was a logical sequence
that they should constitute, as was provided, the reserves of the
National Banks, the liabilities of which equalled $1,900,000,000.
If reserves equalling 25 per cent. of their immediate liabilities
were to be provided, the legal tender notes of the Government, including those of 1890, equalling $500,000,000, were ample therefor
without the provision of a dollar in gold. As by the act of 1890
it became the duty of the Government to make good the dollars
coined under the act of 1878, as well as the certificates issued against

the same, its own immediate liabilities, payable in gold, were increased to $830,000,000. To the above sums were to be added the issues, $700,000,000, of State Banks, bankers, and trust companies, serving as money, the aggregate being $3,400,000,000, all resting possibly upon an assumed provision of $100,000,000 in gold, the reserves of the Government, such sum by drafts upon it being, at one time, in 1894, reduced to the pitiful sum of $41,348,181. Such was the financial structure which Mr. Sherman above all others contributed to rear, to the support of which he seems to be fully committed.

Another purpose of Mr. Sherman was to increase the value of silver in order, in concert with other nations, to maintain the two metals at their legal parity. Why should we wish to increase the value of silver in order to maintain the parity of two metals, one of which is never again to be used as money ?   As silver is never again to be used as money, the lower the price, from reduced cost, the greater the general welfare, from the wider use in the arts of so valuable an article. With the same sense Mr. Sherman might call for a convention of nations to restore the price of copper to the old figures in order to bring it into use as money and maintain its " parity with gold."

The third purpose of Mr. Sherman, which will be considered further on, was the establishment of " Bi-metallism."

The effect of the large increase, due to the act of 1890, of Government notes, for the retirement of which no provision was made, which largely served as the reserves of banks, and were greatly instrumental in drawing gold from the treasury, was to increase the apprehension which had prevailed, and which became so intense as to lead to the act of Nov. 1, 1893, for the repeal of the preceding act. This act failed to bring the expected relief, from the following recitation it contained :

It is hereby declared to be the policy of the United States to continue the use of both gold and silver as standard money, and to coin both gold and silver into money of equal intrinsic and exchangeable value, such equality to be secured through international agreement, or by such safeguards of legislation as will insure the maintenance of the parity in value of the coins of the two metals and the equal power of every dollar at all times in the markets and in the payment of debts. And it is further declared that the efforts of the Government should be steadily directed to the establishment of such a safe system of bi-metallism as will maintain at all times the equal power of every dollar coined or issued by the United States in the markets and in the payment of debts.

"The chief merit of this law," said Mr. Sherman, "was that it suspended the peremptory coinage of the silver purchased under it into silver dollars which could not be circulated, but were hoarded in the Treasury at great cost and inconvenience. It required the monthly purchase of a greater amount of silver than before, but that could be held in the form of bullion, and could be paid for by treasury notes equal in amount to the cost of the bullion, the whole of which was held in the Treasury as security for the payment of the notes. If silver bullion did not decline in market value it could, if necessary, be coined without loss, and thus the parity of the notes with gold could be readily maintained according to the declared policy of the law.

As Mr. Voorhees, Chairman of the Committee of Finance of the Senate, reported the bill for the act of 1893, which was supported by great numbers of members of Congress as pronounced silver men as himself, the conclusion is irresistible that it was from the conviction that its repeal was to be speedily followed by one for unlimited coinage of silver.

For the repeal of the act of 1890 the vote in the Senate was 43 to 32, and in the House 194 to 94. Mr. Sherman, then member of the Senate, voted for the repeal.

THE LATE ADMINISTRATION.

The situation, already sufficiently set forth, may again be briefly stated — $830,000,000 of Government notes, all payable in gold, not one of which came into being as an instrument for the distribution of merchandise, the only reserves provided for their conversion into coin being the assumed amount of $160,000,000, the amount at times falling below one-half that sum. Of the whole amount some $500,000,000 are legal tender in the payment of all debts, public and private, and serve as the reserves of the National Banks, the issues of which, with those of the State Banks, bankers, and trust companies, made an aggregate of $3,400,000,000. The gravity of the situation is greatly increased by the general assumption that no substantial reform is required ; that all that is wanted is the maintenance of the *status in quo ;* that no danger is to be feared so long as the amount of government money is not increased. There is little recognition of the disturbing and disastrous effect in affairs of the issue, on a colossal scale, of debt to serve as money. So long as there is none no measure of reform will ever be entered upon. Such was the position of the late administration; such that of the present one. That of the former was well set forth by the late Secretary, Mr. Carlisle, in a circular letter addressed by him to Mr. J. J. Helm, of Kentucky, under date of Sept. 15, 1896 :

Your letter asking how the silver dollars, which contain a quantity of bullion commercially worth only about 53 cents each, are maintained at a parity with gold, notwithstanding the fact that the Government does not directly redeem them, or the certificates issued upon them, in gold, is received, and as a great many inquiries upon the same subject are addressed to me daily from different parts of the country, which it is impracticable to answer in detail, I will take advantage of your favor to answer them all at once :

All the standard silver dollars issued from the mint since the passage of the act of 1878, now amounting to more than $433,000,000, have been coined on public account from bullion purchased by the Government, and are legal tender in payment of all debts, public and private, without regard to the amount, except when otherwise expressly stipulated in the contract between the parties.

The Government has made no discrimination whatever between the coins of the two metals, gold having been paid on its coin obligations when gold was demanded and silver having been paid when silver was demanded.

Under this policy the coinage has been so limited by law and the policy of the Treasury Department that the amount coined has not become so great as to drive the more valuable coin, gold, out of use, and thus destroy the basis of our monetary system ; and so long as the two metals are of unequal commercial value, at the ratio established by law, this limitation upon the coinage is, in my opinion, absolutely essential to the maintenance of their parity in effecting exchanges.

If the limitation were removed, confidence in the ability of the Government to preserve equality in the exchangeable value of the coins would be destroyed, and the parity would be lost, long before the amount of silver coinage had become really excessive.

With free and unlimited coinage of silver on account of private individuals and corporations, the Government would be under no moral obligation to maintain the parity, and, moreover, it would be unable to do so, because the volume of overvalued silver forced into the circulation by a legal tender provision would soon expel gold from the country, or put such a premium upon it that it would be impossible to procure and hold in the Treasury a sufficient amount to provide for the redemption of silver on presentation.

In order to maintain the parity under such conditions, the Government would be compelled from the beginning to exchange gold for silver dollars, or their paper representatives, whenever demanded, just as it now exchanges gold for its own notes when demanded ; and as the coinage of silver dollars would be unlimited, and therefore constantly increasing, a point would soon be reached where it would be impossible to continue the process of redemption.

The implied obligation of the Government to preserve the value of the money which it coins from its own bullion and for its own use, and which it forces the citizens to receive in exchange for their property and services, has been supplemented by two statutory declarations, which substantially pledge the public faith to the maintenance of that policy.

The act of July 14, 1890, after providing that the Secretary of the Treasury should, under such regulations as he might prescribe, redeem the treasury notes issued in the purchase of silver bullion, in gold or silver coin at his discretion, declares that it is " the established policy of the United States to maintain the two metals on a parity with each other upon the present legal ratio, or such ratio as may be provided by law," and the act of Nov. 1, 1893, again declares it to be " the policy of the United States to continue the use of both gold and silver as standard money, and to coin both gold and silver into money of equal intrinsic and exchangeable value, such equality to be secured through international agreement or by such safeguards of legislation as will insure the maintenance of the parity of value of the coins of the two metals and the equal power of every dollar at all times in the markets and in the payment of debts."

It is not doubted that whatever can be lawfully done to maintain equality in the exchangeable value of the two metals will be done whenever it becomes necessary, and although silver dollars and silver certificates have not, up to the present time, been received in exchange for gold, yet, if the time shall ever come when the parity cannot be otherwise maintained, such exchanges will be made.

It is the duty of the Secretary of the Treasury, and of all other public officials, to execute in good faith the policy declared by Congress, and whenever he shall be satisfied that the silver dollar cannot be kept equal in purchasing power with the gold dollar except by receiving it in exchange for the gold dollar when such exchange be demanded, it will be his duty to adopt that course.

But if our present policy is adhered to, and the coinage is kept within reasonable limits, the means heretofore employed for the maintenance of the parity will doubtless be found sufficient in the future, and our silver dollars and silver certificates will continue to circulate at par with gold, thus enabling the people to use both metals instead of one only, as would be the case if the parity were destroyed by free coinage.

Under the acts of 1878 and 1890 more than 433,000,000 of silver dollars, said the Secretary, had been coined, a large amount of silver bullion purchased under the act of 1890 remaining in the Treasury as bullion and represented by notes. At the time of his circular letter the Government made no difference whatever between the coins of the two metals. As the coinage of silver had been on account of the Government, the amount had been so limited that it had not, the Secretary declared, driven the more valuable metal, gold, out of circulation, thus destroying the basis of our monetary system, the parity of the two metals being maintained. Thrown open to the public, the

Government would be under no obligation to, nor could it, maintain such parity. The effect would be that the least valuable would drive the most valuable out of circulation, or raise its price so high as to put it beyond the reach of the Government. The implied duty to preserve the parity of all money issued by it was, said the Secretary, supplemented by the acts of 1890 and 1893, both of which have been sufficiently described. The act of Jan. 14, 1875, for the resumption of specie payments, recited that, "to enable the Secretary of the Treasury to prepare and provide for the redemption in this act authorized or required, he is authorized to use any surplus revenues, from time to time, in the Treasury not otherwise appropriated, and to issue, sell, and dispose of, at not less than par, in coin, either of the descriptions of bonds of the United States, described in the act of Congress, approved July 14, 1870, entitled "An act to authorize the refunding of the National Debt." With the Secretary provision for the maintenance of the parity of all the issues of the Government was made by the above act and by no other. When he became satisfied that the silver could not be kept equal in purchasing power to the gold dollar except in receiving it in exchange for the gold dollar, such exchange would be made, the parity of the metals being thereby maintained. If his position was a correct one, then there should still be a steady increase of government money of some kind to meet the wants of the people increasing at the rate of 1,600,000 annually. Assuming that' the proper amount of money in actual circulation would be $25 a head, the annual increased amount required would equal $40,000,000, which might be in the form of silver represented by notes, the only care being that the amount should not exceed the wants of an increasing population. Such ratio being preserved, there would be no difficulty in maintaining without further provision of reserves the value of the whole mass of our currency at the par of gold. Of course the fallacy arose from the assumption that value, either intrinsic or representative, was no necessary attribute of money.

The purpose of giving in this connection the circular letter of the Secretary is to show the position of the sound-money wing of the Democracy, the other, and the dominant one, being fully committed to the free and unlimited coinage of silver at the old ratio. From the former no help is to be expected for the reform of the currency, as, taking the Secretary's authority, it has no adequate conception of the situation nor of the conditions necessary for its restoration. The Secretary in his Annual Reports warmly recommended the retirement of the gold-bearing notes of the Government, so excessive was the annoyance caused in providing the means for their redemption. During his administration of the finances he was driven into the street to raise therefor some $293,000,000. It was natural that he should wish to avoid such mortifying alternatives. But he must have known that a recommendation to retire the legal tender notes of the Government would not for a moment be listened to unless some provision was made to fill the vacuum that would be created. He proposed no such measure. He did indeed recommend in his Report for 1895 an amendment of the banking laws so that the notes to be issued under it should equal the nominal value of the bonds put up for their security. But such provision would only add a few million dollars to the currency. A proposition for calling in the Government notes with nothing to take their place would have instantly precipitated a currency panic. Before any steps are taken for the retirement of a currency, colossal in amount like that of the United States, the alternative must be alike adequate and palpable. He could not propose any, as he was committed to the maintenance of the system of National Banks, and, of course, from the traditions of his party, wholly against a National one. He accepted the situation as it was, his only care being its maintenance. In his Report for 1895 he was for maintaining the whole amount of silver notes in circulation, of which some $433,000,000 had been issued. The reason why the silver notes caused no annoyance was that they were not legal tender. They were not held by banks and bankers, consequently were not used for drawing gold out of the Treasury. They remained almost wholly in the channels of circulation, banks and bankers sedulously avoiding them, although, according to the Secretary, they were payable in gold. But these notes, apparently so harmless, were the chief cause of the embarrassments and annoyances to which the Government was subject. Being receivable in the payment of all the dues, they cut it off wholly from all power to demand gold in their collection. But for them the revenues would have been paid in gold, or in the gold notes of the Government; such employment so far as the latter were used adding to their value. They were paid in gold, or in gold notes, until from the great increase of silver notes and the consequent distrust excited, the latter wholly superseded the former mode of payment. According to Mr. Carlisle, every dollar of the public revenues may be payable in silver notes, the acceptance of which cannot be forced upon a single creditor of the Government! With a Treasury overflowing with silver notes it might not be able to use a single dollar for any purpose whatever except to draw silver coins out of the Treasury. And yet this is the monetary system which Mr. Carlisle would set up as an institution for our people.

In his annual message under date of Dec. 7, 1896, Mr. Cleveland said :

I believe our present tariff law, if allowed a fair opportunity, will, in the near future, yield a revenue which, with reasonable economical expenditures, will overcome all deficiencies. In the meantime no deficit that has occurred or may occur need excite or disturb us. To meet any such deficit we have in the Treasury, in addition to a gold reserve of $100,000,000, a surplus of more than $128,000,000, applicable to the payment of the expenses of the Government, and which must, unless expended for that purpose, remain a useless hoard, or, if not extravagantly wasted, must, in any event, be perverted from the purpose of its exaction from our people. The payment, therefore, of any deficiency in the revenue from this fund is nothing more than its proper and legitimate use. The Government thus applying a surplus fortunately in its Treasury to the payment of expenses not met by its current revenues is not at all to be likened to a man living beyond his income and thus incurring debt or encroaching on his principal.

During his last administration Mr. Cleveland was incessant in his demands for the retirement of the gold-bearing notes of the Government, the sole cause, he declared, of the disastrous condition of affairs that prevailed. For their retirement, by his direction, bonds to the amount of $262,000,000, producing $293,000,000, were issued. The amount of the notes taken in was equal to the proceeds of the bonds. Of these $165,000,000, up to Dec. 7, 1896, had been paid out for the current expenses of the Government. The notes, Mr. Cleveland declared, were an endless chain for pulling money out of the Treasury. The only way to break it was to render the Government self-supporting from its revenues — a proposition which he persistently refused to countenance. The endless chain was consequently allowed to run with full force. If by means of it gold could be pulled out of the Treasury, a bigger sum could be put in by borrowing. The whole proceeds, $293,000,000, of the loans, or the amount on hand at any one time, became a " surplus in the Treasury," to be applied to the wants of the Government. Otherwise it would be squandered or stolen. To what better purpose could the Government put its money — " an exaction from the people " — than by means of it to defray the expenses of the Government of the people ! The idea of retiring the notes, if it were ever entertained, seemed wholly lost. But not a dollar could be raised by the issue of bonds for the support of the Government. In his annual message for 1895 Mr. Cleveland expressly declared that "the Secretary of the Treasury has no authority whatever to issue bonds to increase the ordinary revenues, or to pay the expenses of the Government." Certainly he could not do indirectly what he could not do directly. Had the Government been self-sustaining from its revenues, every note taken in could have been held in the Treasury, — in effect, retired, — no occasion arising for its reissue. In using the surplus $128,000,000 in the Treasury, "the Government was not to be likened," said Mr. Cleveland, "to a man living beyond his means by incurring a debt or encroaching upon his principal." But in what form was the $128,000,000, the surplus in the Treasury? In that of promissory notes payable in gold on demand, for the discharge of which debts in another form had to be contracted. Is the power to create a debt a surplus in the Treasury? It is difficult from its wildness and incoherency to reply to Mr. Cleveland's statement. In making it he was mentally widely astray.

THE SOUND MONEY WING OF THE DEMOCRACY.

The principles of the Sound Money wing of the Democracy were set forth in the platform adopted at its National Convention, held at Indianapolis, Sept. 3, 1896. Its first declaration was against " Paternalism and all class legislation." In reference to the currency, it said :

> The experience of mankind has shown that by reason of their natural qualities, gold is the necessary money of the large affairs of commerce and business, while silver is conveniently adapted to minor transactions, and the most beneficial use of both together can be insured by the adoption of the former as a standard of monetary measure, and the maintenance of silver at a parity with gold by its limited coinage under suitable safeguards of law.

> Thus the largest possible enjoyment of both metals is gained with a value universally accepted throughout the world, which constitutes the only practical bi-metallic currency.

The substance of this is that gold is to be the standard of value, but silver money is also to be provided, its value to be maintained at the standard of gold by limiting its coinage. In this way, "the largest possible enjoyment of both metals is gained" — in other words, practical bi-metallism will be secured. The statement begs the whole question. Coinage imparts no value to that which will never be used. Debased subsidiary coins are maintained at the value of gold for the reason that they serve equally with gold in the payment of the revenues, in the purchase of postage stamps, for example. They are constantly returning to the Government to be again paid out in exchange for gold, or its equivalent. But silver dollars will never be used in the payment of the revenues on any considerable scale, as a more convenient kind of money will necessarily be provided. They never will be used as the ordinary instrument of exchange from the inconvenience of their use and uncertainty as to their value. They are a wholly superfluous form of money with every commercial people, who, on a large scale, will have only two kinds — gold as a standard of value, and paper, the symbol of merchandise, as the instrument of its transfer. The Sound Money wing of the Democracy is still a victim to the old delusion that money derives its value from the necessity of a medium of exchange — that anything may serve as such if the amount be not excessive. It differs from the Free Coinage wing, not in principle, but in the matter of quantity. It says there may be too much of one kind of money, silver; that perhaps $500,000,000 would not be too much, while $1,000,000,000 would be. The reply of the other wing is if $500,000,000 are good money to-day, $1,000,000,000 will be by the time that that amount could be coined. Before any ordinary audience — before that composed of the people of the United States — the Free Coinage wing of the Democracy would carry the day, the question turning wholly upon quantity, every one wishing to see that increased. As it is, the Sound Money wing, instead of leading the way, is the great obstacle to any adequate measure of reform. Their first purpose is to discharge " Paternalism " from Government. But the exercise of a great deal of " Paternalism " will be required before we can be placed upon firm and solid ground. Mere negation will never place us there.

THE FREE COINAGE DEMOCRACY.

The principles of the Free Coinage wing of the Democracy —
the unlimited coinage of silver at the ratio of sixteen to one — are
too well known to require statement here.   That it has an illustrious
ancestry is well shown by a letter addressed by its great leader, Hon.
William J. Bryan, late candidate of the Democracy for the Presidency, in reply to an invitation to the banquet, Jan. 8, 1897, of
the " Jackson Democratic Association," of the District of Columbia.
In it he said :

I regret that circumstances prevent my celebrating Jackson Day with you.
We have reason to commemorate the virtues of the hero of New Orleans. His
courageous defence of the rights of the people against the assaults of consolidated
capital made him the idol of his party, and the remembrance of his achievements
should inspire the Democrats of this generation to renewed devotion to a government of the people, by the people, and for the people. His final triumph in a
struggle similar to that in which the Democracy was engaged this year gives the
encouragement and hope of ultimate success.

THE ADMINISTRATION.

In his inaugural message, March 4, 1897, President McKinley
said :

The country is suffering from industrial disturbances from which speedy relief
must be had.   Our financial system needs some revision ; our money is all good
now, but its value must not further be threatened. It should all be put upon
an enduring basis, not subject to easy attack, nor its stability to doubt or dispute.
Our currency should continue under the supervision of the Government. The
several forms of our paper money offer, in my judgment, a constant embarrassment to the Government.

Therefore I believe it necessary to devise a system which, without diminishing
the circulating medium or offering a premium for its contraction, will present a
remedy for those arrangements which, temporary in their nature, might well in the
years of our prosperity have been displaced by wiser provisions.

With adequate revenue secured, but not until then, we can enter upon such
changes in our fiscal laws as will, while insuring safety and volume to our money,
no longer impose upon the Government the necessity of maintaining so large a
gold reserve, with its attendant and inevitable temptations to speculation.

Most of our financial laws are the outgrowth of experience and trial, and
should not be amended without investigation and demonstration of the wisdom
of the proposed changes. We must be both '' sure we are right '' and '' make
haste slowly.''

If, therefore Congress in its wisdom shall deem it expedient to create a commission to take under early consideration the revision of our coinage, banking,

and currency laws, and give them that exhaustive, careful, and dispassionate examination that their importance demands, I shall cordially concur in such action.

If such power is vested in the President, it is my purpose to appoint a commission of prominent, well-informed citizens of different parties, who will command public confidence, both on account of their ability and special fitness for the work. Business experience and public training may thus be combined, and the patriotic zeal of the friends of the country may be so directed that such a report will be made as to receive the support of all parties, and our finances seem to be the subject of mere partisan contention. The experiment is, at all events, worth a trial, and, in my opinion, it can but prove beneficial to the entire country.

The question of international bi-metallism will have early and earnest attention. It will be my constant endeavor to secure it by coöperation with the other great commercial powers of the world. Until that condition is realized when the parity between our gold and silver money springs from and is supported by the relative value of the two metals, the value of the silver already coined, and of that which may hereafter be coined, must be kept constantly at par with gold by every resource at our command. The credit of the Government, the integrity of its currency, and the inviolability of its obligations must be preserved. This was the commanding verdict of the people, and it will not be unheeded.

In asserting that our money is all good money, but that its value must not be "threatened," the President begged the whole question. Instead of being good money, greenbacks, silver certificates, and silver notes are all bad money. None could be worse. By declaring that the value of our money must not be further "threatened" he gives away his whole case. The value of gold money cannot be "threatened," for the reason that with all nations it is the highest form of capital. The value of symbolic money cannot be "threatened," as its nominal value does not exceed the value of its constituent certain to be speedily taken for consumption that society may exist. The value of silver is always "threatened" by the constant variation in its value. As it is no longer money, the more its value is "threatened" the greater the public gain from its widely increased use in the arts. No advantage could be greater than, from reduced cost of production, to have the price of silver fall to that of steel. The notes issued against it have the same infirmity as their constituent. The value of the gold-bearing notes of the Government is constantly "threatened," for the reason that previous to their issue no adequate provision was made for their retirement. Such provision may never be made ; or made only at a far distant day. As no provision for an issue on a large scale will ever be made, the fear that a large amount of notes will be presented for redemption is enough of itself to produce a panic. Money of our banks to the amount of $200,000,000 is daily presented for redemption, but such presentation is no threat against it, as before its issue ample means are provided for its retirement. Nor by such presentations is the amount of bank money reduced, as new issues are being constantly made to symbolize new creations of merchandise to take the place of the old. If our Government were suddenly called to take in, say, $10,000,000 of the $830,000,000 of its notes now outstanding, it would send a cold chill throughout the country, the value of the whole volume being seriously "threatened." Should an equal amount be drawn for ten consecutive days, the Government might be without a dollar in its vaults, with $730,000,000 of its notes still to be provided for. Does not this statement show the wide difference between a currency of banks and that of the Government, and that comparatively the latter is a very bad one? That money may be free from "threats," Government should have nothing to do with its creation. Its money will never be kept within bounds, as not a dollar of it has a right to be. There cannot be too much of the money of commerce. Metallic money is capital. Government concerns itself merely about its weight and fineness. Symbolic money is as firmly based as metallic money, barring the accidents incident to all human affairs, the purpose of gold as money being to reach some other kinds of merchandise. The real makers of the money of the country are the producers of the country. It arises from the discount of the bills issued in the distribution of their products. If sales are slow no new purchases will be made until the old stocks are run off. With cessation of demand production ceases, or products are stored. Symbolic money only measures the amount of merchandise in process of distribution.

The President would " devise a system which, without diminishing the circulating medium or offering a premium for its contraction, will present a remedy for those arrangements which, temporary in their nature, might well in the years of prosperity have been displaced by wiser provisions." This statement, with all due respect to the President, requires no reply, as it has no meaning. He has to enter the world of reality before he can enter upon any work of reform.

The statement that " with adequate revenue secured, but not until then, we can enter upon such a change in our fiscal laws as will, while securing safety and volume to our money, no longer impose upon the Government the necessity of maintaining so large a gold reserve, with its attendant and inevitable temptation to speculation," is putting the cart before the horse, or sacrificing the more to the less important. We may for years be without an adequate revenue without affecting injuriously the business operations or credit of the country. An expenditure of $100,000,000 in excess of our income might be no cause of alarm, as it would be well understood that it was in our power, any day, to provide an adequate revenue, fund arrearages, and provide for their payment, certain that such measures would be taken before any disorder resulted. But a vicious currency is a poison in our system, a terrible one, and, when it has reached the magnitude of our own, its removal is the *first*, not the second, duty. In its retirement the question of the revenues need not necessarily be considered. Every dollar of the $830,000,000 of government notes can be discharged without the interposition of a dollar of gold. The matter of great concern is, with its discharge, the provision of an adequate currency to take its place.

The recommendation of a commission "to take under early consideration the revision of the coinage, banking, and currency laws " is an excellent one, although there should be no more reason for it than one to determine whether for the last fifty years the sun has risen and set on regulation time. Every one in affairs should be as familiar with our history as with the rising and setting of the sun. We send commissions to unearth the past of Egypt and Assyria. Why not create one to explore our own soil and recover from it monuments far more priceless than those of ancient civilization? — monuments buried as deep from the inroads of barbarians led by General Jackson as are the treasures of the Old World. Such a commission, well discharging its duties, would bring to light a perfect currency long passed from sight and memory. Whether we have the sense or manhood to restore the severe and simple style, when discovered, of the past, is quite another question. From the time of Jackson the nation has been taught that " consolidated capital " is the enemy of mankind. But "consolidated capital" is to supply our currency if we are to have one worthy of the name. The poison is so deep and widespread that the whole world of the United States seems to be entering on a grand crusade against this common enemy of the race, displaying already the great vice of democracies, hatred and jealousy of everything above the common level, and that a very low one.

BI–METALLISM.

"It will be my constant endeavor," said Mr. McKinley in his inaugural message, "to heartily coöperate with other great commercial powers of the world for the establishment of bi-metallism."

This reference to bi-metallism is to be regretted at this critical time as tending to divert public attention from the all-important matter, the reform of the currency, for notwithstanding the attention it is attracting, bi-metallism seems hardly worthy the serious notice of a great commercial people like our own. Its claims are based upon the assumption, wholly without foundation, that by means of it the amount of money may be increased. Instead of this the greater the amount of metallic money in circulation the less the amount of other kinds, and the less the aggregate. Capital discharged from the exchanges finds its proper employment in production. If merchandise is abundant, the instruments of its distribution — money — will be abundant. Such instruments or processes are now so perfect that metallic money has been almost wholly discharged from use. In ratio thereto production has been increased and prices reduced, the advantage inuring to consumers; the returns of capital, from its abundance, being no greater with low than with high prices. The advantage to capital is the enlarged field. So great have been the improvements in the methods of production that a day's work to-day produces fifty times the quantity of steel that it did fifty years ago. Results almost equally marvellous have been accomplished in distribution as in production. During the past year 1,000,000,000 tons of merchandise, having an estimated value of $20,000,000,000, were distributed by means of written or printed instruments, costing nothing in themselves, but serving in distribution all the uses of metallic money, being at the same time far more convenient of use. We can no more return to the old methods of distribution by metallic money, whether silver or gold, than to the old crucible process in the production of steel. But with the discharge of both metals as instruments of exchange, one must be retained as the standard at the value of which that of all other articles is to be rated and all contracts solved; and which, consequently, as the universal equivalent, must serve as the reserves of the issuers of paper money. As gold has a value thirty-two times greater than silver in ratio to its weight, and sixty-four times greater in ratio to its bulk, it can be cared for and moved from place to place at a far less cost than an equal value of silver. Its value is more uniform than silver from the greater uniformity in its production and in the demand therefor. As the cost of standards of value and of reserves, whatever the metal used, is the same, gold, for the reasons given, has necessarily the preference. There can be no deliberation as to the kind to be used. Is gold in sufficient abundance for the purposes which it has to serve? A standard of value does not ordinarily interpose in affairs like those of extension or weight. It is a final arbiter seldom appealed to. If in the opinion of one proposing to purchase merchandise its value is up to the price demanded, he will take it; if not, not. If the price offered is not up to its value measured by its cost and a fair profit added, it will not be accepted. Not in one transaction in a million does the standard of value interpose. Not in one transaction in a million does the idea of a standard of value ever suggest itself. Merchandise is sold by the delivery of what may be termed the title deeds to the same, the possession of which secures to the holder the right to its constituent. Although every contract is in terms payable in gold, not one in a million is solved by it, creditors taking their equivalent in some other kind of merchandise, to reach which gold, as money, would be used. In affairs gold is demanded only as the universal equivalent when the paper money of commerce cannot be converted into the kind of merchandise desired. Were no paper money issued that did not represent an equal value of merchandise, metallic money would be almost wholly discharged from affairs. The tendency is steadily and necessarily in such direction, even in the United States, possessed of the worst monetary system ever devised,— the National Government making vast issues of notes to serve as money for the retirement of which no adequate provision is made; the notes of banks being limited to 90 per cent. of the nominal value of the bonds put up as security therefor, no restrictions being imposed as to the subject of their loans. The want of a competent system with us has been partly made good by the establishment of Clearing Houses at every considerable place of trade, the members of which are compelled to discharge daily in coin, or in lawful money, all balances found against them. In this way the rule of the strong becomes that of the weak. It is at these houses that the amount of

balances arising in the domestic trade of the country is determined
and discharged. The amount daily arising at the present time
averages about $14,000,000, the exchanges daily taking place equal-
ling $200,000,000. The first sum measures that required in the
domestic trade of the country, creditors at the Clearing Houses one
day being debtors the next. Of course a much larger sum would
under all conditions as a matter of caution be maintained. Should
we return to a normal system, the amounts required at the Clearing
Houses would be greatly reduced. With such, no considerable
balances to be discharged in gold could arise in the foreign trade
of the country, the instruments of expenditure never exceeding the
means of the people. Up to a comparatively recent date the average
amount of gold held by the Bank of England as the reserves of all
the issuers in the United Kingdom, their issues largely exceeding
those of our own institutions, was about $110,000,000, or, say,
£22,000,000. This has been lately largely increased, in common
with the action of all the great Continental powers, in view of military
and political complications. With an adequate system $100,000,000
in gold would be ample for all the purposes which, with us, it would
be called upon to serve. With it we could presently discharge from
use some $500,000,000 of gold, assuming the amount in the country
to be $600,000,000 ; and an equal nominal amount of silver, the
whole to be applied to production and distribution. As the world's
stock of gold exceeds $4,000,000,000, and as the annual product,
rapidly increasing, exceeds $200,000,000, our own share exceeding
$50,000,000, and as with us gold money has but one use, to serve
as the reserves of the issuers of paper money, we have no more
reason to trouble ourselves about the adequacy of the amount than
about the adequacy of rainfall, or of the vital air, to meet the wants
of our increasing numbers ; and no more concern about the restoration of silver as money than that of old mechanical contrivances long
since relegated to the scrap heap.

We have briefly summarized the laws and attributes of money as
illustrated by our history — a history which fortunately has solved
every question that can arise in reference thereto. At the outset
bi-metallism was attempted, to fail with the attempt. Thereafter no
thought of the reconciliation of the coin value of the two metals
was ever entertained. For forty of the first years of our existence
as a people silver was our proper metallic money. In 1834 gold,

by its deliberate debasement, took the place of silver. Neither metal, while serving as the standard of value, was ever the instrument, on a large scale, of exchange. In 1830, for the first time from the establishment of the Government, attention was turned to the subject, and on the 23d of December of that year a special committee of the House, of which Campbell P. White, a member from the city of New York, was chairman, was directed to inquire into the expediency of adopting as our own the coins of the newly established Spanish-American Governments, the people of which were the great producers of the precious metals; and also to inquire whether any additional provisions were necessary in relation to the coinage of foreign silver at our own mints. The committee reported, February 23, 1831, that of coins having a value of $37,-000,000 that had issued from our mints, of which $27,000,000 were silver, only about $7,000,000 in value of the latter were in circulation; $4,000,000 being in the hands of the banks, the coin reserves of which equalled $22,114,917; and about $3,000,000 in the hands of the people. The total amount of metallic money in their hands did not exceed $5,000,000, or 30 cents per head. Of the gold coin, $9,000,000, not a dollar remained in circulation. If we could not retain our own coinage, if we made no difference between it and that of other nations, why not, it was asked, adopt their coins as our own, saving thereby a large annual outlay? In view of a suggestion so reasonable, the committee recommended that the silver dollars of Mexico, Central America, Peru, Chili, and Brazil, and the five-franc pieces of France, be adopted as our own, provided that they were of standard fineness. For such a recommendation precedents of our use of the metallic moneys of Great Britain, Portugal, France, and Spain were cited. As was proper, the committee recommended that subsidiary coins should issue from our own mints, the annual amount not to exceed $200,000 or $300,000. The conclusions to which it came were summarized as follows:

" 1. That the operations of commerce will assuredly dispense to every country its useful and equitable proportion of the gold and silver in currency, if it is not repulsed by paper or subjected to legal restrictions.

" 2. That it cannot be of essential importance to any State whether its proportion of the money of commerce thus distributed consists of gold or of silver, or of both metals, it being the instrument of exchange, but not the commodity really wanted.

" 3. That there are inherent and incurable defects in the system which regulates the standard of value in both gold and silver : its instability as a measure of contracts, and mutability as the practical currency of a particular nation, are serious imperfections, whilst the impossibility of maintaining both metals in concurrent, simultaneous, or promiscuous circulation appears to be clearly ascertained.

" 4. That the standard being fixed in one metal is the nearest approach to invariableness, and precludes the necessity of further legislative interference.

" 5. That gold and silver will not circulate promiscuously and concurrently for similar purposes of disbursement. Nor can coins of either metal be sustained in circulation with bank notes, possessing public confidence, of the like denominations." [1]

The report of the committee was conclusive of the whole subject — that the operations of commerce will assuredly dispense to every country its useful and equitable proportion of the silver and gold in currency (silver from the small transactions taking place being at the time equally convenient in use as gold and equally uniform in value) ; that, although the two metals were at the time nearly uniform in value, they could not be so reconciled that they would circulate side by side ; that the standard of value must be fixed in one metal alone, and that from the use of paper money neither metal could be maintained in circulation as the ordinary instrument of exchange. The conclusions of the committee had all the force of mathematical demonstration, and served implicitly as our guide down to 1878, when Congress, with incredible recklessness and levity, restored the coinage of silver at the old ratio, although the value of the silver dollar had fallen to 89 cents in gold. The bill was vetoed by the President, Mr. Hayes, as a flagrant act of improvidence and bad faith. It was held in the debate that the coinage of metals at a rate widely differing from their commercial value would have the effect to reconcile their value at any ratio that might be established, although all history had demonstrated that the insignia of governments has no effect to increase the value of the metal on which it is impressed. It was most unfortunate that precedents long established, and which carried the force of demonstration,

---

[1] See page 50.

should have been wantonly thrown aside. It was still more unfortunate that the nature of the act should have been concealed by an issue of notes assumed to be promises of the Government to pay gold. As the coinage was on account of the Government, it was held bound to sustain all its issues at the par of gold, no matter how much they might differ from it in value. It is hardly too much to say that no such purpose was ever really entertained when the act of 1878, or that of 1890, was passed, as otherwise some provision would have been made to maintain the value of the coinage. It is not too much to say that, from the absurdity of the proposition, no provision will ever be made for the maintenance of the debased silver coin at the par of gold. The cost of such maintenance would fully equal a provision of gold, to which is to be added the cost of the machinery that would be required. All this talk about the maintenance of the coins of the two metals at certain ratios is without a particle of sense or reason. We have reached a point in which we can no longer afford to indulge in such idle vaporings. Unless some remedial measures are speedily taken, the consciousness, only partially defined, that our monetary system is a false one, that Government may be speedily called upon for large sums of gold, its inherent weakness as an issuer of paper money being thereby disclosed, is certain to lead to a panic, Government and people being alike involved in a common catastrophe.

Apart from the absurdity of bi-metallism as a proposition, the appointment of a Commission to treat with other great powers should be deprecated, unless we are prepared to meet them on equal terms. While, from the force of laws which no intelligent people can long resist, other powers have been busy in discharging themselves of their useless loads of silver, we have been piling it up till our purchases have reached 459,946,701 ounces, at a cost of $464,210,262. Assuming the silver to be worth 66 cents the ounce, the loss on our purchases already equals $160,000,000. The interest on them equals, say, $140,000,000, the total loss so far being $300,000,000. With such a load on our own, should we appeal to other great powers for the establishment of bi-metallism, the natural inference would be that our purpose was to throw a part of it upon their shoulders. Should we expose ourselves to such insinuations? As evidence of our sincerity, let us meet the great powers, if we are to meet them, on equal terms.

If our currency was wholly symbolic, we might with safety dally with the subject of bi-metallism, certain that it would never come to anything but speculation and talk ; but as it is largely one of Government notes, the consideration of this subject as a serious proposition has the direct effect. to delay the inauguration of any measures of reform.   If by international agreement the value of silver as money can be doubled, certainly by compact among ourselves the value of Government notes can be maintained at the par of gold.   One assumption being correct, the other by necessary consequence must be.   It is here that our danger lies.   Years may be required to secure an international compact for the use of silver as money.   Till that great stumbling-block is removed, it is hardly possible that any steps by way of reform will be taken.

THE REMEDY.

The remedy : A return to a symbolic currency alike for the Government and the people.   What is the situation ? — $830,000,000 of government notes, for $346,000,000 of which only a small provision is made, and, say, $484,000,000 of silver notes assumed by the Government to be payable in gold, their constituent, unless converted into gold, being wholly unavailable for their discharge.

The first step, to quiet alarm, is provision for funding all the notes into bonds having a value in gold equal to their nominal amount.   The terrible tension would be instantly relieved.   Every man and every industry in the country would spring to its feet.   The echo of the acclaim would go around the world, everywhere carrying hope and joy, for if one great nation like our own be in distress all alike share.   Such a provision would be the equivalent of placing $830,000,000 of gold in the Treasury.   We cannot now even deliberate without creating alarm.   We cannot expose the situation without the danger of exciting a run upon the Government that would force it into a suspension of specie payment, and with it the people, as the entire monetary fabric of the country rests upon that of the Government.   The present secure, we could proceed at leisure.

The second step would be to return to the people the power of creating everywhere their own money by removing the tax upon the circulation of the State Banks.   Its imposition was a flagrant act of despotism by a gross infraction of the Constitution.   The State

Banks were suppressed that a crowning wrong, the substitution of a currency of the Government, of debt, for one the symbol of capital, might be perpetrated. State Banks were in existence before the Constitution was framed. Their right to exercise all functions proper to them, among these the issue of notes, was supported by precedent of seventy years. Mr. Madison, who earnestly controverted the right of Congress to create the Bank of the United States, declared that precedent of twenty years' standing, unsupported by judicial decisions, settled the question of its constitutionality. Under our dual system precedent should run as much against as in favor of the National Government. If the latter could purposely by a tax destroy one of the functions of a bank, it could in the same way destroy every other. If it could destroy their banks, it could destroy every function necessary to the existence of the States. The elevation of the author of such a doctrine as this to the Chief Justiceship of the Supreme Court of the United States shows how little we have mastered the principles upon which stable and well-ordered governments must rest. Not to be controlled by precedent established under conditions perfectly free is to have no anchorage whatever. The common law of a people is that which best expresses and best guards their life. Every one having merchandise fitted for consumption is competent to issue instruments, of the value of gold, for its distribution. All the qualification required to issue the money of commerce, and good money, is the instinct that demands an equivalent in the sale of a horse. If the people of Kansas want cheap money, let them have it by the cart-load. But they would want no such thing for their own use. The provision of such money would always be for people other than themselves. Whatever the kind, none would be created for domestic use but the best. They could no more afford to have poor money than poor instruments for the cultivation of their farms. The people of Mississippi might well be entrusted with the creation of their money. As they no longer have the power to swindle outsiders, they will be very careful not to swindle themselves. The creation of their own money might well be left to the people of States wholly Populistic, with the certainty that they will be most scrupulous in providing a good one. It is only for outsiders that base money is ever provided; but in this matter outsiders would prove quite competent to take care of themselves. When it is analyzed it will be seen that one kind of money for one class, and another for another, is a thing that defies human ingenuity, for the reason that to every transaction there must be two parties, each one demanding an equivalent for that with which he parts. It is upon this instinct that society itself rests. The people of the silver-producing States left to themselves will no more adopt silver as their standard money than those of Great Britain, for the reason that a better and less costly one is to be had; no more than they would adopt iron in the place of steel in their mining operations. A proposition that the people of Colorado imitate the example of the United States, that silver, supported by gold, be their money, would be received by them with jeers of derision and contempt. "We are not," would be the universal exclaim, "such shams and fools as this." With a proper system the money of each State would result from, and be the measure of the value of, the products of each. That of Colorado would measure the value of the products of her mines; of Kansas, that of her corn and hogs; of the Dakotas, that of their wheat; of Mississippi, that of her cotton; of Pennsylvania and Ohio, that of their coal and iron; of the Eastern States, that of the products of their manufacturing establishments — all the equivalents of gold. The proper measure of the money of every commercial community like the United States is the value of its products, whether of gold, silver, copper, iron, cotton, or corn. It makes no difference which. What more can be asked? The producers of silver say that the price of a product is measured by the uses to which it can be put. Very true. The use of silver as money once sustained its value. But its use has been superseded by more convenient and less costly instruments of exchange. Its value now rests upon the uses to which, like steel, it can be put in the economy of life. Like steel it is now merchandise, not money. By no possibility can it be restored as money unless inconvenient and costly methods are preferred to convenient and cheap ones. The value of money must be intrinsic or representative. When this lesson is learned the people of the South and West, instead of spending their time in railing at "consolidated capital," will seek by proper methods to become "consolidated capitalists" themselves. But they are in distress. They think they see the way out of it in the situation in which the Government is placed in having in its vaults some 400,000,000 of silver dollars, full legal tender, but worth only one-half their nominal value. If these could be had at their real value, and used by them in the payment of debts at their nominal value, all, they think, would be well. But in obedience to an instinct which would be as strong with them the moment they began to reflect and act for themselves as with the people of Massachusetts and New York, they would soon see that neither silver nor gold was to be their ordinary money; that the cost of the provision of a standard of value, whether silver or gold, would be the same, the choice turning upon the relative fitness of the two. But the silver dollars in the Treasury are to be had only by "bursting" the Government. The people will never take any steps in such direction, always preferring government notes to gold. The classes that will "burst" the Government, if this is to be done, will not be the people, but drawers of exchange, and great bankers, in position to see how the current is running and take instant advantage of it.

The third step would, by necessary sequence, be the return to the National Banks of the bonds put up by them as security for their notes. As these and the State Banks began the issue of notes, the holders of those of the Government would instinctively begin their conversion into its bonds, the conversion going on in ratio as the money of commerce was supplied to take their place.

When such a stage in the process of reform is reached the inquiry would naturally suggest itself, Why, if the money of commerce is to be that of the people, should it not be that of the Government, issued by a bank of its own creation? The National and State Banks might indeed supply an adequate amount, but Government would want something more — a custodian of its revenues which would be receivable in its notes and disbursed by means of cheques upon it, precisely as the National Banks now serve as the custodians of the money, utilized by means of cheques, of the people. A surplus of, say, $50,000,000 in the Treasury would be hardly entrusted to a bank in the city of New York, the great point of the collection of the revenues, the share capital of none exceeding $5,000,000. To distribute the amount among half a dozen of the strongest institutions would be a favoritism that would hardly be tolerated. To deal out a portion to each in ratio to its share capital would involve the opening of a great number of accounts, some with banks hardly to be trusted with the public moneys. The State Banks, if emancipated from the burdens now imposed upon them, would properly come in for their share. But State Banks, the right to issue notes restored, would be as free from the direct control of the Government as they were before the establishment of the present Safety Fund System. Institutions over which the Government has no direct control should certainly not be entrusted with its funds. The custodian of these should be always subject to restrictions which would not only render loss impossible, but which would make the issues of all other banks as good as its own. As a National Bank would necessarily in the course of business receive on deposit, and in the payment of the revenues, the notes of all issuers and cheques upon them, it would for its own safety require the daily discharge in gold of all balances found in its favor. By such means the restrictions imposed upon it would in effect be imposed upon all other issuers. A perfectly safe currency would by such means be everywhere provided. As the National Bank would make loans based upon the deposits of the Government for which the latter had no immediate use, as upon those of its ordinary customers, all balances that could be safely spared would be promptly returned to the channels of production and trade from which they were drawn, not a dollar being allowed to lie idle. With a National Bank, the Independent Treasury would naturally be discontinued as wholly superfluous, the bank assuming all its functions, the saving being a half a million annually. By means of it metallic money as capital would, except in the form of small coins, be wholly discharged from the operations alike of Government and people. From the restrictions imposed upon it, and through it upon all other issuers, no balances could arise either in the foreign or domestic trade of the country requiring any considerable provision of gold for their discharge.

The reasoning here is without a flaw; what is better, it is supported by precedent of forty years. Why was it that a system so beneficent in its results was overthrown? From fear of "consolidated capital," that arch enemy of the race, certain, if allowed to have its way, to reduce the great mass of the people to the condition of serfs and slaves! In the second Bank capital was consolidated on a vast scale. From its alleged use in oppressing the people it was overthrown. From its overthrow General Jackson was hailed as the savior of his country. From that time the danger of "consolidated capital" was the constant theme of the great political party which so long dominated the country. Mr. Van Buren, who immediately succeeded General Jackson, thanked Heaven in one of his messages that the great monster was at last under the sod. It was the constant theme of succeeding presidents down to and including Mr. Buchanan. With Mr. Voorhees the oppressions of " consolidated capital" had been such that the value of a day's work was reduced to ten cents and that of a horse to ten dollars ! With Mr. Carlisle, after fifteen years of weary warfare with " consolidated capital," the people stood on the very verge of financial ruin. But in describing the oppressions of this terrible monster Mr. Cleveland bore off the palm. In his annual message for 1888 he said :

Our cities are the abiding places of wealth and luxury. Our manufactures yield fortunes never dreamed of by the fathers of the republic. Our business men are madly striving in the race for riches, and the immense aggregations of capital outreach the imagination in the magnitude of their undertakings. By a more careful scrutiny we find the wealth and luxury of our cities mingled with poverty and wretchedness and unremunerative toil. We discover that the fortunes realized by our manufacturers are no longer solely the reward of sturdy industry and enlightened foresight, but that they result from the discriminating favor of the Government, and are largely built up by undue exactions from the masses of our people. The gulf between employers and employed is constantly widening, and classes are rapidly forming, one comprising the very rich and powerful, while in another are found the toiling poor. As we view the achievements of aggregated capital we discover the existence of trusts, combinations, and monopolies. While the citizen is struggling far in the rear or is trampled to death under an iron heel, corporations, which should be the carefully restrained creatures of law and the servants of the people, are fast becoming the people's masters.

Never before in history was such a picture drawn, and that by a president of a great republic, of avarice and brutality on one side and of degradation and suffering on the other. If true, it shows a republic to be the worst form of government, being wholly unable to protect the people, stamped to death under the iron heel of selfishness and greed. But is the picture true? How is " consolidated capital," from the experience of its use, viewed? Suppose a charter for a National Bank, providing for a capital $100,000,000, to be offered to the highest bidder. Chicago would instantly step forward with her millions to secure the prize which in her estimation would stamp her as the imperial city of the world. The most rampant Populist would vie with the hardest-headed man of affairs in his earnestness and contributions. Not a suggestion would arise from any quarter that the bank could be an instrument of oppression, or that by means of it any private ends could be secured. A single common and honorable impulse would be that of every citizen from the highest to the lowest — the honor and greatness of Chicago ! No one not entitled to the money of the bank could get a dollar of it. No one who could not offer an equivalent therefor could get a dollar of it. For a bank not to demand an equivalent when a loan is made is, ordinarily, to make a loss equal to the amount — an offence against society, as its welfare is in ratio to the amount of capital usefully employed. As the demand for its money, and consequently the returns upon it, would be in ratio as the people were industrious, intelligent, well-to-do,, and free, the bank would have every motive to promote their industry, intelligence, welfare, and freedom. It would be a moral institution of high value in the example set by it for all others, as well as an indispensable one in affairs.

As the act for the creation of the bank would provide for numerous branches, the same contest would arise for their possession as for that of the parent bank. If ten branches were assigned to Illinois, fifty places would be earnest competitors for one of them, well understanding the benefits that would arise therefrom in the increased provision for symbolizing their products as well as from the prestige and preëminence it would secure. In the struggle to secure a branch, political distinctions, so pronounced in other matters, would be wholly forgotten.

As on a great, so on a small scale. From the sense of the advantages derived from them our present National Banks are eagerly welcomed by every community throughout the land. In welcoming these all political distinctions are also forgotten. All make contributions for their establishment according to their means. They immediately become the custodians of the surplus cash of the people, their issues serving as instruments for turning into potential money all products prepared for market. Their management is intrusted to boards of directors, to "committees of safety," composed of discreet and prosperous citizens familiar with the character and means of every person likely to apply for loans. The "committees of safety" are usually large owners in the share capital of the banks whose operations they conduct, a guarantee for their proper management. Any loss that may be made comes largely out of their own pockets. With such a committee always on the alert, loans would seldom be made for the payment of which adequate provision in merchandise was not previously provided. Such institutions are so essential to the general welfare that the appointments of no considerable community are complete without them. Their success is a matter of satisfaction and pride to all, whether or not they have any interest in them.

With a proper system, that is, with a National Bank, free issue to be allowed to all others, State and National, it is not probable that one-twentieth part of the currency would be supplied by the National one, each section of the country creating its own. No monopoly, consequently, of issue could exist.

And how about manufacturing establishments in which capital must be massed on a vast scale, and remain massed in corporations having a perpetual existence, being dedicated to purposes as enduring as society itself? There is not a community in the United States in which such works are not warmly welcomed by gifts in the form of sites, material, money, or the remission of taxes for a series of years, the degree of welcome being in ratio to the amount of capital to be employed. They at once, wherever they go, set everything in motion, add largely to the value of real property, give new opportunities for the employment of labor at rates far above those which had previously prevailed, and create, at largely increased prices, a domestic market for products which previously had none. They must be large purchasers of labor and material from those under no obligation to make any return in kind. There is hardly a municipality in the Northern States that is not authorized by law to offer inducements of the kind described from a sense of the advantages to be secured. In welcoming them all party distinctions are forgotten. The people of Kansas, were they able, could well afford to contribute $100,000,000 for the purpose of attracting manufacturing establishments which would supply their wants by direct exchange for the products of their soil. A sense of their value is rapidly travelling southward, the State of Alabama having recently authorized her municipalities to offer substantial aid to secure them. While the necessary effect of every establishment of the kind is to advance the price of labor and of the products of the community in which they are domiciled, its tendency, from an increased supply and from the improved methods brought into use, is always to reduce the price of its peculiar product. Take the case of steel. There is no branch of industry which requires a greater massing of capital ; there is none in which greater skill and training are required. Its manufacture in this country since 1862 has been protected by prohibitory duties. If monopoly or oppression were possible anywhere it would be here. Yet with the most persistent efforts of manufacturers to maintain them, prices have fallen from $140 the ton in gold, in 1867, to $20 in 1897. The increase of product in the same period has been from 17,000 to 6,114,834 tons. In the same period the wages of labor employed in its manufacture have been doubled from the enormously increased demand therefor. From their fall in price steel have taken the place of iron rails on our railroads, the gain to the public being many hundred millions annually. The example, a striking one, is true of every other department of production. Every one seeks to get, as he should, the most out of his business. If he begins with, or realizes, large profits, competition is certain speedily to reduce them to the common level, as capital, the supply being unlimited, eagerly seeks investments that will yield five per cent. One cannot enter upon any branch of production on a large scale and make a success in it without reducing the price of the product, being thereby a public benefactor. He is subject to a law higher than his own. The more intent upon gain, the more effectually does he serve others rather than himself. In the nature of things it is impossible that, in a country like the United States, where the field is open to all, corporations should oppress, though they may not reduce prices fast enough to suit the popular idea.

As with manufacturing establishments, so with railroads entered upon as an investment of capital. The advantage to those who have no pecuniary interest in them is fifty-fold greater than to their promoters. They create values on an enormous scale by opening markets for products otherwise without them. In some systems hundred of millions of dollars are massed — the greater the amount, the better the service and the less the charge. Were monopolies possible it would be in such lines as the New York Central and Pennsylvania, but there is hardly a pound of freight moved by either that is not fiercely competed for by numerous other lines. So great have been the improvements in the methods used, and so fierce the competition, that there is not a railroad in the United States that has not, within a comparatively short period, with an enormous increase of traffic, in some cases five or ten fold, been compelled to reduce rates on merchandise to one-quarter those charged twenty-five years ago ; and to such an extent that the return on the investments in these works is far below the average of those in other departments of industry or enterprise. The most promising field of all at the outset is that in which capital has suffered the most. The only function in a government like that of the United States, where the supply of capital and raw material is unlimited, is to see to it that opportunity is alike open to all. With such provision society may rest assured that capital will be always working for its welfare, and never for its harm; that it is amply protected by a law far higher and more exacting than any of human contrivance.

It may be urged that corporations will combine to put up prices. They cannot by combination put up prices so that, where the conditions, as in the United States, are perfectly free, profits in any line will exceed the average of other departments of enterprise and industry, as capital, the supply of which is unlimited, always flows in the direction which promises the best return. It is for the interest of the public that corporations, by restricting production, for example, should combine so that profits in any one line may not fall below the average. If from want of adequate returns any go out of operation, the survivors, the field remaining to them, will naturally put up prices. But the moment that their profits exceed the general average, competition comes in as the natural and inevitable corrective. It is better for society that the number in operation be maintained than that any should be compelled to go out of business, their places in time to be supplied by new ones, involving new outlays of capital to meet the increase of consumption by a steadily increasing population. Society need not be under the slightest concern that all service, so far as it is rendered by capital, whatever the form, will not be at the lowest cost. That side of life, without any interposition of Government, is wholly secure.

There is undoubtedly a great deal of ill-gotten capital that most offensively flaunts itself. But for such the laws enacted by the people are chiefly responsible. Capital honestly acquired and honestly employed is an essential condition of human progress. Vast fortunes have been made by those who control improved processes in production and distribution. The law here stands for twenty years their friend. But where one is the measure of their gain, a thousand is that of the public, of which the case of steel may again be cited. Vast fortunes are made by combination by which

capital, in ratio to the result secured, is discharged from use, the benefit inuring far more to the public than to those who exploit the new
methods. The laying by of a dollar a day is equivalent to a fortune
at the end of a long life. The beneficence of capital is shown by the
struggle for its possession by all engaged in production and distribution, more being made by its use than the charge for its use. When
massed in corporations pursuing legitimate industries, it is always
beneficent, as in ratio as it is massed is cost of production reduced,
the demand for labor, the only factor short in supply, and with it
the compensation, being greatly increased. Much discontent still
prevails by those whose hours of labor have been shortened, their
compensation being largely increased, the price of all articles essential to their comfort and welfare being greatly reduced. Contrasts
in society still exist and will exist so long as difference in faculty or
desert exists. But there must be incentives to an industrious and
honorable life in its rewards. Without them society would sink to
the level from which it rose. The lesson to be learned by those who
have excelled in the race is to extend a helping hand to those less
fortunate than themselves. But this opens a chapter not here to be
entered upon.

To conclude : In discussing the currency we must start from the
premise that paper money, in some form, is always to be that of our
people, as it must be that of every great commercial community.
No other kind can be afforded. No matter how unsound it may be
there will be no thought of returning to metallic money, the use
of which would reduce transactions to one-fifth or one-tenth their
present volume. When paper money is most depreciated a better
kind will always be sought, but never a return to one of capital.

The second proposition is that the money of the people must be
that of the Government. There may be a good currency without
the interposition of law. Every person possessed of merchandise
is competent to issue instruments for its distribution, and would
issue them but for the reason that a better way is provided by
means of corporations dedicated to a particular purpose and not
subject to the risks of production and trade, their issues to be
measured by the nominal value of the merchant's bills held by
them. Good local currencies may be provided, but with all the
safeguards which State legislation and careful supervision would

throw round them, the National Government could not directly commit itself to their use. It must have an institution of its own creation to stand between it and all other issuers throughout the country — one which would in the course of business receive the notes and credits of all other issuers in the payment of the public revenues, on deposit, and in the payment of its bills. The National Bank would prefer to have its bills paid and revenues collected in the issues of other banks rather than its own, as in ratio as the former were received its own would remain in circulation. It would protect itself against loss by demanding that all balances arising in its favor be daily discharged. By the provisions described the issues of every bank throughout the country, in good standing, would, in effect, be received in the payment of the revenues, payments being made in kind, as it were, in the symbol of the particular product of the section where they were collected. A currency common alike to Government and people would thus be provided ; a currency never in excess ; always retired by its use ; a currency which, through the value of its constituent, would wholly supersede gold, metallic money, as the ordinary instrument of exchange: If gold were wanted by the Government or people it would be supplied by the banks out of their reserves. With a National Bank restricted in its discounts to bills of exchange, the Government would have no more occasion to concern itself about the solvency of the currency than about the solvency of the makers of bills upon which it was based ; no more than about the solvency of drawers of exchange, or of railroad or manufacturing corporations, as no currency that was not retired by its use, the crucial test, could get into circulation. Successful issuers should no more be compelled to make up the losses of the unsuccessful, than successful merchants should make up those of the unsuccessful and incompetent ones. If the principle upon which the national banking system is based be correct, then Government should in the same way place itself behind every industry and enterprise in the land. With a National Bank full and adequate provision for a sound currency would be made previous to its issue. It is easy to prevent the perpetration of a great wrong. It may be impossible to repair its effects. We are oppressed by a great wrong that should never have been committed. Jackson did his work so well that as a people we have never recovered our sense or reason, so completely was the example of the past effaced from memory. That we should have dethroned Hamilton and put Jackson in his place as our oracle and mentor in the matter of money shows our immeasurable folly, and how incapable we are to deal with matters that most intimately concern our highest welfare. The necessary consequence has been that our history, so far as money has been concerned, from the time of Jackson has been one of alternations, on a vast scale, of farce and tragedy.

Why should not a return be made to a currency common alike to government and people — a currency founded in the very nature of things, the soundness and value of which have been demonstrated by precedents of forty years, and which can only be provided by a National Bank? In the way stand the history and traditions of a great party, now broken into two wings, that its creation transcends the power of the Government, its existence being incompatible with the liberties of the people. There is no evidence that either wing has receded from a position which both in common so long held. With the Sound Money wing of the Democracy, the creation of a National Bank would be an act of " Paternalism " by no means to be permitted. With it salvation is to come, if at all, from accident, from drifting, not from forecast or method. The Free Coinage wing wants money that costs little, the less the better, but issued in ratio to the needs of the people. The money of banks could be had only at its value. Hence all of it must be issued by the Government.

The great party now in control insists, with plenty of unmeaning platitudes, that the present situation be maintained ; that all the money we have is good money, and that all that is wanted is a little patching by which its value may be no longer " threatened." Should not the use of such an ominous word have suggested to its chief that money the value of which can be threatened is not good money, and the remedy for money that is not good? With him all kinds now in circulation, gold, silver, issues of Government and banks, have an equal standing in the courts of reason and law. There is no hint of reformation in its proper sense. So far as Congress is concerned its attention is engrossed by the crowning piece of tomfoolery of modern times, Bimetallism, — the Senate, by unanimous vote, declaring itself in its favor, and the House by a vote of 279 to 4. In the meantime matters are steadily going from bad to worse. The tariff is its panacea for all evils. It is well to have the National Government self-supporting. Had it been so for the last four years, the greater part of the legal tender notes could have been safely locked up in the Treasury. But the new tariff, while it will improve, will not restore the situation. Without a reform of the currency, the clouds, now deep on the horizon, will only grow darker and more portentous. One that is neither capital nor the symbol of capital always exacts a penalty, and when issued on a vast scale, an enormous one. The penalty is not so much the final catastrophe as the long and lingering illness which necessarily precedes it.

There is one bright spot on the horizon. The Secretary of the Treasury is a man trained in affairs, and should know the difference between palaver and "cash down." He may not be a Hamilton, but if he restore the work of Hamilton he will be second only to his illustrious predecessor in deserving and receiving the grateful homage of an emancipated people.

NOTES AND ILLUSTRATIONS.

In 1696 the silver currency of England (the only one then in use) had become so reduced in value, from clipping and wear, as to cause the greatest inconvenience in all the operations of society. The coins in use, no matter how light, could still be used in the payment of debts and of the taxes due the government. The latter attempted for a long time to correct the evil, by causing large quantities of silver to be coined of the standard weight and fineness; but as the old coins, with one-quarter or one-fifth less of pure metal, were used as currency equally with the new, the latter were immediately taken up and melted down, or exported at their value as bullion or merchandise, so that no progress whatever was made in remedying an evil which had become well-nigh insupportable.

"The financiers of that age," says Macaulay, in his graphic picture of it, "seem to have expected that the new money, which was excellent, would soon displace the old money, which was much impaired. Yet any man of plain understanding might have known that, when the State treats perfect coin and light coin as of equal value, the perfect coin will not drive the light coin out of circulation, but will itself be driven out. A clipped crown, on English ground, went as far in the payment of a tax or a debt as a milled crown. But the milled crown, as soon as it had been flung into the crucible or carried across the channel, became much more valuable than the clipped crown. It might therefore have been predicted, as confidently as anything can be predicted which depends on the human will, that the inferior pieces would remain in the only market in which they could fetch the same price as the superior pieces; and that the superior pieces would take some form or fly to some place in which some advantage could be derived from their superiority.

"The politicians of that age, however, generally overlooked these very obvious considerations. They marvelled exceedingly that everybody should be so perverse as to use light money in preference to good money. In other words, they marvelled that nobody chose to pay twelve ounces of silver when ten ounces would serve the turn. The horse at the Tower still paced his rounds. Fresh wagon-loads of choice money still came forth from the mill; and still they vanished as fast as they appeared. Great masses were melted down; great masses exported; great masses hoarded; but scarcely one new piece was found in the till of a shop, or in the leathern bag which the farmer carried home from the cattle fair. In the receipts and payments of the Exchequer the milled money did not exceed ten shillings in a hundred pounds. A writer of that age mentions the case of a merchant who, in the sum of thirty-five pounds, received only a single half-crown in milled silver. . . .

"The evils produced by this state of the currency were not such as have generally been thought worthy to occupy a prominent place in history. Yet it may well be doubted whether all the misery which had been inflicted on the English nation in a quarter of a century by bad kings, bad ministers, bad parliaments, and bad judges was equal to the misery caused in a single year by bad crowns and bad shillings. Those events which furnish the best themes for pathetic or indignant eloquence are not always those which most affect the happiness of the great body of the people. The misgovernment of Charles and James, gross as it had been, had not prevented the common business of life from going steadily and prosperously on. While the honor and independence of the State were sold to a foreign power, while chartered rights were invaded, while fundamental laws were violated, hundreds of thousands of quiet, honest, and industrious families labored and traded, ate their meals and lay down to rest, in comfort and security. Whether Whigs or Tories, Protestants or Jesuits were uppermost, the grazier drove his beasts to market ; the grocer weighed out his currants ; the draper measured out his broadcloth ; the hum of buyers and sellers was as loud as ever in the towns ; the harvest-home was celebrated as joyously as ever in the hamlets ; the cream overflowed the pails of Cheshire ; the apple-juice foamed in the presses of Herefordshire ; the piles of crockery glowed in the furnaces of the Trent ; and the barrows of coal rolled fast along the timber railway of the Tyne. But when the great instrument of exchange became thoroughly deranged, all trade, all industry, were smitten as with a palsy. . . .

" Since the Revolution the state of the currency had been repeatedly discussed in Parliament. In 1689 a committee of the commons had been appointed to investigate the subject, but had made no report. In 1690 another committee had reported that immense quantities of silver were carried out of the country by Jews, who, it was said, would do anything for profit. Schemes were formed for encouraging the importation and discouraging the exportation of the precious metals. One foolish bill after another was brought in and dropped. At length, in the beginning of the year 1695, the question assumed so serious an aspect that the Houses applied themselves to it in earnest. The only practical result of their deliberations, however, was a new penal law, which it was hoped would prevent the clipping of the hammered coin and the melting and exporting of the milled coin. It was enacted that every person who informed against a clipper should be entitled to a reward of forty pounds, that every clipper who informed against two clippers should be entitled to a pardon, and that whoever should be found in possession of silver filings or parings should be burned in the cheek with a red-hot iron. Certain officers were employed to search for bullion. If bullion were found in a house or on board of a ship, the burden of proving that it had never been part of the money of the realm was thrown on the owner. If he failed in making out a satisfactory account of every ingot he was liable to severe penalties. This act was, as might have been expected, altogether ineffective. During the following summer and autumn the coin went on dwindling, and the cry of distress from every county in the realm became louder and more piercing.

" But, happily for England, there were among her rulers some who clearly perceived that it was not by halters and branding-irons that her decaying industry and commerce could be restored to health. The state of the currency had, during some time, occupied the serious attention of four eminent men closely connected by public and private ties. Two of them were politicians who had never in the midst of official and parliamentary business ceased to love and honor philosophy ; and two were philosophers in whom habits of abstruse meditation had not impaired the homely good sense without which even genius is mischievous in politics. Never had there been an occasion which more urgently required both practical and speculative abilities ; and never had the world seen the highest practical and the speculative abilities united in an allegiance so close, so harmonious, and so honorable as that which bound Somers and Montague to Locke and Newton. . . .

" In whatever way the restoration of the coin might be affected, great sacrifices must be made, either by the whole community or by a part of the community, and to call for such sacrifices at a time when the nation was at war, and was already paying taxes such as, ten years before, no financier would have thought it possible to raise, was undoubtedly a course full of danger. Timorous politicians were for delay ; but the deliberate conviction of the great Whig leaders was that something must be hazarded, or that everything was lost. Montague in particular is said to have expressed in strong language his determination to kill or cure. If, indeed, there had been any hope that the evil would merely continue to be what it was, it might have been wise to defer till the return of peace an experiment which must severely try the strength of the body politic. But the evil was one which daily made progress almost visible to the eye. There might have been a recoinage in 1694 with half the risk which must be run in 1696 ; and great as would be the risk in 1696, that risk would be doubled if the recoinage were postponed till 1698.

" Those politicians whose voice was for delay gave less trouble than another set of politicians who were for a general and immediate recoinage, but who insisted that the new shilling should be worth only ninepence or ninepence halfpenny. At the head of this party was William Lowndes, Secretary of the Treasury, a most respectable and industrious public servant, but much more versed in the details of his office than in the higher parts of political philosophy. He was not in the least aware that a piece of metal with the king's head on it was a commodity of which the price was governed by the same laws which govern the price of a piece of metal fashioned into a spoon or a buckle, and that it was no more in the power of Parliament to make the kingdom richer by calling a crown a pound than to make the kingdom larger by calling a furlong a mile. He seriously believed, incredible as it may seem, that if an ounce of silver were divided into seven shillings instead of five, foreign nations would sell us their wines and their silks for a smaller number of ounces. He had a considerable following, composed partly of dull men who really believed what he told them, and partly of shrewd men who were perfectly willing to be authorized by law to pay a hundred pounds with eighty. Had his arguments prevailed, the evils

of a vast confiscation would have been added to the other evils which afflicted
the nation; public credit, still in its tender and sickly infancy, would have been
destroyed, and there would have been much risk of a general mutiny of the fleet
and army. Happily Lowndes was completely refuted by Locke in a paper drawn
up for the use of Somers. Somers was delighted with this little treatise, and
desired that it might be printed. It speedily became the text-book of all the
most enlightened politicians in the kingdom, and may still be read with pleasure
and profit.''

The proposition of Lowndes was for a recoinage of the currency
with one-fifth less metal than the standard of the old coins; to raise,
to use his own words, " the value of the silver in the coins to the
foot of 6s. 3d. in every crown, because the price of standard silver
in bullion is risen to 6s. 5d. an ounce." Locke was called upon to
prove, and did prove most conclusively, that silver coins only
equalled in value similar weights of the metal in bullion; and, consequently, that nothing could be gained, at home or abroad, by alter-
ing the standard, as the coins, both at home and abroad, would pass
only at their value measured by weight and fineness. It would seem
that the conclusions to which Locke came might have been assumed
as axioms from which he might have commenced his argument. If
so, the statement of the question contained its own answer. Locke
was not content with this. He prepared a pamphlet of more than
a hundred pages in which he reënforced his argument by a wealth
and conclusiveness of illustration which should have put the question
forever at rest. He did, indeed, carry the government with him,
but by no means the general sense of mankind.

The plan of relief finally adopted by the English government
provided that the money of the kingdom should be recoined
according to the old standard of weight and fineness; that all the
pieces should be milled, and that the loss on the clipped pieces
should be borne by the public. A time was fixed after which no
clipped money should pass, except in payments to the government;
and a later time after which it should not pass at all. To provide
for the loss on the clipped coins, the Bank of England undertook,
on the security of the window tax, to advance the government
£1,200,000. This advance, however, afforded but a partial relief.
Full relief could only be had when the new silver (the metal chiefly
in circulation) came in in sufficient abundance to fill up the vacuum
made by calling in the old.

" Saturday, the second of May," (1696), said Lord Macaulay, " had been fixed as the last day on which the clipped crowns, half-crowns, and shillings were to be received by tale in payment of taxes.   The Exchequer was besieged from dawn till midnight by an immense multitude.   It was necessary to call in the guards for the purpose of keeping order.   On the following Monday began a cruel agony of a few months, which was destined to be succeeded by many years of almost unbroken prosperity.

" Most of the old silver had vanished.   The new silver had scarcely made its appearance.   About £4,000,000, in ingots and hammered coin, were lying in the vaults of the Exchequer ; and the milled money as yet came forth very slowly from the Mint.   Alarmists predicted that the wealthiest and most enlightened kingdom in Europe would be reduced to the state of those barbarous societies in which a mat is bought with a hatchet, and a pair of moccasins with a piece of venison.   There were, indeed, some hammered pieces which had escaped mutila-tion, and sixpences not clipped within the innermost ring were still current.   This old money and the new money together made up a scanty stock of silver, which, with the help of gold, was to carry the nation through the summer.   The manu-facturers generally continued, though with extreme difficulty, to pay their work-men in coin.   The upper classes seem to have lived to a great extent on credit. Even an opulent man seldom had the means of discharging the weekly bills of his baker and butcher.   A promissory note, however, subscribed by such a man, was readily taken in the district where his means and character were well known. The notes of the wealthy money-changers of Lombard street circulated widely. The paper of the Bank of England did much service.   .   .   .

" The directors soon found it impossible to procure silver to meet every claim which was made on them in good faith.   They then bethought them of a new expedient.   They made a call of twenty per cent. on the proprietors, and thus raised a sum which enabled them to give every applicant fifteen per cent. in milled money on what was due to him.   They returned him his notes after making a minute upon it that part had been paid.   A few notes thus marked are still preserved among the archives of the Bank, as memorials of that terrible year.   The paper of the corporation continued to circulate ; but the value fluctuated violently from day to day, and indeed from hour to hour ; for the public mind was in so excitable a state that the most absurd lie which a stock-jobber could invent sufficed to send the price up or down.   At one time the dis-count was only six per cent., at another time twenty-four per cent.   A ten-pound note, which had been taken in the morning as worth more than nine pounds, was often worth less than eight pounds before night.   .   .   .

" Meanwhile, strenuous exertions were making to hasten the recoinage. Since the restoration the mint had, like every other public establishment in the kingdom, been a nest of idlers and jobbers.   The important office of warden, worth between six and seven hundred a year, had become a mere sinecure, and had been filled by a succession of fine gentlemen who were well known at the hazard-table at Whitehall, but who never condescended to come near the Tower.   This office had just become vacant, and Montague had obtained it for Newton.   The ability, the industry, and the strict uprightness of the great philos-opher speedily produced a complete revolution throughout the department which was under his direction. He devoted himself to his task with an activity which left him no time to spare for those pursuits in which he had surpassed Archimedes and Galileo. Till the great work was completely done, he resisted firmly, and almost angrily, every attempt that was made by men of science, either here or on the Continent, to draw him away from his official duties. The old officers of the mint had thought it a great feat to coin silver to the amount of fifteen thousand pounds a week. When Montague talked of thirty or forty thousand, these men of form and precedent pronounced the thing impracticable. But the energy of the young chancellor of the Exchequer and of his friend the warden accomplished far greater wonders. Soon nineteen mills were going at once in the Tower. As fast as men could be trained to the work in London, bands of them were sent off to other parts of the kingdom. Mints were established at Bristol, York, Exeter, Norwich, and Chester. This arrangement was in the highest degree popular. The machinery and the workmen were welcomed to the new stations with the ringing of bells and the firing of guns. The weekly issue increased to sixty thousand pounds, to eighty thousand, to a hundred thousand, and at length to a hundred and twenty thousand. Yet even this issue, though great, not only beyond precedent, but beyond hope, was scanty when compared with the demands of the nation. Nor did all the newly stamped silver pass into circulation ; for during the summer and autumn those politicians who were for raising the denomination of the coin were active and clamorous ; and it was generally expected that, as soon as Parliament should reassemble, the standard would be lowered. Of course, no person who thought it probable that he should, at a day not far distant, be able to pay a debt of a pound with three crown pieces instead of four, was willing to part with a crown piece till that day arrived. Most of the milled pieces were, therefore, hoarded. May, June, and July passed away without any perceptible increase in the quantity of good money. It was not till August that the keenest observer could discern the first faint signs of returning prosperity." [1]

The parallelism between the situation in the United States to-day and that in England two hundred years ago, both countries suffering from a similar cause, a vicious currency, one of the greatest calamities that can befall a people, is very striking. Macaulay states that of the receipts into the English Treasury when the currency there was at its lowest value not over one-half of one per cent. was in money of full weight. The receipts into the Treasury of the United States are now almost wholly in the form of silver certificates, universally regarded as of " light weight," as the least valuable of the various kinds of money with us in circulation. In spite of the protestations of our Government that every kind of money issued by it is equally good, the better sense of the people tells them that there is a wide difference in value between them. Greenbacks, the highest

---

[1] Macaulay's " History of England," Volume IV.

form of Government paper money, are legal tender, and are in terms payable in gold, of which reserves equal to twenty-five per cent. of their amount are assumed to be provided. The notes of 1890, constituting the second form of paper money, are also legal tender, which implies an obligation on the part of the Government to pay them in the kind of money demanded by the holder. They are also supported by a declaration of Congress that they are to be paid in gold at the option of the holder. But such a declaration has not the force of positive law. For these Government does not assume to provide any reserves whatever. The third form are the silver notes of 1878 to which it is assumed that the declaration of Congress in favor of the notes of 1890 applies. They are not legal tender, and it is purely optional with the Government whether it will make any provision for them other than the silver which they represent, the value of which somewhat exceeds fifty per cent. of their nominal amount. So far as reserves are concerned the silver notes are the best secured of all. Although the notes of all still circulate at the nominal value of gold, banks and bankers are very careful never to have any considerable amount of notes of 1878 on hand. They are not available for settlements of balances at the clearing houses in the leading cities, especially in the city of New York. Silver dollars, a fourth kind of debased money, worth less than one-half their nominal value, are scrupulously avoided by all classes for fear that any day they may circulate at their real value. The result is, that instead of one kind of debased money, as in England, we have four in the United States : United States notes — the greenbacks, — the silver certificates of 1878, the silver notes of 1890, and silver dollars, all with a well-marked difference in value. By means of them almost all the business operations of the country are carried on. All are inflations of the currency for the discharge of not one of which in gold any adequate provision has been or ever will be made. With so many different kinds of money differing in value, is not the paralysis resting upon all business affairs, extending backwards through several years, readily accounted for? The condition of things in England two hundred years ago, described so graphically by Macaulay, was normal compared with the confusion and chaos that exist here. Can the crisis here be met with the sense and courage which was displayed in a similar one two hundred years ago ? Is the officer who presides over the department of the Treasury of the United States, like the one who presided over a similar department in England, ready to declare his determination to "kill or cure"? The motives that press upon him are ten-fold more urgent. In the place of 7,000,000 people we have here 70,000,000 groaning under the evils of a vicious monetary system, all apprehensive of the crowning disaster which may happen at any moment — suspension of specie payments alike by the Government and people. The operations of society here resting upon a debased currency are twenty-fold greater per head than they were two hundred years ago. The boon which he would confer should he succeed in the great task before him is beyond estimate, and would entitle him to the highest position among those who have deserved well of their country.

PAPER MONEY IN FRANCE. — THE MISSISSIPPI SCHEME.

One of the most striking and instructive examples of a *credit* currency was that of France, under the leadership of the celebrated John Law. He proceeded upon the assumption that "as the credit of a merchant amounted to ten-fold his capital, that of a bank might be still greater; while there was no limit to that of a State or a king;" that as money is that which sets everything in motion, the prosperity of a people or State is in ratio to its amount; and metallic money receives its value from the insignia of Government. He began his vast schemes by securing (May 7, 1716) an edict for the establishment of a private institution called "La Banque Générale." As at the outset it was conducted in a business-like manner, it met with great success, increasing the supply of money, and thereby reducing by one-half the rates previously paid. Its capital consisted of 6,000,000 livres (the equivalent of about $1,200,000), divided into shares of 5,000 livres each. Its capital was paid one-fourth in coin and three-fourths in Government funds. On the 10th of April, 1717, an edict was passed ordering the collectors of taxes to receive in their payment the notes of the bank, thereby securing for them a large circulation. From the uses they served their amount was presently increased to 60,000,000 livres.

A high credit having been secured by such measures for his bank, Law proceeded to the development of his grand schemes of controlling, through the money supplied by it, the whole machinery of society and state. In August, 1717, he procured an edict for the establishment of the "Compagnie des Indes-Occidentales," which secured to him the virtual sovereignty of the most fertile portions of the continent of North America. This was the beginning of the famous " Mississippi scheme," of which so much has been written and said. The capital of the new company was 100,000,000 livres ($20,000,000), divided into shares of 500 each, payment being made one-fourth in coin and three-fourths in government funds. On the fourth of September, 1718, the bank became a government institution, under the title of " La Banque Royale," of which Law retained the management, the king guaranteeing its notes, the stockholders of the old bank being paid off in coin. To increase the importance of the bank the transfer of money between the cities in which it had branches was forbidden. The bank now allied itself to the Mississippi Company, which became the great instrument of Law in carrying out his vast schemes, its issues being increased to 110,000,000 livres. In 1719 the East India and Senegal Companies of France were united with the Mississippi Company, a union which secured to the latter the greater part of the foreign trade of the kingdom. From the assumed advantages that would result, the stock of the Mississippi Company rose to a premium of 450 per cent. In August, 1719, the company undertook to advance to the Government, at the rate of 3 per cent., the sum of 1,500,000,000 livres for the payment of the public debt, which had previously borne interest at the rate of 5 per cent. As a part of the transaction the farming of the revenues was conceded to the company in consideration of the annual payment of 52,000,000 livres. The coinage was also conceded for a period of nine years in consideration of the payment of 5,000,000 livres.

The stock of the Mississippi Company now rose to a premium of 1200 per cent. To aid it in its various undertakings the bank increased its issues to 1,000,000,000 livres. Money became so abundant that lands sold at fifty years' purchase. From November, 1719, to April, 1720, the market value of the stock of the company rose to a premium of 2050 per cent. Law, capable of giving to the most worthless substances the value of gold, became the greatest figure in Europe. Its proudest aristocracy bowed in humble reverence at his feet, while the favor and admiration of the masses was won by his liberal use of his apparently boundless wealth, the creation of the printing-press. He was now made Controller-General of the finances of the kingdom, one of its most distinguished citizens being compelled to make way for him. As Paris was the theatre of this vast creation of apparent wealth, all France literally flocked to it as the place where money was to be had for the asking. Trade received a mighty impulse. Everybody seemed to be getting richer and richer, and no one poorer. It was the halcyon era of pure populism. The market value of the shares of the bank reached 10,000,000,-000 livres. Upon such a sum a revenue of 500,000,000 was necessary to pay 5 per cent. Its whole income from all sources did not equal one-sixth part of that sum. As was inevitable, the more reflecting classes began to exchange their shares for other kinds of property. The example was contagious, and shares began to fall rapidly in price. To meet the fall a series of edicts was rapidly issued, one of which provided that the notes should command a premium over gold, the use of which was to be greatly restricted, every one being forbidden to have any considerable amount in his possession. All such measures only served to accelerate the decline. To arrest it the gross value of the shares was fixed at 9,000,000,000 livres, the company being required to purchase and sell at that rate. To add to the confusion and distress metallic money was not to be had, the greater part of that previously in circulation having been sent out of the kingdom. Universal disaster and distress took the place of the extravagance and waste which had so recently prevailed. The money of the bank became almost wholly valueless. The untold wealth of the Mississippi Company was seen to be only a dream. Great masses of people who had invested their all in Law's schemes were reduced to abject want. The vast fabric that was reared and the terrible catastrophe that followed were rendered possible only through the issue of a "credit currency" precisely similar in kind to the United States notes. With the turn of the tide, Law, speedily stripped of all his offices and honors, fled secretly and in disgrace from France, never to return. To restore the situation in part, the government again assumed the charge of the public debt, the interest on it being reduced about half — to 40,000,000 in the place of 80,000,000 livres. The charter of the bank was abrogated, and the famous Mississippi Company, divested of all its vast powers, was reduced to the condition of a private and insignificant trading corporation. That the issue of United States notes, a currency precisely similar in kind to those of the Bank of France, has not been followed by calamities similar to those which overtook Law's bank, is due to the fact that it has not been made the basis of vast speculative operations, its orderly retirement being still within our reach.

But France, as well as England, had an illustrious citizen, Turgot, capable of demonstrating, and who did demonstrate most conclusively, the laws and nature of money, whether metallic or paper. To Law's assumption that

These two metals — gold and silver — are only the *signs* that represent real wealth, that is to say, commodities. A *crown* is a note conceived in these terms: "Any seller shall give to the bearer the article or merchandise of which he may have need, to the amount of three livres, for as much of another merchandise which has been delivered to me;" and the effigy of the prince stands for the signature. Now what does it signify whether the sign be of silver or of paper? Is it not better to choose a material that costs nothing and which we are not obliged to withdraw from commerce where it is employed as merchandise, — one, in fine, that is fabricated in the kingdom and does not subject us to a necessary dependence on foreigners and owners of mines, who greedily profit by the seduction into which, by the glamour of gold and of silver, other nations have fallen, — a material which we can increase according to our needs, without fear of its ever being deficient? Paper has all these advantages which render it preferable to hard money.[1]

Turgot replied:

Here would be a benefit as grand as the philosopher's stone if all these reasonings were just. We should have need of neither gold nor silver to buy all kinds of commodities. But has it been left to Law to remain ignorant that gold falls in value like everything else by becoming more plentiful? If he had read and studied Locke, who wrote twenty years before him, he would have known that all commodities of a country are balanced between themselves, and with gold and silver according to the proportion of their quantity and the demand for them; he would have learned that gold has not a value which corresponds always to a certain quantity of merchandise, but that when there is more gold it is cheaper, and gives more of it for a determinate quantity of merchandise; that thus gold, when it circulates freely, suffices always to the need of the State, and that it becomes a matter indifferent to have one hundred millions of marks, or one million, if we are to buy all commodities dearer in the same proportion. It is ridiculous to say that metallic money is only a *sign* of value, the credit of which is founded on the stamp of the king. *This stamp is only to certify the weight and the title. Even in its relation to commodities the metal uncoined is of the same price as that coined.* The marked value is simply a denomination. This is what Law seems to have been ignorant of in establishing his bank.

It is then as *merchandise* that coined money is, not the sign, but the *common measure*, of other merchandise, and that not by an arbitrary convention,

1 Stephens' "Life of Turgot," page 206.

founded on the glamour of that metal, but because, being fit to be employed in different shapes as merchandise, and having on account of this property a salable value, a little increased by the use made of it as money, and being besides suitable of reduction to a given standard and of being equally divided, we always know the value of it. Gold obtains its price from its rarity, and so far from its being an evil that it is employed at the same time as merchandise and as money, these two employments maintain its price.

Supposing that the king could establish paper money, which, with all his authority, would not be easy, let us examine what he would gain by it. First, if he increased the quantity he would lower the value by the same act; and as he reserves the power to increase it, it is impossible for people to consent to give their commodities, at the same nominal price, for a bill, when by a stroke of the pen that could be made to lose its real value. " But," says Law, " the king, to preserve his credit, is interested in restricting the paper within just limits, and this interest of the king is sufficient to establish public confidence." What should the just limits be, and how are they to be determined? Let us follow out the system into the different suppositions that may be made, and let us see in each case what would be its solidity in respect to the utility it proposes.

I observe, first of all, that it is absolutely impossible for the king to substitute the use of paper for that of gold and silver. Gold and silver themselves, regarding them only as signs, are, by the fact of their circulation, actually distributed among the public according to the proportion of the commodities, of the industry, lands, and real wealth of every kind existing. Now, this proportion can never be primarily known, because it is hidden, and because it varies continually by a new circulation. The king will not proceed to distribute his paper money to each person in the proportion that he holds gold and silver money, forbidding him at the same time to employ the metal in commerce ; it would be necessary for the king to take to himself the gold and silver of his subjects, giving them his paper in their place. . . . But it is a point, equally of theory and of experience, that the people would never receive the paper except as representing real money, and consequently convertible into it.

One of the ways in which the king could draw to himself metallic money in exchange, and perhaps the only way, would be for him to take back his notes, conjointly with the coin, but to give out only his notes, while keeping the coin. Then he would choose between these two expedients: either to melt the coin in order to use it as merchandise, reducing his subjects to the use of paper, or to leave the coin and to circulate conjointly with it the paper as representatives of each other. I commence by examining this last supposition.

I assume, then, that the king puts into circulation a quantity of paper money equal to that of coin (Law would have put ten times more). Now, as the total quantity of signs (instruments of exchange) always balances itself with the total of commodities, it is plain that the sign will be worth the half less, or, what is the same thing, commodities will be worth as much again more. But independently of their function as signs of value, gold and silver possess their real value as articles of merchandise, a value which also balances itself against the commodities proportionately to the quantities of these metals, and which they do not lose by their function as money, but on the contrary ; that is to say, their value will be balanced with more merchandise as metal than the paper can be with which it was balanced as money, and, as I shall afterwards show, the king being always obliged to increase the number of his notes if he would not have them rendered useless, this disproportion will go on increasing to the point when specie and paper will be no longer reciprocally convertible, and the paper must become discredited from day to day, while the value of metallic money will be always sustained.[1] .   .   .

If more than forty years afterward (said Dupont in his "Works of Turgot") the majority of the Constituent Assembly had had as much enlightenment upon this question as Turgot already had shown while almost a youth, France would have been saved from the *assignats*. In the United States, after the experience of nearly two hundred years, Law instead of Turgot, upon the subject of money, is still our mentor and guide.

ADAM SMITH.

The theory of money which now obtains in the United States was formulated by Adam Smith, who was a follower of Law in assuming that it circulated from the necessity of a medium of exchange, and that without any other support it would continue to circulate and perform all the functions of metallic money provided it was not in excess; that is, provided that the amount did not exceed that of the metallic money which had circulated in its place. Costing nothing in itself, it was a very proper substitute for metallic money, the value of which was intrinsic. In his great treatise, "Wealth of Nations," he said: .

The substitution of paper in the room of gold and silver money replaces a very expensive instrument of commerce with one much less costly, and sometimes equally convenient. Circulation comes to be carried on by a new wheel, which it costs less both to erect and maintain than the old one. But in what manner this operation is performed, and in what manner it tends to increase either the gross or the neat revenue of the society, is not altogether so obvious, and may, therefore, require some further explication.

There are several sorts of paper money, but the circulating notes of banks and bankers are the species which is best known, and which seems best adapted for this purpose. When the people of any particular country have such confidence in the fortune, probity, and prudence of a particular banker as to believe that he is always ready to pay upon demand such of his promissory notes as are likely to be at any time presented to him, these notes come to have the same

---

[1] Stephens' "Life of Turgot," page 206.

currency as gold and silver money, from the confidence that such money can at any time be had for them.

A particular banker lends among his customers his own promissory notes, to the extent, we shall suppose, of a hundred thousand pounds. As those notes serve all the purposes of money, his debtors pay the same interest as if he had lent them so much money. This interest is the source of his gain. Though some of these notes are continually coming back upon him for payment, part of them circulate for months and years together ; though he has generally in circulation, therefore, notes to the extent of a hundred thousand pounds, twenty thousand pounds in gold and silver may frequently be sufficient provision for answering occasional demands.

Let us suppose, for example, that the whole circulating money of some particular country amounted at a particular time to £1,000,000, that sum then being sufficient for circulating the whole annual produce of their land and labor. Let us suppose, too, that some time thereafter different banks and bankers issued promissory notes payable to the bearer, to the extent of £1,000,-000, reserving in their different coffers £200,000 for answering occasional demands. There would remain, therefore, in circulation, £800,000 in gold and silver and £1,000,000 of bank notes, or £1,800,000 of paper and money together. But the annual produce of the land and labor of the country had before required only £1,000,000 to circulate and distribute it to its proper consumers, and that annual produce cannot be immediately augmented by the operations of banking ; £1,000,000, therefore, will be sufficient to circulate it after them. The goods to be bought and sold being precisely the same as before, the same quantity of money will be sufficient for buying and selling them. The channel of circulation, if I may be allowed such an expression, will remain precisely the same as before. One million pounds we have supposed sufficient to all that channel. Whatever, therefore, is poured into it beyond that sum cannot run in it, but must overflow : £1,800,000 are poured into it ; £800,000, therefore, must overflow, that sum being over and above what can be employed in the circulation of the country. But though this sum cannot be employed at home, it is too valuable to be allowed to lie idle. It will, therefore, be sent abroad, in order to seek that profitable employment which it cannot find at home. But the paper cannot go abroad, because at a distance from the banks which issue it, and from the country in which payment of it can be exacted by law, it will not be received in common payments. Gold and silver, therefore, to the amount of £800,000 will be sent abroad and the channel of home circulation will remain filled with £1,000,000 of paper instead of the £1,000,000 of those metals which filled it before. . . .

When paper is substituted in the room of gold and silver money, the quantity of the materials, tools, and maintenance which the whole circulating capital can supply may be increased by the whole value of gold and silver which used to be employed in circulating them. The whole value of the great wheel of circulation and distribution is added to the goods which are circulated and distributed by means of it.

What is the proportion which the circulating money of any country bears to the whole value of the annual produce circulated by means of it, it is, perhaps, impossible to determine. It has been computed by different authors at a fifth, at a tenth, at a twentieth, and at a thirtieth part of that value. But how small soever the proportion which the circulating money may bear to the whole value of the annual produce, as but a part, and frequently but a small part, of that produce is ever destined for the maintenance of industry, it must always bear a very considerable proportion to that part.

The whole paper money of every kind which can easily circulate in any country can never exceed the value of the gold and silver of which it supplies the* place, or which (the commerce being supposed the same) would circulate there if there were no paper money. If twenty-shilling notes, for example, are the lowest paper money current in Scotland, the whole of that currency that could easily circulate there cannot exceed the sum of gold and silver which would be necessary for transacting the annual exchanges of twenty shillings' value and upwards usually transacted in that country. Should the circulating paper at any time exceed that sum, as the excess could neither be sent abroad nor employed in the circulation of the country, it must return immediately upon the banks to be exchanged for gold and silver. Many people would immediately perceive that they had more of this paper than was necessary for transacting their business at home ; and, as they could not send it abroad, they would immediately demand payment for it at the banks. When this superfluous paper was converted into gold and silver, they could easily find a use for it by sending it abroad ; but they could find none while it remained in the shape of paper. There would immediately, therefore, be a run upon the banks to the whole extent of this superfluous paper; and, if they showed any difficulty or backwardness in payment, to much greater extent, the alarm which this would occasion necessarily increasing the run.

What a bank can with propriety advance to a merchant or undertaker of any kind is not either the whole capital with which he trades, or even any considerable portion of that capital, but that part of it only which he would other-wise be obliged to keep by him unemployed, and in ready money for answering occasional demands. If the paper money which the bank advances never exceeds this value, it can never exceed the value of the gold and silver which would necessarily circulate in the country if there were no paper money. It can never exceed the quantity which the circulation of the country can easily absorb and empty.

When it was observed that, within moderate periods of time, the repayments of a particular customer were upon most occasions fully equal to the advances which a bank had made him, it might be assumed that the paper money which had been advanced to him had not at any time exceeded the quantity of gold and silver which he would otherwise have been obliged to keep by him for answering occasional demands ; and that, consequently, the paper money which had been circulated by his means had not at any time exceeded the quantity of gold and silver which would have circulated in the country had there been no paper money. The frequency, regularity, and amount of his repayments would sufficiently demonstrate that the amount of the advances made had at no time exceeded that part of this capital which he would otherwise have been obliged to keep by him unemployed, and in ready money for answering occasional demands. . . .

The advances of the bank paper, by exceeding the quantity of gold and silver, which, had there been no such advances, he would have been obliged to keep by him for answering occasional demands, might soon come to exceed the whole quantity of gold and silver which would have circulated in the country had there been no paper money, and, consequently, to exceed the quantity which the circulation of the country could easily absorb and employ ; and the excess of this paper money would immediately have returned upon the bank to be exchanged for gold and silver.

The increase of paper money, it has been said, by augmenting the quantity, and consequently diminishing the value, of the whole currency, necessarily augments the money price of commodities ; but as the quantity of gold and silver which is taken from the currency is always equal to the quantity of paper which is added to it, paper money does not necessarily increase the quantity of the whole currency.[1]

With Smith money arose from the necessity of a medium of exchange, value, either intrinsic or representative, being no necessary attribute of it. Metallic money, first in use, was a very costly "wheel of circulation," for which another "wheel," costing nothing, paper money, was "substituted," a corresponding amount of capital being thereby discharged from unproductive to be applied to productive uses. To secure the acceptance of the "substitute," all that was required was good credit on the part of the issuer. The process was a very simple and safe one, as the amount of the "substitute" could never exceed that of the metallic money displaced, the excess, for which there was no use in the channels of circulation, returning immediately to the issuer. At the time Smith wrote there was no money of the kind described. It is easy to see how his mistake arose. He saw that the notes of the Bank of England were uniform, or nearly so, in amount; and that only a small provision by way of reserves appeared to be made therefor. He inferred, consequently, that they were accepted and maintained in circulation upon the credit of the issuer; and that the reserves were provided only to meet "occasional calls" for coin, and to take in any "excess." He wholly overlooked the fact that the notes of the Bank were issued in the discount of bills, which in the place of coin served as the instruments for the distribution of merchandise from producer to distributer, the notes serving for the distribution of the same merchandise directly to consumers. The notes were money

---

[1] "Wealth of Nations," Book II., Chapter II., et seq.

for the reason that, from their representative value, they performed
all the functions of metallic money. The term "money" might in fact
be well applied to bills of exchange, — instruments of distribution, —
these, like the notes issued in their discount, being retired by their
use. Such instruments of distribution, from the greater safety and
convenience of their use, were preferred to metallic money irrespective of the saving effected thereby. As already shown, the
process of issue is a mutual exchange of obligations; of payment,
the mutual cancelling of the same obligations. As the bills discounted by the Bank matured within periods of, say, sixty days, the
notes issued in their discount and used in their payment were
necessarily returned within similar periods, and without any interposition on its part, its bills, representing merchandise in demand
for consumption, being certain to be paid. Issues made in the discount of fictitious paper were, from the credit of the Bank, accepted
by the public equally with those issued in the discount of business
paper. Both alike were treated as capital. But issues made in the
discount of the former would not, for the want of means on the part
of their makers, be returned by them in its payment, but by other
issuers into whose hands they would fall, who would demand the
daily discharge in coin of all balances in their favor. Against such
issues the Bank would have nothing by way of offset but its own
capital in the form of coin. For reasons well understood it would,
as a rule, lose an amount equal to that of fictitious paper discounted. If it discounted none other it would, in spite of its reserves, speedily become bankrupt.

That Smith's theory of "credit money" never obtained in England
was due to the fact that the Bank of England was forbidden by its
charter to deal in anything but bills of exchange and gold and
silver bullion. It would never, unless imposed upon, exchange its
obligations based upon capital but for those equally well based.
If possessed of capital, no conditions, in fact, need be imposed upon
issuers, as their chief care will always be its preservation. The Bank
of England, exacting daily settlements with all other issuers (it alone
having the prerogative of issuing notes), virtually imposed upon all
the restrictions imposed by law upon itself. As the Bank of England
was a permanent institution, Smith's "credit money" never had a
foothold in that country. It never had any in the United States during
the existence of the two National Banks, both being based on capital,

and both being restricted in their operations to bills of exchange and to gold and silver bullion. As they greatly ranked, in means and influence, all other institutions of the kind ; as they had branches in every considerable place of business ; and as they received on deposit, and in the payment of their bills, and of the public revenues of which they were the custodians, the notes and credits of all similar institutions, occupying positions in reference to the Government similar to that now occupied by the Independent Treasury, but receiving every kind of money, they necessarily, for their own protection, enforced daily settlements with all other issuers, in this way imposing upon all the restrictions imposed by law upon themselves. During their existence the currency, whoever the issuer or wherever issued, was, as in England, always the equivalent of coin, being always based upon capital, and in great part upon merchandise in process of distribution.

The winding-up of the first Bank was the first opportunity for Smith's "credit money" here. In a very short time after its charter expired the issues of the State Banks, subject to no proper restraint, rose speedily from $80,000,000 to $300,000,000, chiefly by the discount of fictitious paper. The second Bank, supplying everywhere, through its branches, good money, and enforcing daily settlements with all other issuers, speedily drove " credit money " out of existence. The second opportunity for this came with its overthrow. General Jackson in his assault upon it, borrowing almost the exact language of Smith, who had drawn his inspiration from Law, declared that the notes issued by it were mere forms of credit, and that the interest charged for their use was pure robbery. The " wild-cat money " of the South and West, and for a time of the whole country, Smith's "credit money," was the result. Within a short period from its overthrow the currency rose from $116,000,000 to $276,000,000, to speedily fall, from its inherent rottenness, to $114,-000,000. Of the terrible disasters that resulted from the use of " credit money " the extracts given from the annual message for 1857, of President Buchanan, present a striking but by no means extravagant picture. In the mania for it vast numbers of banks were created like those described by the governor of Indiana, having no offices or places of business but saddle-bags.

As the people, left to themselves, always seeking the best methods to given ends, will never long tolerate a vicious currency of banks, the situation when the war of the Rebellion broke out was, through the operation of what may be termed natural laws, in great measure restored. The Independent Treasury, established by the Government to avoid the use of Smith's "credit money," and into which nothing but metallic money was to enter, unfortunately remained. In the payment of the loans negotiated on a large scale with the Banks for carrying on the war, the Secretary, Mr. S. P. Chase, would accept nothing but metallic money. The result was, as already shown, the speedy suspension by them of specie payments. Their suspension, accompanied by the refusal to use the money of banks, necessarily led to the issue for the first time in our history of Smith's "credit money" by the Government.

It was to avoid the use by the Government of "credit money" that the Independent Treasury was established. Its establishment forced in the end the adoption of the very kind of money sought to be avoided. The remedy for a vicious currency of banks will, sooner or later, always be applied, as no one will understandingly accept anything in exchange but an equivalent. But a remedy so effectual in correcting a vicious currency of banks cannot be so readily applied to the notes of a government armed as they are with the legal tender attribute. When one refuses the note of a bank, for the reason that it is not good money, he has his own immediate interest only in view. He is indifferent as to the effect of his refusal in curtailing the currency. When the same person is called upon to take action to retire, as it were, the great mass of currency in circulation, he naturally hesitates, from the consequences involved. He may, he fears, be for a time without any medium of exchange whatever. This is the reason why the retirement of a currency of Government notes is so difficult a matter. This hesitation will give place to action when it is seen that the reform of the currency is a matter of absolute necessity, and that, with provision for funding the notes of the Government, the amount of the currency remaining in circulation will never fall below that necessary for the distribution of the products of the people, than which nothing more is to be asked.

The amount of the advances in the form of credits to be made by banks and bankers to merchants or undertakers was not, said Smith, to equal the whole amount of the capital of the former, but only an amount equal to that of the gold and silver they would be obliged to keep on hand to meet occasional calls. But banks and bankers are never to advance to merchants or undertakers any portion of their reserves, the chief function of the former being to issue instruments of distribution. To make advances of their credits to serve as the reserves of others in affairs would be to bring speedy ruin upon themselves. Every one in affairs is to provide his own reserves, but those of merchants and undertakers may be in the form of the products in which they deal and which are to have the value of an equal nominal amount of metallic money.

What, asks Smith, is the proportion which the circulating money of any country is to bear to the whole value of the merchandise to be circulated by it? And he replies by stating that it may equal a fifth, a tenth, a twentieth, or a thirtieth of the value of such merchandise. The inquiry and reply show his profound ignorance upon the subject on which he wrote. In commercial countries, like Great Britain and the United States, merchandise entering into consumption is moved by the issues of banks and bankers which, from the services they perform, are called money, the nominal value of one equalling the actual value of the other.

As Smith's " credit money" is, from its very nature, always an instrument of fraud and waste ; as hardly a day passes that does not, in this country at least, show its real character in the disasters that follow its use (for it may be in the form of cheques as well as notes), how is it that he is still the unquestioned authority? The reason is, that as one with money is possessed of everything else, he who can show how it is to be had in abundance is sure of the popular ear. If one scheme fail, another is certain to take its place, as upon this subject there is no end to human credulity. Smith, the greatest schoolman of modern times, and one of the greatest of all times, dreaming away his life in his closet, showed how money was to be had for nothing. The scholasticism of the middle ages was almost unhesitatingly adopted by modern universities, over which, till within a recent period, men of affairs have had no control. The graduates of these, armed with the lessons taught them by schoolmen, became the teachers of our youth, entered into the halls of legislation, and have had almost the entire direction of the popular mind. All "learned men," so far as money was concerned, were naturally followers of Smith. By all, " fiat money " is held to be good money. Of this, one illustration will suffice. In the " Popular Science Monthly " for December, 1883, Professor Taussig, who now fills the •chair of Political Economy in Harvard University, said :

Paper money, though of the purest *fiat* character, with no hope or promise for its redemption in specie, may yet perform with reasonable efficiency, the functions of a circulating medium.